P9-DXE-849

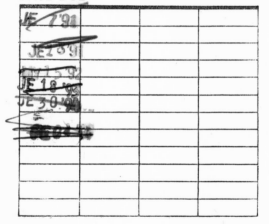

DATE DUE

JE 7'91			
JE 28'91			
JE 18'92			
JE 30'94			

Women Composers, Conductors, and Musicians of the Twentieth Century:

Selected Biographies

Volume III

by

Jane Weiner LePage

The Scarecrow Press, Inc.
Metuchen, N.J., & London
1988

Library of Congress Cataloging-in-Publication Data
(Revised for vol. 3)

LePage, Jane Weiner, 1931-
  Women composers, conductors, and musicians of the
twentieth century.

  Includes indexes.
  1. Women musicians--Biography. I. Title.
ML82.L46   780'.92'2   80-12162
ISBN 0-8108-2082-X

Dedicated to my husband,
William E. LePage

CONTENTS

Acknowledgments   vii

Preface   ix

GRAZYNA BACEWICZ   1

BETTY BEATH   18

ANNE BOYD   37

SYLVIA CADUFF   56

ANN CARR-BOYD   67

GLORIA COATES   80

SELMA EPSTEIN   104

NICOLA LEFANU   115

PRISCILLA McLEAN   129

ELIZABETH MACONCHY   147

MARY MAGEAU   165

URSULA MAMLOK   178

PRIAULX RAINIER   198

SHULAMIT RAN   215

RUTH SCHONTHAL   235

MARGARET SUTHERLAND   250

JOAN TOWER   264

GILLIAN WHITEHEAD   281

Index   299

ACKNOWLEDGMENTS

It was an inspiring experience to work with the composers, conductors, and musicians presented in this book. Their willingness to share personal experiences as well as to give their attention to detail and authenticity made possible a thoroughly documented publication. To these women I am deeply grateful. At the end of each biography, the selected lists of compositions were chosen by the composer. It is neither desirable nor practical to list every composition written by each artist; music catalogues are readily available for this purpose.

My heartiest thanks are due to all writers and publishers for allowing me to make use of their ideas and words. Full references are provided with quotations.

My research was facilitated by many library staffs, and I am especially grateful to those of North Adams State College, Williams College, Bennington College, New York Public Library and the University of New South Wales, Australia.

The assistance I received in Australia was overwhelming; Roger Covell, Fred Blanks, and James Murdock, authorities on music, especially Australian music, were most gracious and supportive. Frank Maietta, director of the Australia Music Centre, and Vicki Jones, information base assistant, were most receptive and helpful during my many weeks of research at 80 George St., Sydney. Helen Lewis, an associate with Arts Management, provided valuable assistance with my research on Gillian Whitehead. My thanks to Peter O'Brien, master of The Kensington Colleges at the University of New South Wales. Wanda Bacewicz, guardian of her sister Grazyna's works, corresponded with me from her home in Warsaw, Poland, for over two years. Hence, the chapter on the great Grazyna Bacewicz was read and approved by her.

A special thanks to Dr. Catherine Tisinger, president of North Adams State College, and Dr. James Roach, president of the University of Maine at Presque Isle, for their encouragement and support, and to Alan H. Green of Williamstown, Massachusetts, for his editing of the manuscript. Dr. Nancy Van de Vate, founder of the International League of Women Composers, and Dr. Kathy Heiligmann of Salem State College have been a source of inspiration and support for over a decade.

I wish to acknowledge my colleagues, Dr. Dwight Killam Dr. Christine Condaris, Dr. Ali Allmaker, Suzanne Kemper, research librarian; Bettina Nadeau, a senior undergraduate student; and the support staff at North Adams State College, especially Carol Robare and Jean Dolle. Without their help this book could not have been completed.

My total absorption in my research, writing, and interviewing was thoughtfully supported by my husband and family. Special thanks to my daughters, Jane Weiner Sumner and Renay LePage Donelan, and to my sons, Bruce Weiner and Buddy Weiner.

PREFACE

Volume III is a sequel to my previous two books, <u>Women Com-</u>
<u>posers, Conductors, and Musicians of the Twentieth Century,</u>
volumes I and II, published by The Scarecrow Press. Bio-
graphies included in volume I are: VICTORIA BOND, AN-
TONIA BRICO, RADIE BRITAIN, RUTH CRAWFORD (SEEGER),
EMMA LOU DIEMER, MARGARET HILLIS, JEAN EICHELBERGER
IVEY, BETSY JOLAS, BARBARA ANNE KOLB, WANDA LAND-
OWSKA, THEA MUSGRAVE, PAULINE OLIVEROS, EVE QUELER,
MARGA RICHTER, LOUISE TALMA, ROSALYN TURECK,
NANCY VAN DE VATE. Volume II includes: BETH ANDER-
SON, DALIA ATLAS, SARAH CALDWELL, POZZI ESCOT,
VIVIAN FINE, KAY GARDNER, MIRIAM GIDEON, PEGGY
GLANVILLE-HICKS, DORIS HAYS, FREDERIQUE PETRIDES,
MARTA PTASZYNSKA, DARIA SEMEGEN, SUSAN SMELTZER,
JULIA SMITH, ELINOR REMICK WARREN, JUDITH LANG ZAI-
MONT, ELLEN TAAFFE ZWILICH.

Reference books and textbooks generally have dismissed
women composers and conductors in a few sentences. My
primary focus is to make readily available the contributions
and accomplishments of some of the gifted women musicians
of the 20th century. The role of women in the arts has been
neglected, and accurate historical information must be collected
if we are to preserve their achievements for posterity.

Ideally, there should be no need to separate the sexes;
merit should be based solely on artistic ability. Unfortunately,
this has not happened, even though recorded history shows
that women have been composing since the third century.
The societal structure did not provide for public presentation or documentation of their work. A few compositions
written by women were performed and published under the
names of their brothers or husbands, or under male pseu-
donyms. The talents of many women have never been preserved

or shared with the world. Society has been the loser because of its failure to recognize these talented and creative women. Negativism should not be accepted, but I do not fault society for its past history. The important issue is to swiftly eliminate the inequities.

My research, interviewing, and writing will continue in the hope of publishing another volume in order to document the contributions of all those women not covered in the first three books.

GRAZYNA BACEWICZ

Composer, Virtuoso Violinist, Pianist

Grazyna Bacewicz was among the most eminent contemporary composers of the 20th century. Known to foreign music critics as the "First Lady of Music," she was one of the most interesting Polish musicians of the century as well as one of its most celebrated artists. Endowed with great talent and versatility, she was a prolific and diversified composer, a remarkable violinist as well as a fine pianist.

The following is an excerpt from Witold Lutoslawski's broadcast over Polish radio on Jan. 1, 1969:

> If Polish musical achievement has won an exception-ally high place in the world it is to great extent due to the personal merit of Grazyna Bacewicz. In the difficult situation of contemporary music, con-stantly bandying new slogans, using new, often shocking means of expression, she could always find her own way. She did not stop, never resting at the stage which brought her international awards, but went forward choosing only that which suited her, only what could be melded by her individual, very personal style. A violinist of highest rank with the fame of virtuoso, she possessed all the secrets of string instruments. And it is probably in this field that her best creative achievements are to be found. But ... the creative talent of Grazyna Bace-wicz was revealed equally in symphonies, stage works, and piano compositions.

The author thanks and is deeply appreciative to Wanda Bace-wicz, sister of Grazyna, and the staff of PWM Edition, whose support and help made possible the presentation of material in this chapter.

GRAZYNA BACEWICZ   Photo by
                                              B. J. Dorys

Grazyna was born in Lodz, Poland, in 1909. Her
Lithuanian father was a teacher who loved music and taught
his four children to play instruments around the age of 5.
Music was cultivated in the home and the Bacewicz family
quartet often performed for family friends. The family artists
include her sister Wanda, a well-known poetess, her brother
Kiejstut, a pianist and music teacher (a second brother,
Witlod, died in the United States in 1970), and her daughter
Alina, a painter.

At the age of 7 Grazyna Bacewicz was performing in
recitals. At age 11 she studied violin and piano at Kijenska's
private Lodz Conservatory. In 1932 she received two diplomas
from the Warsaw Conservatory of Music: violin under Professor Józef Jarzebski and composition under Kazimierz Sikorski,
a professor who nurtured the creative talents of many of the
young gifted Polish composers of the time, including Bacewicz, Krenz, Malawski, Palester, Panufnik, Serocki and
Spisak. She also studied piano with Jozef Turczynski and
philosophy at Warsaw University.

Bacewicz continued her compositional studies in Paris
with the famous Nadia Boulanger, then assistant and friend
of Igor Stravinsky. Boulanger's international reputation as
a teacher of composition and strict musical disciplinarian is
fondly remembered in Poland as the teacher of the Poles. She
helped shape the compositional thinking of several generations
of Polish composers including Bacewicz, Szeligowski, Perkow-
ski, Rudzinski, Zulawski, Krondracki, Spisak, Serocki, and
Skrowaczewski. Many of America's 20th-century composers
would also claim Boulanger as their teacher.

The young Bacewicz continued her violin studies under
the tutelage of André Touret and with the world-famous violinist Carl Flesch. Following two years of study in Paris,
which included first prize at the Young Composers' Competition for her wind quintet in 1933, she embarked on an international career as a concert violinist while continuing her
composing.

Before and after World War II she toured as a violinist
throughout most of Europe appearing under conductors Paul
Kletzki, Gheorge Georgescu, Herman Abendroth and Con-
stantin Silvestri. In 1946 she played Karol Szymanowski's
Violin Concerto in Paris with Paul Kletzki conducting. Those

familiar with this work can appreciate the degree of difficulty
and applaud Bacewicz's virtuosity.

In 1934 the first concert of Grazyna Bacewicz as a
composer took place in Warsaw and in 1939 a similar concert
was held in Paris. She gave public performances of her compositions for violin as well as piano. It is generally agreed
among music critics that her interpretation of her own works
for violin has never been equalled in brilliance. She continued to study the secrets of symphonic orchestration by
playing first violin with the Polish Radio Orchestra of Warsaw.
The group was founded and conducted by Grzegorz Fitelberg
after his ouster from the Warsaw Philharmonic over a dispute
about modern Polish music.

In 1936 Grazyna Bacewicz married physician Andrzej
Biernacki, later a professor at the Medical Academy and the
Secretary of the Polish Academy of Science. Their only child,
daughter Alina, was born in 1942.

Despite the horrors of the war and Nazi occupation,
she was active in the underground musical life of Warsaw
both as composer and performer. She continued her writing,
according to Wanda Bacewicz, after the tragedy in Warsaw
during the August 1944 uprising. She survived being de-
ported from the camp at Pruszkow to Germany because she
was caring for her seriously wounded sister and small daughter. Like other Poles, after the uprising, she experienced
a long period of homelessness in various towns in Poland.
She gave solo concerts and together with her brother, Professor Kiejstut Bacewicz, a pianist, performed other programs
for the Main Council of Relief.

In 1945 Bacewicz returned to Warsaw and to her career
as a violinist in Poland and other countries, winning critical
acclaim for her performances of both classical music and her
own compositions. She continued to compose since this afforded her the opportunity to express her personal feelings
as an artist.

Historians generally agreed that the first three decades
of modern Polish music were influenced by neoclassicism and
the works of Karol Szymanowski. Although the first stage
of Bacewicz's composing career was a period of youthful and
somewhat fresh vanguard searches, she, like all young Polish

composers of the time, was under the influence of Szymanowski. She realized that in order to find her own musical language she had to rid herself of this influence. Her studies
in Paris helped her to expand her compositional skills and
her first style period characterized her development of neoclassical forms. Three of the most noteworthy compositions
of this period were: Quintet for flute, oboe, clarinet, bassoon and horn in 1932, first prize at the Young Composers'
Competition in Paris, in 1933; Trio for oboe, violin and
violoncello in 1935, second prize at the Publishing Polish
Music Society in Warsaw, 1936; Overture for orchestra in
1943, recorded on MUZA XL 0274.

Overture was premiered in America on Nov. 11, 1975,
by the New York Philharmonic conducted by Sarah Caldwell,
in the Celebration of Women Composers Concert. Andrew
Porter, writing in The New New Yorker, considered the
piece as "one of those bright, undemanding eight-minute
pieces for full orchestra which make a good start to a concert." In 1945 S. K. Tygodnik Powszechny wrote of the same
composition: "... Short, sparkling with life, and hastening
as if on wings of rhythmical temperament, the Overture by
Grazyna Bacewicz has a clear, simple, and gay theme, com-
pact form and instrumentation full of uncommon ideas." The
Celebration of Women Composers included three generations
of Nadia Boulanger students including her sister Lili (1893),
Bacewicz (1909), and Thea Musgrave (1928). Other composers
presented on the program were Ruth Crawford Seeger and
Pozzi Escot.

Immediately following World War II, both the political
and social conditions had a strong impact on creativity. The
burden of the occupation had influenced many composers and
they had the need to express in music their emotional response, given the nature of the difficult previous years.

Thus began the second period of Bacewicz's composing
career, reflecting a neoclassical counterpoint and the folk
music style and neoexpressionism of the early postwar years.
In 1948 she received distinction in London for Olympic
Cantata; in 1949 the City of Warsaw Prize for all of her artistic activities as well as a prize for her Piano Concerto; in
1950 she received a State Award for her famous Concerto for
String Orchestra, which was premiered in the United States
in 1952; in 1951 the prestigious International Composers

Contest, First Prize in Liège, Belgium, for her String Quartet No. 4. She went to Belgium to receive the prize and to
perform her Violin Sonata No. 4 accompanied by a Belgian
pianist. Krakow, October 8, 1950, a part of the review of
the piece that would receive a State Award in 1952:

> ... This composition, together with an undoubted
> monumentalism, has a simple, clear, and economical
> texture; the attention is drawn by the piano part,
> not overloaded but expressive, excellently contrast-
> ing with the violin. Dramatic expression and grand-
> iloquence are achieved here with unusually simple
> means, this being particularly striking in the second
> movement.... This work is exceptionally mature
> probably; in form, simply excellent; pliability, unity,
> homogeneity of narration--these are its great achieve-
> ments.

The following is part of a review by Milton Berliner for
the Washington Daily News, Dec. 31, 1952, for Concerto for
String Orchestra (1948):

> Woman--in spirit and in person--dominated last night's
> National Symphony Orchestra concert at Constitu-
> tional Hall. Howard Mitchell opened the program
> with the American premiere of Grazyna Bacewicz's
> Concerto Grosso for Strings and the French pianist,
> Lelia Gousseau, was soloist in the numbers that fol-
> lowed. Actually, there was nothing feminine about
> Mrs. Bacewicz' piece. It was vigorous, even virile,
> with (in the first movement) a pulsing, throbbing
> rhythm and bold thematic material. It was either
> conservatively modern or radically classical. In any
> case it was worth listening to.

Grazyna Bacewicz received the prize of the Minister of
Culture in Arts in 1955 for her Symphony No. 4 written in
1953. The review by L. A. in Dziennik Polski, Krakow, Jan.
19, 1954, included among other things the following:

> What are the features of Grazyna Bacewicz's Fourth
> Symphony? Above all the power of dramatic expres-
> sion. There is simply no passage in which something
> of importance does not happen: constant movement,
> ever new emotions.... All this is carried out by
> means of masterly techniques....

At the height of her career as a violin virtuoso in 1955
she gave up her career as a performer to devote her life to
her first love in music, composing. Her list of compositions
is imposing in both quality and diversity.

The reader will be interested and perhaps a bit amused
to read the following excerpt from Etude, Vol. 73, March 1955,
written by Nicholas Slonimsky. The article was titled "Musical Oddities":

> Feminism in musical composition is still a cause that
> needs its suffragettes. True, musical ladies have
> created some dainty piano miniatures and some very
> appealing songs, but not as many among them have
> written full-fledged symphonies. Mrs. Beach wrote
> a Gaelic Symphony that had performances in Europe
> and America; Dame Ethel Smyth of England wrote
> symphonies and opera. Among forgotten women com-
> posers is Aline Hundt, pupil of Liszt. She conducted
> her Symphony in G Minor in Berlin in the spring of
> 1871....
> The world record for composition, publication,
> and performance of the feminine symphonies belongs
> to the contemporary Polish composer Grazyna Bace-
> wicz.... Perhaps the most remarkable quality of the
> music by Grazyna Bacewicz is that she writes mostly
> absolute music, without reliance on the literary as-
> sociations. This constitutes a definite break in the
> feminist musical tradition, the mainstay of which has
> always been pragmatic music.

As in many countries the Polish composer depended on
subsidies from the government in order to live. As is often
the case, policy, publication, and performance are often dictated by those who award the commissions. But this was to
change when the first postwar festival was held in 1956 in
Poland. Today this festival, Warsaw Musical Autumns, is
highly respected as a leader in contemporary musical thought.
Even more important is the availability of recordings by
Polish composers within two days of performance at the festival. If only other countries would follow this example there
could easily be a wealth of contemporary literature readily
available.

Tadeusz Marek and Bacewicz's sister Wanda both describe

the long hours Grazyna spent each day in her study, working
in solitude and with maximum concentration and subjected to
the greatest strain to write her compositions. She set rigor-
ous standards for herself and in spite of her impressive list
of compositions, composing did not come easily to her. Like
every honest artist, she concentrated on perfecting her form
and strove for the maximum and true artistic expression.
From 1955 her work showed gradual evolution to modern music
declaration.

In her String Quartet No. 6 (1960) she expressed a new
approach and explained that she was drawn to the serial technique principally because she expected to learn from it "a
new rigor of form, a new discipline which would be far more
attractive than the conventionalized discipline of the tonal
world." Tadeusz Zielinski describes the quartet in Przeglad
Kulturalny (Warsaw), Aug. 6, 1960 (excerpt):

> Bacewicz's Sixth Quartet is a work of great inven-
> tion and interesting imagination, and at the same
> time a demonstration of impressive technical and con-
> struction craftmanship. Surely we have not heard
> such an excellent quartet since the times of Szyman-
> owski!

Before this time Grazyna Bacewicz wrote one of her
most important and best-known compositions, Music for Strings,
Trumpets and Percussion, 1958. It has received performances
in Warsaw, Amsterdam, Paris, Chicago, New York, Moscow,
Sofia, Cologne, Budapest, Frankfurt, Rome, London, and
Sydney, among other places. In 1960 this work of Bacewicz's
was awarded third place, overall, at the International Composers Tribune, and first prize in the orchestral division at
UNESCO in Paris. It is recorded on Polish-label record
MUZA SXL 0171, XW 567 and Philips monophonic PHM 500-141
or stereo PHS 900-141, Melodiya D 013193-6 (USSR). The
latter was recorded by the Warsaw National Philharmonic Symphony Orchestra conducted by Witold Rowicki. Titled Contemporary Polish Music, the disc includes: Penderecki, To
the Victims of Hiroshima--Threnody for 52 String Instruments;
Bacewicz, Music for Strings, Trumpets and Percussion; Baird,
Erotica; Serocki, Sinfonietta for Two String Orchestras.

Music for Strings, Trumpets and Percussion was performed by the BBC Symphony Orchestra conducted by Rudolf

Schwarz in 1961. One reviewer called the work a curious piece and described it as "ably written, highly dynamic and full of tension and excitement, and the percussion was treated in such a way that it seemed an integral part of the composition and not a mere accessory."

When Music for Strings, Trumpets and Percussion was introduced in New York under the baton of conductor Victoria Bond in 1976, one of the leading music critics in this country described the piece as follows: "It is spiced by fragments of a jazz character, which gives her formulation an identity of its own." Unfortunately this critic was unaware that the composer had been dead for several years, since he referred to her as a Polish composer "now" in her 60s.

It is of interest to the reader to note and compare comments of other music critics to those written by Tadeusz Zielinski in Ruch Muzyczny, April 30, 1961:

> Musique pour Cordes, Trompettes et Percussion
>
> The first part is something of a revelation: excellent concerting of the rhythmic elements as such as we have not yet had in Polish music, delicious rhythms with subtle nuances with great hidden dynamism, which is in general an essential characteristic of the work, something even reaching a power worthy of the Miraculous Mandarin....

Bacewicz received two other awards in 1960, the Award of the Union of Polish Composers and the prize of Radio and Television for her comic opera, The Adventures of King Arthur, written in 1959, with libretto by Edward Fischer.

During the final years of Bacewicz's young life her compositions brought her new honors, recognition and awards. She went through a serious crisis combining her compositional skills with a sensitivity to new tonal qualities, technical development and the use of numerous new percussion instruments. Her rich, artistic output during this period was an exquisite example of her inexhaustible creative energy.

The mature style of Bacewicz's final years included numerous compositions that combined a new tonal color and texture with deep emotionalism. She was widely considered

the most gifted composer of her time. Her compositional output during this period was extensive and covered a wide
range of works.

Pensieri Notturni for chamber orchestra (1961) was
awarded the 1962 prize of the Minister of Cultural Arts.
Tadeusz Marek described the work: "The poetry of this is
fascinating in its unusual atmosphere. The music shimmers
with a rich range of elegant, varying and tempered shades."
This eight-minute composition has been performed in over 12
countries throughout the world including the United States.

In 1965 Grazyna Bacewicz received the prestigious Gold
Medal prize of the Belgian government at the Queen Elisa-
beth International composers Competition for her Violin Concerto No. 7. The concerto was premiered on Jan. 14, 1966,
in the grand auditorium of the Palais des Beaux Arts of Brussels. The violin soloist was the noted Augustin Leon Ara,
with Daniel Sternefeld conducting the Belgian Radio and
Television Orchestra. The work received critical acclaim from
many sources including a reviewer for La Libre Belgique who
wrote:

> The concerto has a disturbing steel sound; it seems
> to evoke, to seek to transpose to the violin the
> sounds of electronic instruments or a magnetic tape
> used in compositions today. That is curious and
> interesting.

Other critical writers noted that the piece was remarkable for its bold and deft style which indicated that the composer was an up-to-date musician. The courage and originality of the modes of expression used in the violin solo as
well as the orchestral score was also an important aspect of
the work.

String Quartet No. 7, written in 1965, has been recorded
four times, three by the Dimov Quartet in Warsaw and Paris,
and once by the Grazyna Bacewicz Warsaw String Quartet.
An excerpt of a review from Ruch Muzyczny, April 1-15,
1969, written by Witold Lutoslawski, said:

> The Seventh Quartet is a new proof of the existence
> of many hitherto unsuspected possibilities lying hid-
> den in this, one would have thought, so well-known

kind of ensemble. From the time of Bartók not many composers have been able to such a degree as Grazyna Bacewicz to penetrate the secrets of quartet texture. The Seventh Quartet, one of Grazyna's last works, will surely travel a long way across the platforms and studios of the whole world.

When the Hopkins Center at Dartmouth College in Hanover, N.H., opened its doors in 1962, it provided a mecca for contemporary composers. Under the direction of Mario di Bonaventura, the eight-week summer contemporary music festival, Congregation of the Arts, received International acclaim. He directed his attention to the 20th-century creator and provided commissions to composers to write for the festival. In addition he personnally auditioned young musicians and chose about 90 of them to participate in the festival each season. The void between 20th-century composers and listeners can only be narrowed if musicians have the opportunity to perform and understand new works. Much credit must be given to Mario di Bonaventura for his accomplishments during his tenure as director of the festival.

In 1966 Grazyna Bacewicz received a commission to write for this festival and her work Contradizione, for chamber orchestra, was premiered in 1967. She joined other notable contemporary composers whose works were performed over a period of time at the Congregation of the Arts including Carlos Chávez, Zoltan Kodaly, Aaron Copland, Peter Mennin, Witold Lutoslawski, Walter Piston, Hans Werner Henze, Henry Cowell, Vincent Persichetti and others.

Her last great work of 1968 was the ballet The Desire, in two acts, after the play by Picasso, Desire Trapped by the Tail, and it represented a protest against war. This was the furthest stage in Bacewicz's stylistic development; it belonged entirely to the world of the latest musical vanguard.

Cultural exchanges between countries have long played a prominent role in the musical life of both the performers and the listening audience. In 1970 the Royal Liverpool Philharmonic Orchestra, conducted by Charles Groves, performed the works of Polish composers Bacewicz and Lutoslawski and British composers Gerhard and Walton in Liverpool. Bacewicz's Concerto for Viola, one of the last works completed before her death, was performed by the orchestra with Stefan

Kamasa as soloist. Scored for a large orchestra with expanded
percussion, the composer showed considerable ingenuity in
writing exciting accompanying textures. Positive reviews
were written in both countries.

Grazyna Bacewicz played a very important role in the
musical life of her country. In addition to her long list of
compositions and performances she was vice-chairperson of
the Polish Composers Union, a member of many artistic coun-
cils and commissions and a member of the jury at many competitions both at home and abroad. She was also a professor
of composition at the State Academy of Music in Warsaw.

She died unexpectedly in the winter of 1969; her death
evoked stunned surprise and then deep grief. The Polish
Radio broadcast the announcement and the country was plunged
into mourning at the loss of one of its most celebrated artists.
Just a few days earlier she had attended a concert in the
National Philharmonic Hall and was planning to work on the
ending of her ballet The Desire.

The biweekly Ruch Muzyczny in 1969 (April 1-15) devoted an issue to the life and accomplishments of Bacewicz.
She was recognized not only as a brilliant creator but also as
a human being of outstanding qualities. A small excerpt from
the writing of Tadeusz Baird from that issue reads:

> She possessed the uprightness of a human being,
> honest to herself, to people, to facts. She embodied
> the simplicity of friendliness stemming from a not
> frequently met ability to understand others, and in-
> stinctive wisdom seeking escape in doing justice. I
> think that she was a good human being, noble and
> beautiful in her very nature.

In honor of her great contributions her countrymen
have named two streets after her, one in Warsaw and a
second in Gdansk. There are also eight schools in Poland
that bear her name. The Polish government pays tribute to
famous people by placing statues in their honor in various
prominent locations in the country. One will find Grazyna
Bacewicz's statue in front of the Baltic Philharmonic in By-
dgoszcz. She was an outstanding creative artist and a unique
human being.

Selected Compositions of Grazyna Bacewicz

(Performing times, where known, are given in minutes.)

Orchestral Works for Solo and Orchestra

1943 Overture, 6.
1948 Concerto, for string orchestra, 15.
1951 Symphonie No. 2, 22.
1952 Symphonie No. 3, 28.
1953 Symphonie No. 4, c. 30.
1955 Partita, 14.
1957 Variations, 12.
1958 Music for Strings, Trumpets and Percussion, c. 20.
1961 Pensieri Notturni, for chamber orchestra, 8.
1962 Concerto, for great orchestra, 20.
1965 Musica Sinfonica in Tre Movimenti, 16.
1965 Divertimento, for string orchestra, c. 7.
1966 Contradizione, for chamber orchestra, c. 16.
1967 In Una Parte, for symphony orchestra, c. 9.
1948 Concerto No. 3, for violin and orchestra, c. 21.
1949 Concerto, for piano and orchestra, 21.
1951 Concerto No. 4, for violin and orchestra, c. 20.
1954 Concerto No. 5, for violin and orchestra, c. 22.
1965 Concerto No. 7, for violin and orchestra, c. 20.
1966 Concerto, for two pianos and orchestra, c. 17.
1968 Concerto, for viola and orchestra, 20.
1951 Concerto No. 1, for cello and orchestra, 22.
1963 Concerto No. 2, for cello and orchestra, 21.

Chamber Music

1938 String Quartet No. 1.
1943 String Quartet No. 2.
1947 String Quartet No. 3, 17.
1951 String Quartet No. 4, 20.
1955 String Quartet No. 5, 22.
1960 String Quartet No. 6, 17.
1965 String Quartet No. 7, c. 18.
1949 Quartet, for four violins, 13.
1964 Quartet, for violoncello, c. 16
1952 Quintette No. 1, for piano and strings, 25.
1965 Quintette No. 2, for piano and strings, c. 18.

1932 Quintette, for flute, oboe, clarinet, bassoon and horn, 10.
1935 Trio, for oboe violin and cello, 10.
1943 Suite, for 2 violins, 13.
1965 Incrustations, for horn and chamber ensemble, c. 15.
1965 Trio, for oboe, harp and percussion, c. 16.
1945 Sonata da Camera No. 1, for violin and piano 18.
1947 Sonata No. 3, for violin and piano, 18.
1949 Sonata No. 4, for violin and piano, 20.
1951 Sonata No. 5, for violin and piano, c. 14.

Works for Solo Instruments

1953 Sonata No. 2, for piano, 14.
1956 10 Concert Studies, c. 18.
1966 Esquisse, for organ, 3.
1958 Sonata, for violin solo, 11.
1968 4 Caprices, for violin solo, c. 10.

Solo Voice, Choir and Orchestra

1938 Three Songs, c. 8.
1948 Olympic Cantata, 7.
1964 "Acropolis" Cantata, 11.

Opera/Ballet

1959 Przygoda Krola Artura, The Adventures of King Arthur, Radio Comic Opera, c. 50.
1953 Z Chlopa Krol, Peasant King, ballet, 60.
1964 "Esik" W. Ostendzie, In Ostend, comic ballet, c. 60.
1968 Desir (Desire), ballet, 84.

Publisher's Address

Sole Exporter of Polish Music
ARS Polona, Foreign Trade Enterprise
Krakowskia Przedmiescie 7
00-068 Warazawa
Poland

Discography

<u>Concerto, for string orchestra</u> (1948).
    Polish Chamber Orchestra, cond. Jerzy Maksymiuk,
        MUZA SX 1256
    Polish Radio Orchestra WOSPR, cond, Jan Krenz MUZA
        XL 0274 (out of print)
<u>Third Violin Concerto</u> (1948).
    Grazyna Bacewicz-violin, Polish Radio Orchestra, cond.
        Grzegorz Fitelberg MUZA (out of print)
<u>Fourth Violin Sonata</u> (1949).
    Grazyna Bacewicz-violin, Kiejstut Bacewicz-piano, MUZA
        XL 0033 (out of print)
    Edw. Statkiewicz-violin, Aleksandra Utrecht-piano,
        MUZA XL 050
<u>A Selection of Short Violin Pieces</u> (1949-52).
    Grazyna Bacewicz-violin, Kiejstut Bacewicz-piano,
        MUZA (out of print)
<u>Music for Strings, Trumpets and Percussion</u> (1958).
    Warsaw National Philharmonic Orchestra, cond. Witold
        Rowicki MUZA SXL 0171 Philips PHS 900-141 or PHM
        500-141
    (1959). Polish Radio Orchestra WOSPR, cond. Jan
        Krenz, recording made during the Warsaw Autumn,
        MUZA W 567.
    USSR Orchestra, cond. N. Anosov, Melodiya DO13193-6
<u>Overture</u> (1943).
    Warsaw National Philharmonic Symphony Orchestra,
        cond. W. Rowicki, MUZA SX 0274, MUZA XL 0274
<u>Pensieri Notturni, for chamber orchestra</u> (1961).
    Warsaw National Philharmonic Symphony Orchestra,
        cond. W. Rowicki MUZA SX 0274, MUZA XL 0274
<u>Concerto, for great orchestra</u> (1962).
    Warsaw National Philharmonic Orchestra, cond. W. Row-
        icki, MUZA SXL 0274
<u>Piano Quintet No. 1 Piano Quintet No. 2</u> (1952).
    The Warsaw Piano Quintet: Igor Iwanow, Jan Tawrosze-
        wicz, Stefan Kamasa, Wladyslaw Szpilman (piano),
        MUZA SXL 0608
<u>Musica Sinfonica in Tre Movimenti</u> (1965).
    Warsaw National Philharmonic Orch., cond. W. Rowicki,
        Warsaw, Autumn 1965, MUZA XW 567
<u>String Quartet No. 3</u> (1947).
    Wilanow String Quartet, MUZA SX 1597
<u>String Quartet No. 5</u> (1955).
    Wilanow String Quartet, MUZA SX 1597

String Quartet No. 4 (1951).
    Grazyna Bacewicz String Quartet, MUZA SX 1598
    Parrenin Quartet, Warsaw, Autumn 1956, MUZA W 180
String Quartet No. 7 (1965).
    Grazyna Bacewicz String Quartet, MUZA SX 1598
    Harmonia Mundi MHS 1889 or HMO 34708 (Paris)
    The Musical Heritage Society MHS 1889 (out of print)
    Dimov Quartet, Warsaw, Autumn 1966, MUZA M-3XW 716
Violin Concerto No. 7 (1965).
    Piotr Janowski, Violin, Warsaw Philharmonic Orchestra,
        cond. Andrzej Markowski, Warsaw, Autumn 1969,
        MUZA 3XW 1183
Divertimento for String Orchestra (1965).
    Teutsch Chamber Orchestra, MUZA SX 1134 (Musica
        Polonica Nova)
Concerto No. 2 for Cello and Orchestra (1963).
    Gaspar Cassado-cello, Warsaw National Philharmonic
        Orchestra, cond. W. Krzemienski, Warsaw, Autumn,
        MUZA W877/8
String Quartet No. 6 (1960).
    Parrenin Quartet, Warsaw, Autumn, MUZA W 679
Quartet for 4 Cellos (1964).
    A. Ciechanski, J. Weslawski, R. Suchecki, M. Radzak,
        Warsaw, Autumn, MUZA W 969

Piano Works

Second Sonata (1953).
Ten Concert Studies (1956).
Little/Small/Triptych (1965).
    Regina Smendzianka, MUZA SXL 0977
Sonata for Piano No. 2 (1953).
    Nancy Fierro (California, U.S.A.), Avant Records AV-
        1012
    Krystian Zimerman, MUZA SX 1510
Little Triptych for Piano (1965).
    Rosario Marciano, Turnabout TV 34685, FONO FSM 53
        0 36
From Ten Studies for Piano (1956).
    Virginia Eskin, Musical Heritage Society MHS 4236
Contradizione, for Chamber Orchestra (1966).
    Warsaw National Philharmonic Orchestra, cond. W.
        Rowicki, Warsaw, Autumn 1967, MUZA 3 XW 890

Esquisse for Organ (1966).
 Jean Guillou, Philips, Paris, 6504-039
Concerto, for Two Pianos and Orchestra (1966).
 Warsaw National Philharmonic Orchestra, cond. Stanis-
 law Wislocki, MUZA SXL 0875
Concerto for Viola and Orchestra (1968).
 Warsaw National Philharmonic Orchestra, cond. Stanis-
 law Wislocki, MUZA SXL 0875
In Una Parte, for Orchestra (1967).
 Warsaw National Philharmonic Orchestra, cond. S. Wis-
 locki, MUZA SXL 0875
Oberek for Violin and Piano.
 Kaja Dancrowska and Yomusr Olejuicrak, VIFON LP 055

Addresses

Avant Records, c/o Crystal Records, 2235 Willida Lane, Sedro
 Woolley, WA   98284.

PWM Editions, Krakowskie, Przedmiescie 7, Warszawa, Poland.
 (Some MUZA records are also available from: Polish
 Record Center of America, 3069 Milwaukee Ave., Chi-
 cago, IL   60618.)

Philips Phonogram Mercury Records, 810 Seventh Ave., New
 York, NY   10017.

Musical Heritage Society, 1710 Highway 35, Ocean, NJ   07712.

Vox-Turnabout, The Moss Music Group, 211 East 43rd Street,
 New York, NY   10017.

BETTY BEATH

Composer, Pianist, Teacher

Betty Beath, a composer of achievement, is a pioneer in Australia where she has worked indefatigably for the acceptance
and the awareness of contempory music written by women.
She is a pianist and educator (at the Queensland Conservatorium of Music, where she lectures in composition and Asian
music, and at St. Margaret's Girls' School, Brisbane, where
she is head of the music department) and in 1986 was appointed
editor of ASMUSE, a publishing body of the Australian Society
of Music Education. As a composer she has produced much
work in the fields of art song, chamber music and music
drama. Her works for children have been performed extensively by amateur and professional theater and opera companies throughout Australia, while her work in art song and
chamber music has been broadcast and performed in recitals
and theatre presentations in Australia, the United States, the
United Kingdom, Mexico and Indonesia.

Australia is isolated by sheer distance from the great
music centers of the world. Until around 1960 it was necessary for composers to receive recognition abroad (especially
in Europe), before their music was accepted at home. It is
a huge and beautiful country with a small population that is
only now emerging from frontier existence. In 1988 Australia will celebrate its bicentennial.

Beath was born in 1932 in the Gooburrum district near
Bundaberg, Queensland. She is the oldest of the five daughters of Edith Mary and Maurice Wilmot Eardley. She says:

> In thinking about the influences in my life, especially
> as they affected my musical development, I have to
> go back to the beginning to my father who was a

18

BETTY BEATH   Photo by
                                David Cox

cane farmer in the Gooburrum district near Bundaberg and to the end of the day and to me the melody
and the sound of his voice was immensely pleasing.
Perhaps my mother noticed my interest for before I
went to the tiny one-teacher school at Welcome Creek
I had already had several years of piano lessons.
She decided that I was musically gifted and arranged
for me to have music lessons with a cousin, Lorna
Pollard, who lived a day's journey from our farm in
the small coal-mining town of Howard.

Pollard was a highly respected teacher and musical
identity. At age 3, Betty was her youngest student and her
memories of those early lessons with Pollard remain vivid because of the imagination, patience, and initiative she shared.
Betty recalls:

> She tied a pink ribbon to my right wrist and a blue
> one to my left. To correspond with the ribbons,
> pink bows were drawn against all the notes of the
> treble staff and blue ones on the bass. She made
> other little drawings above the notes, for example,
> E was a bird, F was a soldier, G was a cat ... and
> all this helped me to follow the music; though, for
> a long, long time, I did believe that the sounds from
> the piano were made by the fairies and spirits I was
> told lived there. For me there was a mix of joy and
> sorrow in my first music study, for it meant that I
> must live for long periods of the year in Howard
> with Lorna Pollard and her mother, my Aunt Edie,
> far away from my family ... and I was only three.
>   I remember I wrote my first composition when I
> was about five years old. It had an odd title Danc-
> ing on the River and was all on the black notes of
> the piano. I didn't think it was very good at all
> and I was embarrassed and surprised when my
> teacher had me play it for the examiner who came
> once or twice a year to our town.
>   The years that followed were spent, musically
> speaking, in developing my piano technique; I also
> began violin and singing lessons. I worked hard.
> They were busy years too with exams, eisteddfods,
> and concerts. I was successful and winning praise
> and I think I was regarded as something of a small
> prodigy.

In many ways Beath remembers her childhood with both
sorrow and pleasure. She was sad to be away from home and
her sisters but nevertheless everyone was very delighted with
her progress. She took her first piano exam before an examiner from Trinity College, London, when she was 4 years
old. It had been a huge preparation for her and when she
scored a 98 on the exam it didn't mean anything to her since
percentages were not part of her study. She did recall kiss-
ing the examiner.

At the age of 13 she was sent as a boarder to St.
Margaret's School in Brisbane to continue her musical education as a student of Nora Baird, M.B.E. (Member of the
Order of the British Empire). The study of music was an
internal part of her life and she passed many of her exams
and diplomas under the guidance of Miss Baird. Yet, the
conflict of again being away from home and not establishing
herself within the family was an extremely stressful situation
for Betty, which was finally solved when the family moved to
Brisbane and she was allowed to live at home and continue
her studies at St. Margaret's.

During her years at the school she longed to compose
and wrote sad little songs inspired by unrequited love. But
her training was in the field of performance and she was a
finalist in the Australian Broadcasting Company's Concerto
Competitions and Vocal Competitions in 1948 and 1949; at that
time she was also regularly presenting recital programs broadcast by the Australian Broadcasting Commission in their Young
Australia and other special studio presentations.

In 1950 she was awarded The University of Queensland
Music Scholarship (the only music scholarship in Queensland
at the time) and this allowed her to study at the Sydney Conservatorium of Music where she renewed her association with
composer Frank Hutchens. She had been performing his
music since she was 6 years old and had been studying with
him over a period of years when he visited Brisbane. Beath
went to the conservatorium for one year and reflects on that
experience:

> I remember the special thrill I had one day when I
> arrived at the door of Mr. Hutchens' studio to hear
> him playing one of my songs. He had altered the
> bass line and I was tremendously impressed with the

new sound and I was also very surprised when I
saw that he had written the whole thing out again
for me. I still have that manuscript and it is one
of my treasures. I was trained as a performer and
it was beyond my wildest dream that I could write
music.

This was an important period of my life, but unfortunately, after a short time it came to an end.

For too long during my childhood I had been
away from home and for too long during the war I
had not seen my father. So I returned home.

She and John Beath were married in 1953 and they went
to Papua, to live on the tiny island of Abau and then, later,
to Kavieng, New Ireland, where he was a patrol officer. It
was unusual at the time for a woman to go on patrol, but
nevertheless that was exactly what Betty did, and this new
life was an experience that changed her way of thinking.
She heard sounds that were new and different and found the
culture extremely colorful and mysterious which excited her.
She recalls: "For some months I was the only white woman
living on Abau and I was privileged to see the natives paint
their bodies and dance to a music that I had never heard
before."

Beath returned to Australia and when her two children
were old enough to attend school she began full-time studies
at the Queensland Conservatorium in 1965. Since there was
no composing major available at the conservatorium she graduated in 1969 with piano and voice as her principal subjects.
She did study counterpoint, harmony, figured bass and orchestration, but all other aspects of the craft of composing
she learned on her own.

Following graduation Beath worked as an accompanist
on the staff of the Conservatorium of Music in Brisbane and
at the same time as a music specialist at her old school, St.
Margaret's.

In 1970 Beath met and later married David Cox, a writer
and artist. All of her experiences influenced her compositions but three events were special; her work with the singers
at the conservatorium, the musical needs of the students at
St. Margaret's, and her meeting with David became an irresistible catalyst which completely changed her direction.

She said: "My serious work in composition then began in
1972 and it is curious and interesting to me that I became a
young composer when I was almost forty years of age."

Betty Beath and David Cox first collaborated on a 40-
minute opera for children titled Marco Polo in 1972. J. Albert
& Son Pty. Ltd, later published a scaled-down version of
Marco Polo and the editor Dr. Franz Holford became friend
and mentor. The work had an auspicious launching when the
Queensland Opera Company directed by John Thompson took
it on tour throughout Queensland during the school years
1973 and 1974. The professional Queensland Opera Company
has a fine reputation for bringing live theater work to the
children and receive part of their support from The Arts
Council of Australia. Program notes are as follows:

> The Strange Adventures of Marco Polo is an enter-
> taining and educational spectacle. The story of his
> journey is told by the old Marco Polo as he recalls
> his youth and desire to travel. As he commences
> his tale, we see him as a young man, together with
> his father and his uncle, leaving Venice and setting
> off for Asia and the exotic East. The story then
> leaps ahead of them and we meet Kublai Khan, the
> first Mongol Emperor of China, in the splendour and
> magnificence of his court. By this time Marco Polo
> and his company arrive at the Khan's court and
> each then tells of an incident in their journey and
> their life in Venice. However, the call of Venice is
> strong and, to the accompaniment of a large ensemble,
> they leave China and set off towards home, after
> an absence of many years.

In 1973 Beath was invited by Josef Aronoff, conductor
of the Conservatorium Chamber Orchestra, to write a work
for solo voice and orchestra. In This Garden, a cycle of
five songs with pianoforte and orchestral accompaniment, received its world premiere in November 1973, with Aronoff
conducting the orchestra and Queensland soprano Jan Delpratt as soloist. The text is by David Cox and the work was
published in 1976 by J. Albert & Son Pty. Ltd., Sydney.
The first song from this cycle, Spider was selected as a
musical work representing a Queensland woman composer and
was performed at the 1976 International Council of Women Conference in Canada. At later dates the cycle was broadcast

on A.B.C. programs with Jan Delpratt as soloist and Beath
as accompanist. The A.B.C. recorded the work in 1978 to
be considered for future processing to disc and commercial
release. She feels the words are simple, yet evocative
and the music captures the essence. In the same year Sea
Watcher with words by David Cox was commissioned for performance at the Wynnum-Manly Eisteddfod, and this was
published by J. Albert & Son Pty. Ltd. in 1974.

Riddles, a cycle of four songs with text by Cox, was
premiered in 1974 by the Queensland Conservatorium Chamber
Orchestra and tenor Gregory Massingham. Josef Aronoff,
who had requested the work, conducted the performance.
Beath explains why she often chooses texts written by her
husband:

> The text is tremendously important to me and David's
> work always delights me. He has an elegance of
> expression, simplicity, deft technique, humor, and
> always a very real feeling for the subject. He has,
> too, a great regard for words, he enjoys his ma-
> terial, works hard at it and plays with it. He makes
> a search, sometimes a very long one, for the simple,
> 'right' way to say something. Actually, what I
> believe he achieves with words (and illustration) is
> what I hope to do in the setting. I am very much
> aware that the quality of the text has a correspond-
> ing relationship to the quality of the music it pro-
> vokes (this is true for me, at any rate).

In 1974 she was awarded, jointly with her husband, a
Southeast Asian Fellowship from the Literature Board of the
Australian Council which allowed them to spend three months
in Java and Bali where she studied traditional, folk and contemporary music. In 1975 they were awarded a grant by the
Australian Council to carry out further research in Bali and
to gather materials for writing. Beath and Cox are pioneers
in their work toward transcultural expressions and they have
co-produced many projects that are unique in bridging the
cultures they have experienced. "Attempts at Bridging Cultures" was the title of a lecture they gave on their work on
Dec. 3, 1979, when they were invited to speak at the
Taman Ismail Marzuki, the Centre of the Arts, Jakarta. They
collaborated on three outstanding theater pieces during this
period, The Raja Who Married an Angel, Abigail and the

Bushranger and Abigail and the Rainmaker. The following
appeared in Opera Australia in December 1979:

MUSIC THEATRE TWIN BILL FOR QUEENSLAND

The intimate setting of the Brisbane Arts Theatre is
the venue for a double-bill presentation of two music
pieces by Brisbane composer, Betty Beath, and her
husband-librettist, David Cox.

Performances of The Raja Who Married an Angel
and Abigail and the Rainmaker are being presented
at the Arts Theatre until December 22, as part of
the pre-Christmas program of the theatre, home of
one of Brisbane's most active drama companies.

The Raja Who Married an Angel is taken from
Indonesian legend and concerns Raja Pala, his faithful servant K'Tut, and the smallest angel, Supraba.

David Cox and Betty Beath were commissioned to
create a music theatre work for schools by the Australian Schools Commission, Canberra. The work
has now been published by Playlab Press.

The composers made two visits to Indonesia
sponsored by the Australia Council, to collect au-
thentic material for their work and to observe the
music, musical instruments, costumes, characteristics
and legends of the people.

Most of the cast of 15 came from the Arts Theatre
junior workshops and include Len Crook (story-
teller), Michelle Searle (old woman), Sean Riordan
(Raja Pala) and Robyn Finken (bride of the Raja).

The same cast makes a quick change of costume
and character to take part in the contrasting work
on the program, Abigail and the Rainmaker, which
is set in outback Australia. It is a happy linking
of cultures through music.

Jonathan Papa, Director of Lyric Theatre at Northern
Iowa University, reviewed The Raja Who Married an Angel
for Opera for Youth News, Volume VI, No. 2, 1983:

The latest offering from Playlab Press of Brisbane,
Australia is The Raja Who Married an Angel, a music
theatre piece for children by Betty Beath and David
Cox. This distinguished husband and wife team is
responsible for several delightful works for young

performers and young audiences, which are fortunately becoming more widely known in this country.
Since this particular piece is based on a Balinese
legend, Beath and Cox were awarded a research
grant from the Literature Board of the Australian
Council for travel to Indonesia where they studied
and absorbed the culture which they subsequently
represented in music and drama.

The story tells us of Raja Pala, an arrogant king,
who while hunting in the forest with his faithful
servant K'Tut comes upon seven angels who have
descended to earth to bathe in a beautiful pool.
While bathing, the angels have hung their wings on
the surrounding bushes. From the moment he sees
her, Raja Pala falls in love with the youngest angel
Supraba. The angels hear the two men and scramble
after their wings. Raja Pala and K'Tut manage to
seize Supraba's wings before she can retrieve them
and she is trapped on earth. Raja Pala offers to
give her back her wings if she will agree to marry
him. Supraba consents, but says that she can only
stay on earth for six years. During her six years
as a mortal wife Supraba manages to bring love to
many people and learns of the beauty of the earth.
After she returns to heaven Raja Pala becomes a
holy man and eventually joins his love.

The Raja Who Married an Angel is written as a
total learning experience for the young performers
and audience. The story is told by three old men
to a circle of Balinese villagers and makes good use
of solo and group numbers (both sung and spoken)
in verse. The characters are well drawn and the
plot is clear and concise with a charming blend of
comedy, romance and local color. Production problems are minimal since the environment is often suggested through actor movement. In fact, librettist
David Cox has illustrated the performing edition with
ideas for settings and costumes which can be easily
and inexpensively procured by students.

The score is written to reflect the music of Bali
and the "orchestra" consists of recorders, gongs,
glockenspiels and other percussion instruments which
suggest the Balinese gamelan. The vocal line is
simple and usually quite lyrical. Students could
easily sing and play the score to The Raja Who

Married an Angel, and in doing so, learn about one
type of non-Western music.

To extend the learning experience, Beath and
Cox have prepared a booklet called Reflections from
Bali which accompanies the performance materials.
This social studies reader introduces students to
Bali, discussing the traditions, culture, livelihoods,
arts and religion of the island. The booklet is quite
well prepared and could function as excellent sup-
plementary material for a complete learning experience
about Bali in conjunction with the production.

The Raja Who Married an Angel is an excellent
educational piece for production by young people
for young people. The show is well written and challenging for students, but at the same time it offers
quality learning experiences and artistic stimulation
to those involved. The target age group for actor
and audience would probably be grades 4-8, although
these parameters might be extended on both ends.
The duration of the piece is about 35 minutes and
the cast size is anywhere from 15 to 25 boys and
girls, equally mixed.

Abigail and the Rainmaker was performed at the Kennedy
Arts Center in the United States sponsored by Opera For
Youth and was included in the 1986 Season of Children's
Theatre at the Brisbane Arts Theatre. The work is published
by J. Albert & Son. The Raja Who Married an Angel has had
numerous performances throughout Australia and the editor
of Book Reviews wrote, "If you are building up a collection
of multicultural resource material, this is a must." The work
is published by Playlab Press, Ashgrove, Queensland.

The slim volume of poems by Carmen Bernos de Gasztold, The Beasts' Choir, was an unexpected gift handed to
Beath as she was leaving a dinner party. She set five of
the 26 poems to music in her song cycle by the same title
that has become one of her most performed works. The world
premiere was given at a Composers' Concert at the Queensland
Conservatorium with Jan Delpratt, soprano and Regis Danillon,
pianist in 1979. Songs From The Beasts' Choir were programmed in Ireland at the Hugh Lane Gallery by the contemporary
chamber music ensemble Concorde directed by Jane O'Leary.
Beath's cycle was the only work presented that was not written by an Irish composer. The program was reviewed in The
Irish Times on Oct. 2, 1984, by James Maguire (excerpt):

Betty Beath's <u>Songs from the Beasts' Choir</u> was of
a neatly complementary character to Mr. Buckley's
item. Faithfully setting a short series of prayers
(written by a nun) in which various members of the
animal kingdom tell God of their plight and their
ultimate ambitions. Ms. Beath catches the innocence
and profundity of each with an almost Brittenesque
feel for words. The composer was sympathetically
served by the delicate and meticulous accounts by
Anne Woodworth (mezzo-soprano) and Jane O'Leary.

Beath was particularly pleased when the songs were
given an American premiere at Carnegie Recital Hall in New
York by Ronana Gales and later performed at Symphony
Space. She received an invitation to be the resident com-
poser for the St. Bernard Performing Arts Ensemble in New
York.

Beath composed <u>Indonesian Triptych</u>, a cycle of three
songs for medium voice and piano to the poems by leading
Indonesian poet, Goenawan Mohamad. The work was performed at the Queensland Conservatorium of Music, Queensland University and the Darling Downs Institute of Advanced
Education. Broadcasts include A.B.C. National program with
Helen McKinnon as soloist, A.B.C. Queensland, with Jan Del-
pratt as soloist and 4MBS and 4ZZZ local stations in Queens-
land. The cycle has been recorded by A.B.C. with a view
to future processing to disc and commercial release.
The first American performance was given by the North-
South Consonance on April 23, 1986, in their Chapel Concert
Series held in the historic First Unitarian Church, Brooklyn
Heights, N.Y.

Betty Beath has been a member of the International
League of Women Composers for many years and has been an
active member of the executive board for the past several
years. In 1982 she developed a project that would have a
far reaching effect on contemporary music in Australia when
she approached Brisbane Radio Station 4MBS-FM, who special-
ize in broadcast of fine music and had previously produced
two programs of her music, to consider a program featuring
the work of women composers throughout the world. She accepted the responsibility of gathering the material and providing appropriate biographical and program notes. Gary Thorpe,
chairman of the Board of Directors, was airing a regular two-

hour monthly series for the International Society of Contemporary Music and was very pleased with Beath's idea and agreed to include a regular segment on the works of women composers. The program was so successful that it was extended to a one-hour time slot during prime listening time.

Unfortunately there has been little composition in Queensland by Queenslanders. Until recently there were no composition degrees offered in the colleges and universities and there are very few opportunities for the publication of serious music. Beath said:

> So, in the end, the purpose in this project of bringing the work of contemporary women composers to my country begins to appear to be not just the edification of the composers whose works are heard, though many, with great humility, express that edification, not simply to bring the music to radio listeners--the end objective, as I see it, is to create an atmosphere in my land where new music can develop and blossom. What will follow? If anything does we shall be grateful to our world of women composers who help to make it possible.
>
> And so, in addition to the broadcasts of discs and tapes sent from abroad, there will also be live performances of the works of international women composers by Australian performers. From the beginning of this project a major ingredient of its success has been the initiative and imagination of Gary Thorpe and his ever-growing interest in the works of women composers.
>
> Another interesting development is that a number of works from the ILWC Project Broadcasts have already been heard a second and a third time. Almost all of the material sent is now lodged in the 4MBS library which provides a unique collection of women's work from women composers around the world. From this collection works are now selected for programming in the station's regular time-table.
>
> Although the project began from 4MBS-FM Brisbane, monthly programs are also broadcast from 3MBS-FM Melbourne. 2MBS-FM Sydney will participate in the ILWC Project with a program broadcast in August 1986.

Kudos to Betty Beath for her work on behalf of women
composers from around the world.   Programs such as those
developed in her project are essential if women composers are
going to take their rightful place on the roster of contemporary
music.   Now, if only other countries will expand on Beath's
project, a powerful network of support will develop.

The Brisbane Baroque Trio commissioned Beath in 1982
to write Piccolo Victory, Images of Colonial Australia.   The
work received its world premiere by Gary Williams, cello,
Adelaide Brown, flute-piccolo and Mary Mageau, harpsichord,
all members of the Brisbane Baroque Trio.   John Villaume
reviewed the concert for The Courier Mail on April 27, 1982
(excerpt):

> Perhaps the most striking piece was Betty Beath's
> Piccolo Victory, Images of Colonial Australia.
>   This sought to play off suggestions of Aboriginal
> music against fragments of the songs the first colo-
> nists brought with them; its effectiveness was en-
> hanced by the unscheduled exposition of the didgeri-
> doo as a prologue.

When the work was recorded by the Brisbane Baroque
Trio for Grevillia Records, Beath wrote a prologue and epilogue which she scored for the didgeridoo played by Harry
Wilson.   The following is an excerpt from program notes written by Dr. Stuart Collins:

> As the title suggests the work evokes a variety of
> images depicting colonial Australia.   The principal
> episodes include the arrival of the first settlers and
> the lament of a convict.   Later there are suggestions
> of folk-melody while, in the penultimate episode the
> cello has a theme derived from Waltzing Matilda.
> The work begins and ends with an Aboriginal theme
> which is also used to link the episodes.   Piccolo
> Victory was originally scored for piccolo, flute,
> cello, harpsichord, rhythm sticks and side-drum,
> though the latter turns out to be the cello in dis-
> guise.   For this recording the opportunity was taken
> of including the didgeridoo as a prologue and epilo-
> gue to the work.   Betty Beath sketches evocative
> images with economy of gesture and empathy.   More-
> over she melds together a variety of diverse musical

materials--modal, whole-tone, diatonic and encompasses them all with the haunting Aboriginal theme
and didgeridoo, resulting in a work that speaks directly and with sympathy.

In 1984 Betty Beath and Ann Carr-Boyd were the two
Australian composers sponsored by the Australian Fellowship
of Composers to attend the Third International Congress On
Women In Music in Mexico City and the Concert Tour and Re-
treat in the State of Zacatecas. The Congress was co-chaired
by Jeannie Poole and Beverly Grigsby from the United States
and concentrated on the work of women composers throughout
the world. Hundreds of composers, musicians and writers
from Mexico, Australia, France, Norway, Germany, Spain,
Japan, Venezuela, the United States and Indonesia were in
attendance making this Congress the strongest and most active organization of its kind in the world today.

Beath and Ann Carr-Boyd presented papers, tapes,
live performances, and introduced a film on outstanding Australian women in music produced by Adele Sztar. Their
presentations were of enormous interest to the delegates including me. I knew then that my series of books on the accomplishments of women in the 20th-century musical arena would
never be complete without the inclusion of the talented Australian women composers. In 1986 I went to Australia to
interview some of their talented composers who will be included in this volume as well as a future volume.

The Australian Fellowship of Composers can be proud
of the work accomplished in their behalf by Beath and Carr-
Boyd at the Congress. It was disappointing to find no representative at the next International Congress held in Atlanta,
Ga. in 1986.

Betty Beath is a remarkable woman who has genuinely
contributed to the artistic growth of her country. Her compositions are transcultural and defy categorization as defined
by Western standards. She has been influenced by her experiences in Indonesia, Bali, Java and indeed Asia but believes her music to be essentially Australian in character.
For whatever reason the listener is attracted to the beauty
and content of her work. She responds to her writing by
saying:

There are always influences and I think we naturally
select what we will use most successfully. I find
myself 'listening' much of the time.... I'm interested
in 'new'work and 'new sounds' a wonderful discovery,
even though they may be ancient--like the gamelan
in Bali and Java or the sounds of a corroboree.

Recent works, Yunggamurra and The Ninya (both works
setting words by the distinguished Australian writer, Patricia
Wrightson, O.B.E.) relate to the Australian Aboriginal culture.

Yunggamurra, for soprano, cello and flute was given a
first American performance when it was included in a recital
program on March 21, 1986 at the Fourth International Congress of Women in Music held in Georgia. The Ninya for
soprano, two-part choir, instrumental ensemble, dancer, tape
and slides was commissioned by St. Margaret's Girls' School,
Brisbane in 1985 and given a first performance in the Festival
of Australian Music, an annual musical event, which takes
place at the school, running over two days in early October.
The Festival was developed to sponsor the work of Australian
composers with the special feature the first performance of a
work commissioned by the school for performance by student
musicians.

On the subject of composers Beath had this to say:

I'm very much aware that there needs to be a good
spirit between the composers of Brisbane--of Queens-
land--of Australia--and then you can establish an
international network too. But I think that because
we are here, say, in Brisbane, we've got to be
concerned with the composers here, they need to
be supported. We should support one another. It
should be very strong and an important thing for
us to know what is happening with our fellow composers, to give opportunities for performance, to
work together, strongly, to create a platform, and
this can be done. I know that it can work successfully ... there is room for each voice to be heard
and I think we should open the doors to create the
possibility for those voices to be heard. I'm sure
that we have a responsibility to bring forward others
working with composition because it will strengthen

that whole area, it will make the public more aware,
there will be the enthusiasm that we muster ... performers, of course, are part of this bringing forward
of new music and the excitement of recreating new
works because they're bringing them forward--they
have a recreational role don't they? One really
can't exist without the other.

Quoting from the closing paragraphs of a Keynote Address by Jeannie Poole, founder of the International Congress
on Women in Music, given at the Opus 3: Women in Music
Conference held at the University of Kansas in March 1985:

We owe these foremothers several things because
they struggled and worked for us on our behalf, as
they created more opportunities for themselves. We
owe them the respect and honor of not duplicating
their efforts. We owe them not to repeat their mis-
takes, but to pursue their honorable and meritorious
goals. We should conduct our activities with dignity
and professionalism, bringing into the service of
our cause that powerful and winning combination of
talent, vision and perseverance.
Among us today are leaders for the movement ...
Nancy Van de Vate, Judith Lang Zaimont, Siegrid
Ernst (Germany), Elizabeth Klein (Norway and Denmark), Betty Beath (Australia), Denise Laroutis
(Paris) and too many more to mention here.

Selected Compositions of Betty Beath

Solo Voice

1974 Seawatcher, for solo voice with words by David Cox,
          published by J. Albert & Son Pty. Ltd.
1975 Three Cautionary Songs, words by David Cox, com-
          missioned by Twelfth Night Theatre, Brisbane.
1978 Given the Time, for solo voice and piano, words by
          Franz Holford.
1978 Songs From the Beasts' Choir, a cycle of five songs
          for voice and piano, translations by Rumer Godden
          of poems by Carmen Bernos de Gasztold.
1978 Indonesian Triptych, a cycle of five songs for voice
          and piano, words by the Indonesian poet, Goenawan
          Mohamad.

1983 <u>Nawang Wulan</u> and <u>Manusia Pertama Di Angkasa Luar</u>,
     settings of two poems by the Javanese poet, Subagio
     Sastrowardojo.

Choral

1981 <u>Walking in Sunshine</u>, six two-part vocalise with piano
     accompaniment, published by ASMUSE.
1985 <u>The Ninya</u>, for soprano soloist, two-part female choir,
     flute, bassoon, piano, cello, double bass, rhythm
     sticks, unpitched drum, triangle, cymbal and tape
     (optional), words by Patricia Wrightson, O.B.E.

Chamber

1975 <u>Askesis</u>, for soprano and piano; also an arrangement
     for soprano harpsichord, cello and percussion, words
     by Günter Grass.
1975 <u>The Cry</u>, for soprano and piano; also an arrangement
     for soprano harpsichord, cello and percussion, words
     by Tadashi Amano.
1976 <u>In This Garden</u>, a cycle of five songs for medium voice
     and piano accompaniment. Also an arrangement for
     solo voice and chamber orchestra, words by David
     Cox, published by J. Albert & Son Pty. Ltd.
1976 <u>In the Carnarvon Ranges</u>, for voice, pianoforte and
     rhythm sticks, words by David Cox.
1977 <u>Poems From the Chinese</u>, for solo voice, clarinet, cello
     and piano, translated from the Chinese by Kenneth
     Rexroth.
1981 <u>Three Psalms</u>, (Psalm 23, Psalm 121, and Psalm 150,
     for voice, flute, harp and cello; also arranged for
     voice and piano.
1984 <u>Yunggamurra</u>, for voice and piano or voice, flute and
     cello, a setting of prose and verse by Patricia
     Wrightson, O.B.E.

Orchestra and Voice

1974 <u>Riddles</u>, a cycle of four songs for solo voice and or-
     chestra.

Instrumental

1982 Piccolo Victory, Images Of Colonial Australia, for pic-
      colo, flute, harpsichord, cello, rhythm sticks and
      side drum, commissioned by the Brisbane Baroque
      Trio.

Keyboard

1983 Black On White, piano piece for left hand. Commis-
      sioned by Shirley Harris, Director, The Harbor
      Conservatory for her second collection of Piano
      music for one hand alone.

Theatre Music

1972 Marco Polo, music drama for children with book by
      David Cox. This work was scaled down from the
      opera The Strange Adventures of Marco Polo, pub-
      lished by J. Albert & Son Pty. Ltd.
1974 Francis, one-act music drama with book by David Cox,
      published by ASMUSE, publishing body of the Au-
      stralian Society for Music Education.
1976 Abigail And The Bushranger, musical story for child-
      ren's voices and percussion, story by David Cox,
      published by J. Albert & Son Pty. Ltd.
1976 Abigail And The Rainmaker, musical story for children's
      voices and percussion, story by David Cox, pub-
      lished by J. Albert & Son Pty. Ltd.
1979 The Raja Who Married An Angel, one-act music drama,
      arising out of research made in Indonesia. The play
      is based on the Balinese version of a folk story
      which is common to all the islands of the Indonesian
      Archipelago, book by David Cox, published by Play-
      lab Press.
1983 Procession, A March Of Celebration ... The March Of
      The Bunyip, a musical event for untrained musicians,
      commissioned and performed throughout Queensland
      by The Children's Activities Groups Association.
1984 Abigail And The Mythical Beast, two-act music drama
      for children, words by David Cox. Work is scored
      for voices and piano and for voices with chamber
      orchestra, commissioned by St. Margaret's Girls'
      School, published by Cockatoo Capers.

1986   Abigail and the Bushranger, arranged in a version for
         voices with piano accompaniment, published by
         Cockatoo Capers.

1986   Abigail and the Rainmaker, arranged in a version for
         voices with piano accompaniment, published by
         Cockatoo Capers.

1986   The Sermon To The Birds/La Predica Agli Uccelli, two
         arrangements of this work. 1. Solo soprano voice
         with alto voice or alto choir and instrumental en-
         semble (flute, amplified acoustic, guitar and strings).
         2. Solo soprano voice with alto voice or alto choir
         and piano accompaniment. Both the English transla-
         tion and the original Italian text are used. Solo
         part is sung in the English translation and the alto
         voice or choir sung in Italian. Words: Giovanni
         Pascoli. English translation--John Gransden.

Addresses of Publishers

ASMUSE, 139 Musgrave Road, Red Hill, Queensland, Australia.

Australia Music Centre, P. O. Box 49, Broadway, NSW 2089,
      Australia.

J. Albert & Son Pty. Ltd., 7-11 Ranger Road, Neutral Bay,
      NSW 2089, Australia.

Playlab Press, P. O. Box 185, Ashgrove, Queensland 4069,
      Australia.

Cockatoo Capers, 8 St. James Street, Highgate Hill 4101,
      Queensland, Australia.

Discography

Piccolo Victory, Images of Colonial Australia. Brisbane Baro-
      que Trio: Adelaide Brown, flute/piccolo; Gary Williams,
      cello; Mary Mageau, Harpsichord; Harold Wilson, did-
      geridoo. Grevillea Records.

Address

Grevillea Records, 26B Wallace St., Albion, Queensland, Australia.

ANNE BOYD

Composer

The vibrant and gifted Ann Boyd was one of the second
generation of Australian-born women to establish her credentials as a 20th-century composer within her own country.
For many years the isolation of the country from the great
music centers of the world was considered to be a detriment
to an artistic career. It had been necessary for older composers to first receive recognition overseas before acceptance
at home. Boyd and her contemporaries realized that the
European cultural tradition was inappropriate for them in
their quest for originality. Australian music flourishes today
because of the commitment of Boyd and her contemporaries to
express in their music the multicultural traditions that exist
in the country. Australian composers found their own individuality only late in the 20th century when they fully
realized that they no longer had to write music in the European tradition to be accepted.

Boyd was born in Sydney, Australia, in 1941 but when
her father died her mother was unable to support the family
of three children and she was sent to live with her aunt at
Maneroo at the age of 3 1/2. Maneroo was an isolated sheep
station in remote central Queensland. The schooling for Anne
and her two cousins who lived on the property was by correspondence which was overseen by Aunt Rita. Boyd said,
"living in that kind of isolation children with creative abilities
develop them because there is little else to do." When she
was 5 years old her sister sent her a recorder and a teach-
yourself book for Christmas. This gift was especially important for the talented young Anne, who taught herself to
play the instrument and to compose her first pieces using
drawings and symbols that to her represented music. Listening to the radio provided her with the only link to the outside

ANNE BOYD   Photo by
                             John Carewe

world for much of each year. Each day she would listen to
the A.B.C. Children's Hour and every Thursday 10 minutes
of Mr. Melody Man. These radio programs were tremendously
important for her and some years later she received the A.B.C.
Children's Hour Commonwealth Music Award for her composition of Air and Variation for flute and piano.

As a child Boyd spent much of the time amusing herself by writing stories, plays, poems and drawing and painting. She said, "I suppose I was a bit of a show-off since I
loved to organize entertainment and plays for special occasions
at Maneroo. The jackeroos who lived on the property came

to a formal dinner once a week and whenever she could make
arrangements she would direct her cousins and any other
willing participants in entertainment and plays for the occasion. Living in the Australian bush provided her an independence in seeking ways to nurture her creative interests.

Her fondest childhood memories were the holidays she
spent once a year with her mother who somehow managed to
save the money, from her meager salary at a private boys
school, to pay her air-fare so they could be together. Her
mother worked at the school so she could provide Anne's
brother with a good education. During these holidays her
mother always encouraged her to continue her musical activities and dramatic presentations and early on predicted that
Anne's career would be in either drama or music.

When Anne was 11 years old she went to Sydney to
live with her mother and began her formal education. Shortly
after she arrived her mother died and it was a tragedy that
would strongly affect her for the remainder of her life. She
was an orphan who had lost both her parents in the first
few years of her life and the isolation which she had learned
to cope with in bush country continued, for she was isolated
in her own world without the love, understanding and encouragement of parents.

She was boarded with friends of her sister so she could
continue with school and the family put together a small fund
for her education including one year of private piano lessons.
She said, "I studied piano with a Hungarian woman who introduced me to Bartok and Bach and I loved it. They were the
first proper music lessons that I had ever had and it was
bliss, absolute bliss."

When she entered Hornsby Girls High School she began
to play the school-owned flute and she gave up her treasured
piano lessons because there was not enough money for her
to continue with both instruments. Playing the flute and
writing music became an emotional outlet that helped compen-
sate for the loss of her mother. These were troubled years
for the young artist and she immersed herself in performing
and writing for every instrument she could find. Her music
teachers were very encouraging, especially Victor McMahon
with whom she studied flute. Although he did not rate her
potential as a flutist as highly as she thought she could

achieve she scored unexpectedly high marks in her school
exams and won a Commonwealth Scholarship to the University
of Sydney where she could have studied any subject she
chose. But McMahon encouraged her to study composition.
He said, "I am not qualified to tell you how far you will go
as a composer but I think it is best suited for your temperament, open your horizons as much as possible and do an arts
degree."

Boyd attended the University of Sydney and studied
English literature, philosophy, psychology and education and
met a variety of interesting people. During her first year
at the university she continued her music lessons at the
conservatory, thinking she might teach music at some point
in the future. Before graduating she took a year off from
the university to play in the Australian Ballet Orchestra.
Of that experience she relates:

> I got it out of my system and found I hated playing
> in the "pit" orchestra. It was boring, hard work
> and I felt drab, uninspired and nothing contributed
> to a creative fire at all. I couldn't wait to get back
> to the university.

The University of Sydney had a fine music department
which was established under Professor Donald Peart whom
Boyd describes as a "marvelous eccentric Englishman who
always encouraged his students to take an imaginative account
of the fact that they were Australians." He also encouraged
them to see music as a world phenomenon and that European
music was only a part of it. For Boyd this proved to be
some of the best advice she had ever been offered.

Boyd received a broad education and was afforded an
opportunity to study with musicians of considerable repute.
When Peter Sculthorpe, a young composer, arrived to take
the post of lecturer in the music department many of the
undergraduate students of composition felt that this was the
most exciting thing that could have happened to them and
the university. Boyd explains:

> Peter Sculthorpe, more than anyone else, showed
> the students what it was to be a living composer.
> Here suddenly there was a live composer working
> in our midst. Composition was always the focus of

what he had to say and he always related music to
his own work as a composer. He was narcissistic
and egocentric but then what composer in the Western world was not narcissistic? From Beethoven on,
Western music has been nutured by the cult of the
ego.

Sculthorpe's classes in composition and ethnomusicology
were of tremendous importance to Boyd's development. The
ethnomusicology class introduced her to a wide spectrum of
non-Western music that has strongly influenced her composing. Studying composition with Sculthorpe was another new
experience for her. Although his teaching and ideas were
most important to Boyd's musical development his personal
philosophy was a detriment to her. When he saw, by chance,
the graphic scores that she had created as a child he was
marvelously encouraging and excited by the fact that a student was writing in this manner without ever having received
instruction. But Sculthorpe proved to be a male chauvinist
and often stated that he did not think women could write
music, although he did agree that Boyd might prove him
wrong, which she did. (When he joined her in a film made
some 12 years later on the accomplishments of women composers, with hindsight he praised her work and her ability
to write with modern structures.) Although Boyd and Sculthorpe have had some differences of opinion she is quick to
defend him as an enormously generous friend and her music
is greatly influenced by his. She said, "Peter is possibly
the most important single influence on my life and work."

Anne Boyd was also discriminated against when the male
students of her generation received all the opportunities to
write for the ABC Orchestra. She said, "I am just as sure,
as I am sitting here, that it was the direct result of sheer
prejudice against women writing music." But Boyd was not
only talented, she was a survivor and graduated with a rare
first-class honors from the university, receiving the Frank
Albert Prize for Music.

Anne Boyd was too good to be denied and her music
was performed and enthusiastically received throughout the
1960s. Exegesis No. I scored for four flutes and two pic-
colos was premiered at the National Music Camp in Geelong
soon after it was written in 1964. The following year her
Trio for oboe, clarinet and bassoon was performed at the

National Music Camp in Melbourne. Before she graduated
from the university she stunned the music department with
her brilliant scoring and notation for Nocturnal Images written
for a collection of junk and objects found in Sydney. In
1965 she wrote The Creation for five recorders and percussion
that was premiered at the Australian UNESCO Seminar and in
1966 The Fall of Icarus, for flute, cello, clarinet and piano
was heard at the prestigious Adelaide Festival of the Arts.

Boyd's early compositions were influenced by the music
and philosophy of John Cage, Asian music, particularly
Japanese, and medieval music since she has written her thesis
on the Medieval Aspects of Contemporary Music. She freed
her music from conventional tonality and the restrictions of
European traditions with her brilliant writing and imaginative
scoring for instrumental combinations. The works she composed during this period were original and memorable; her
music flourished as Australian music flourished with a taste
and character of its own.

During this period she spent an enormous amount of
her time and energy in behalf of all kinds of musical organizations for she knew that any changes in Australian music
would need to begin with the grass roots approach. She
served as the secretary of the Pro Musica Society of the university, organized concerts for the local chapter of International Society for Contemporary Music, arranged the first
experimental concert based on the philosophy of John Cage
where she performed the Australian premiere of his classic
example of pure nonmusic, 4'33", in which the role of silence
and the unpredictable background noises are always present.
In 1968 she devoted her energy to preparing, in collaboration
with Professor Donald Peart, Australia's first contemporary
music journal, Music Now.

Boyd's compositional output was rather large during
the 1960s as she wrote some 30 chamber works including the
music for a 30-minute documentary, Shineberg, for the ABC.
She was commissioned by Ballet Australia to write The Stair-
way, based on a story by Charles Higham. Alma Redemptoris,
written for two choirs and two pianos, was premiered in 1968
at the Adelaide Festival of the Arts, at an International Society of Contemporary Music concert, was considered by many
music critics to be her most impressive work incorporating
medievalism and Asian music.

She was active in the Vietnam Moratorium movement
and was commissioned by the Vietnam Arts Festival in Sydney
to compose a work, Tu Dai Oan, (The Fourth Generation), a
string quartet based on a Vietnamese folk song which Boyd
wrote for the festival. She sets the record straight with
the following comments:

> The critics wrote that I had found my style with
> this piece but that was not true, I found my style
> with a later work. I actually wrote the quartet in
> a response to a challenge that Peter Sculthorpe
> sent me. I still don't believe in the piece, I think
> it's much too derivative of Webern.
> Tu Dai Oan is a semi-serial technique in the
> service of an Asian theme. It's really serialization
> of a Vietnamese folk song, five notes and seven
> notes and built upon five transpositions. I serialized
> the rhythm as well and it is a very intricate piece.
> It was the first time I serialized anything because I
> didn't believe in it as a technique which suited me.

In 1969 Anne Boyd received the first Commonwealth
Overseas Grant for composition and she chose to study for
her Doctor of Philosophy degree at York University in Great
Britain because Wilfrid Mellers was the professor who had
been in Australia in 1965 encouraging students to attend
York. Boyd said, "There weren't many schools at the time
where one could go and compose for three years." She admired Mellers' interest in Australian composers and the university hosted several of them when Boyd was in attendence.
The university was a wonderful and exciting place for her to
be and she was determined, like most Australian musicians of
her generation, not to subscribe to what was European musical convention but rather to find a way to express in her
work the Australian culture.

The music department at the university had many young
composers on the staff including Bernard Rands, a recent
recipient of the Pulitzer Prize in the United States. Although
Rands was a bit hesitant to work with Boyd because of her
already established reputation as a composer, she found working with him important and stimulating.

Under Rands' guidance, she wrote what she considers
to be her most important piece of music using Etenraku as

the major source of inspiration. The Voice of the Phoenix is
scored for orchestra, amplified solo piano, guitar, harp,
harpsichord, 10 percussion players, augmented woodwinds
and an electronic musical instrument designed for live performance. When Boyd heard the premiere performed by the
York University Orchestra in 1971 conducted by Bernard
Rands, she knew she had found her voice as an Australian
composer, what she had to say, and how to express it. The
excerpts from her program notes on The Voice of the Phoenix:

> I first conceived the idea of writing an orchestral
> work based on gagaku, the ancient court music of
> Japan, about five years ago when I was a student
> in Peter Sculthorpe's ethnomusicology class in the
> Music Department at the University of Sydney. Dur-
> ing a course on Japanese music he played a record-
> ing of the gagaku orchestra of the Imperial Japanese
> Court performing Etenraku. I was immediately fasci-
> nated by the strange, centuries-old, yet somehow
> timeless, static quality of this music; by the weirdly
> beautiful and exotic sonorities of an orchestra com-
> prised of wind, string and percussion instruments
> which, unlike the instruments of our Western sym-
> phony orchestras, have remained in a non-evolu-
> tionary state in some cases for thousands of years.
> I was struck too by the perfection and subtlety of
> the performing technique of the musicians dedicated
> to the preservation of this ancient and beautiful
> music.
>
> My impression of this music seemed to me to be
> related to my experience as a child in the landscape
> of out-back Australia, a feeling of remoteness in the
> harsh yet compelling beauty of an ancient continent
> in which man and his imported animals and machines
> battled for survival against the much stronger ele-
> mental forces of the natural environment. The
> phoenix, the mythical bird which is destroyed by
> fire and is re-created from its own ashes seems to
> me to symbolize this life-death struggle of man to
> achieve harmony within the mysterious cycle of na-
> ture. It is this concept which underlies my or-
> chestral piece The Voice of the Phoenix.

As the result of this premiere two important musicians
of the time, the American composer Morton Feldman and

British composer Harrison Birtwistle, became interested in
her career and gave her support and encouragement. Birtwistle conducted The Metamorphoses of a Solitary Female
Phoenix, which she wrote in 1971, at the important Dartington Summer School of Music and at the equally important 40th-
anniversary season of the Macnaghten Concerts on Oct. 5,
1971. Leslie East reviewed the concert for Music and Musicians, v.20, January 1972 (excerpt):

> ...The most impressive works were two that exploited
> the instruments' intrinsic qualities. And, as a mere
> male, it is a pleasure to be able to report that both
> were by women. Anne Boyd's The Metamorphoses of
> a Solitary Female Phoenix was one work in which ef-
> fects did not seem forced and self-conscious and
> she evidently has an ear for pleasing unhackneyed
> sonorities which in Metamorphoses are attuned to a
> fascinating formal progression.

An important work completed at York was The Rose
Garden, an hourlong experiment in music theatre work to
a text by the English poet Robin Hamilton. The musical
drama is scored for several groups of performers, including
electronic sequences, double choirs, solo soprano, speaking
voices, percussion, organ, guitars, flutes and actors. The
following is the first paragraph of Boyd's extensive program
notes for The Rose Garden:

> The Rose Garden is intended as a ritual concerned
> with the search for a higher spiritual meaning or
> purpose in life and in death. The performers are
> the celebrants, the audience are the participants
> and these two are linked in an inseparable relation-
> ship with the Rose who is both high priestess and
> incarnation of the absolute. The Rose can be imag-
> ined to symbolize achievement (of artistic beauty,
> absolute truth, ultimate sorrows). TO BE. The
> Searcher symbolizes all those who strive for the
> achievement of an ideal--the performers, the audi-
> ence. TO BECOME. The Garden is where the Rose
> is to be found. The world. In the Garden also
> are found all the obstacles which will impede the
> search for the Rose, IS.

In July 1972 the University of York conferred the Doctor of Philosophy Degree on Anne Boyd and she was appointed

as lecturer at the University of Sussex. Boyd's music changed
after she left York.

Although she was never a Zen Buddhist by any stretch
of the imagination, the philosophy of Buddhism did have a big,
influence on her and she has always been interested in reli-
gions of all kinds. Since her interest in music had been very
spiritual it was easy for her to write in a meditative style
during her tenure at the University of Sussex. She said, "I
began to think of music as a tool rather than an art form, a
tool for meditation. If you listen to Angklung which I wrote
in 1974 you will know what I mean."

Angklung was written for pianist Roger Woodward for
whom it is dedicated. It uses only four notes, Bb, Ab, Eb
and Fb and was premiered by Woodward at the 1974 Edinburgh Festival. According to Boyd, "Angklung in its own
curious way is the only perfect piece I ever wrote." When
Katherine Ryder performed the work in Sydney, Australia,
music critic Roger Covell reviewed the concert for The Morning Sydney News, April 9, 1978 (excerpt):

> It is certainly among the most restrained and fasti-
> dious pieces that have ever been written: concede
> physically with it, as if fined to four pitches (one
> of them evidently tuned away from the norm) and
> their octave extensions, in the spirit of a particular
> variety of Indonesian music for shaken bamboo tubes.
>   The composer talks of it as a process of tuning--
> for player and listeners. It is a means of shifting
> our attention from the vast batteries of sound and
> noise that constantly assail us and attending to
> small, limited musical events.
>   A listener with an irreverent turn of mind might
> compare its purgative function with Rossini's sly
> title for one of his late pieces, Hygienic Prelude for
> Morning Use. Angklung is also very beautiful, as
> finely calculated as one of those ancient Chinese or
> Japanese paintings that record the fall of an autumn
> leaf.

Boyd's meditative work for unaccompanied choir, As
I Crossed the Bridge of Dreams, was commissioned under the
terms of the 1975 Radcliffe Trust. The work refers to three
of the dreams from the journal of an 11th-century Japanese

writer, Lady Sarashine, who was interested in spiritual en-
lightment. Musically the work is based on the sound of the
sho, the Japanese mouth organ, which is the background
sonority to the gagaku and influenced by Etenraku. It was
first performed in Wigmore Hall, London by the John Alldis
Singers, who also performed it during their tour of Australia
several months later. It has been recorded on the EMI label,
number OASD-7629 by the Chamber Choir of the University
of Sydney, conducted by Nicholas Routley.

As I Crossed the Bridge of Dreams marked the end of
Boyd's meditational period and she did not write anymore
significant pieces in that genre. She considers this piece
the culmination of one period of her writing and the beginning
of a search for new expression.

She resigned her lecturing post at the University of
Sussex when she received a Special Purpose Grant from the
Music Board of the Australia Council in 1977. Boyd returned
to Australia, after having lived abroad for eight years, and
came to live in the tiny seaside town of Pearl Beach, about 50
miles north of Sydney. Her challenge was to try to survive as
a freelance composer. Here she met the Korean-born writer,
Don'o Kim, who was a near neighbor. She said, "I was immediately excited by the unique qualities of his writing within which I found a genuine and fertile synthesis of East and
West. His prose, immediate, vital, extraordinarily sensitive
and fascinating in its concise and precisely ordered imagery,
leans toward poetry in spirit." Over a period of time Boyd
and Don'o Kim collaborated on several exciting works.

Boyd felt that the meditative works she had been writing in England would not be well-received in Australia and
she was tired of the style. She was searching for fresh new
inspiration and the works she wrote show quite a stylistic
change. She started to write real melodies, although still
quite pentatonic, usually based on Asian scales, and her
music became much more rhythmic.

In 1978 she was commissioned to write for the Sydney
University Musical Society Centenary Festival and at first
thought she might write a requiem for humanity and civiliza-
tion for the occasion. However, she finally made the decision that the festival should be a celebration and she composed her first major choral work, an oratorio on a text by

Don'o Kim, <u>The Death of Captain Cook</u>. The work is scored
for soprano, tenor, and baritone soloists, three small choirs,
large SATB chorus and full orchestra. She chose Captain
Cook because she loved him dearly as a character and he was
very much alive in her mind. She said, "I think he was a
most beautiful man and I would have loved to have known
him. The sort of man I would have trusted completely--and
there are so few of them."

Not wanting to present just Cook's voyages she and
Don'o Kim spent considerable time on the rocks at Pearl
Beach, bringing the piece to fruition. Their Captain Cook
was an 18th-century view of him as a scientific explorer
mixed with an Aboriginal and Hawaiian perspective and what
drove him as an individual.

Roger Covell who reviewed the premiere for <u>The Sydney</u>
<u>Morning Herald</u>, on Sept. 4, 1978, said in part:

> It represents a growth in vocabulary and scope in
> this composer's career. The choral-orchestral writ-
> ing is uninhibited in colour and emphasis, generous
> in style and forthright in tactics.
> There are fanfare patterns, a metrically taut Ab-
> original section which deliberately approaches Ab-
> original music through European sensibilities, and
> orchestral collision between two disjunct variants of
> <u>Rule, Britannia</u> in the manner of Charles Ives, and
> some sturdy choral marches in nineteenth century
> style. The Hawaii section includes some dazzling
> instrumental constructions.
> The composer and her librettist, Don'o Kim, have
> avoided anything like explicit chronology and nar-
> rative. The six sections of the work take us through
> the moral dilemmas and the violence prompted by
> Cook's explorations in or around Australia, Hawaii
> and Antarctica.
> Writer and composer approach the end of their
> own journey of exploration with settings of the
> phrase "to live and live well together," seeming to
> aspire to the effect of a tentative benediction.
> The musical seed of the work is a little phrase
> in which the eager onset of the first two notes is
> inverted a half-step higher. The impression given
> is of enthusiasm immediately turning over on its

back and disclosing despair. The phrase permeates
the whole score; its verbal counterpart is the word
"information," set and combined in many different
ways.

Her children's opera in two acts, The Little Mermaid,
with text by Robin Lee (English) after Hans Christian Andersen, was completed in 1978. It is a brilliantly atmospheric
adaption of Hans Andersen's well-known story set to music
with strong Asian rhythmic and melodic influences. It was
premiered under the aegis of the University of Wollongong in
1981 and music critic Roger Covell ranked the opera with the
Adelaide Festival performance of Peter Maxwell Davies' work
The Two Fiddlers. He wrote, "It outranks it in some ways,
among other things it provides evidence that an Australian
composer has created one of the best of children's operas,
a work potentially of lasting and universal appeal."

When the opera was presented at the Sydney Opera
House in 1985 it was a sellout well in advance of the six performances. Dr. Covell again reviewed The Little Mermaid
for The Sydney Morning Herald on Aug. 30, 1985 (excerpt):

> Anne Boyd's music makes effective and appropriate
> use of Indonesian gamelan (gong orchestra) pat-
> terns and timbres. When her pentatonic melody
> shapes are transferred to strings they have a ten-
> dency to sound more like Vaughan Williams. The
> song tunes and ensembles are clear, bright, well-
> shaped.
>   This is an attractive score by a gifted Australian
> composer, characteristic in its marriage of candid
> invention with a rather endearing hint of technical
> awkwardness and sufficiently true to its poetic vision
> to rank as one of the most distinguished of child-
> ren's operas.

My Name is Tian for soprano, flute, viola, harp and
percussion was commissioned by the Seymour Group with
financial assistance from The Music Board of the Australian
Council. It is based on the novel by Don'o Kim published
by Angus and Robertson in 1968. It is set in Vietnam from
the days before the defeat of the French at Dien Bien Phu
in May 1954 to the arrival and advance of the Americans from
the early 1960s.

Boyd feels that the innate music in Kim's work provided
her the possibility of a genuine collaboration such as is rare
between artists and they completed four works together. In
this piece, according to Boyd, the music takes as its starting
point the "Tu Dai Oan' melody which threads its way throughout each of the five sections. Each of these is based upon
a single musical mode and arranged around a centrally placed
symmetrical axis. The work is conceived as a simple three-
part song form, A-B-A. Each section is, similarly, a ternary
structure.

The Seymour Group performed My Name is Tian in its
concert titled Music of Many Cultures. The program was reviewed by Fred Blanks for The Sydney Morning Herald on
Aug. 11, 1979 (excerpt):

> The major work, a premiere, was My Name is Tian
> by Anne Boyd--based on a poem about a boy in
> Vietnam by Don'o Kim, and scored for soprano,
> flute, viola, harp and percussion.
>   The treatment is typical of the composer. The
> idiom is Indonesian, with airy, simple, lucid melodies
> which at their best are alluringly pretty and evoca-
> tively poetic, but which practice a frugality of notes
> and originality which sometimes suggests Balinese
> Muzak. Kathy Marsh was the clear, sympathetic
> singer, Graeme Leak the percussionist who drummed
> lively, haunting rhythms.

Her choral symphony Coal River was commissioned by
the Newcastle City Council for the golden jubilee of the Civic
Theatre, Newcastle and scored for orchestra, brass band, a
hundred voice choir and soloists. Boyd again chose Kim as
librettist and the setting depicts Newcastle as a brave city,
the ethos of the working man and pragmatic. Boyd wrote,
"It is, I hope, more than a vehicle for the story of a brave
city. It is my metaphor for hope."

The symphony was premiered in Newcastle and reviewed
by T. H. Naisby for the Newcastle Morning Herald on Nov.
26, 1979:

> Coal River encompasses the growth of the Hunter River
> from its first droplets to its powerful surge into the
> ocean. Moments of lyricism contrast with quite

impressionistic comments on, for instance, Aborigines
and machines.

Indeed, the machine section was marked by a
robot-like precision and monotony in the choir allied
with jazz-like elements in the orchestra.

Details which remain with me are many. I have
three for mention.

There was the most imaginative section, The
Promised Land, a swelling node in the work, in
which Waltzing Matilda was used with unusual apt-
ness. The second was the exciting battle of the
bands in, appropriately, Cartels and Cartels, Unions
and Unions. The third was the unaccompanied vocal
section, Our Earth in Our Care, which was sensi-
tively scored.

The musical thread in the composition was a de-
scending four-note motif that unified the entire
work.

Anne Boyd was commissioned to write a public
piece. That she avoided vulgarity on the one hand
and obscurity on the other indicated an admirable
artistic integrity. [Review courtesy of The Newcastle Herald.]

In 1984 the Flederman Ensemble, specialists in new
music, premiered Boyd's Aboriginal-inspired Kakan for flute,
marimba and piano. In this chamber piece she combines an
impression of Aboriginal music with the landscape of the outback which she is so familiar with from childhood. She loves
the Australian landscape and there is nowhere in the world
that she feels so in tune.

Dr. Anne Boyd was appointed Head of the Music Department at the University of Hong Kong in 1981. She is
ideally placed to bring together the Eastern and Western influences on her music as a teacher and as a composer. In
a short five years the department has developed under her
leadership and now offers a full music degree, the history
and criticism of music from the Renaissance to the present
and the language of music involving both the theoretical and
practical skills. Students can choose among performing, composing and history. She possesses tremendous organizational
skills so necessary in building a solid music department in a
university that had never offered a music major prior to her
appointment.

With her university responsibilities and the birth of
her own daughter Helen-Louise Freda in Hong Kong in 1983,
and the duties of raising her child as a single parent, she
had precious little time to compose. She speaks of her daughter:

> It's hard to quantify Helen-Louise's influence but it
> is certainly the overwhelming important emotional ex-
> perience of my life after the death of my mother
> from which I've still not recovered.
>
> Helen-Louise has already brought me incalculable
> joy and I sometimes tell people that I have to juggle
> four careers simultaneously: mothering, university
> teaching and administration, composing and music
> criticism. I review an average of six concerts per
> month both for the main English language news-
> paper in Hong Kong, The South China Morning
> Post and I have my own column on the Hong Kong
> Philharmonic Orchestra in the TV Times. During
> the recent fascinating and inspiring First Contempo-
> rary Chinese Composers Festival held here, I re-
> viewed all six concerts on consecutive nights.
>
> I've just today (July 18, 1986) completed my
> first composition dedicated to Helen-Louise, A Rain
> Song written for the Hong Kong Children's Choir
> forthcoming tour of Australia. I have plans for
> more compositions I know she would enjoy for this
> medium.
>
> You may note a significant number of my compo-
> sitions in the past have been for children, whom I
> have always loved.
>
> Through Helen-Louise I have discovered LOVE
> which is also linked to the renewal of my Christian
> faith.

She did complete one commission for the Hong Kong
Arts Festival but had to give several commissions away. Her
music is being performed in many countries and she is now
looking forward to the time when she can devote more of her
energies to writing again. When I spoke with Dr. Boyd in
Hong Kong in 1986 she told me:

> I can't tolerate music that doesn't show sensitivity
> to the timbre of the instruments it's written for.

(I insist on this with my students.) One characteristic of my music which is traditional with Asian
composers is that timbre is as important to organization as harmony in the West. The sensitivity to the
color of the instrument must be built into the fabric
of the whole work and that is tremendously important.

Our Vice-Chancellor, to whom the department of
music here at the University of Hong Kong owes its
existence, recently retired and to honor this occasion I composed my first setting of Cantonese Western orchestra and chorus. It was well-received and
will have a very large impact on my future music
written in Hong Kong.

Anne Boyd is the epitome of the 20th-century enlightened woman. She is well-educated, a fine musician, a respected professor and a talented composer. Her music speaks
for itself. I've listened to many of her works; she is a creative discoverer in the musical culture and such expertise is
limitless.

Selected Compositions of Anne Boyd

Chamber

1968   String Quartet No. 1 (Tu Dai Oan).
1971   Voice Of The Phoenix, for woodwind, brass, tympani,
      ten percussion, harp, piano, harpsichord, electric
      guitar, (all amplified) strings, VCS 3 synthesizer.
1971   Metamorphoses Of The Solitary Female Phoenix, for
      wind quintet, piano, and percussion.
1973   As It Leaves The Bell, for piano, two harps and four
      percussion.
1976   As All Waters Flow, for five female voices, seven high
      wind instruments, piano, three tuned percussion and
      gong, text in Sanskrit.
1976   Summer Nights, for alto or counter-tenor, harp, four
      percussion, and strings, text by Christopher Wallace-
      Crabbe.
1977   Bencharong, for strings, seven violins, two viola, two
      violoncellos and double bass.
1978   Goldfish Through Summer Rain, for flute and piano.

1979 My Name is Tian, for soprano, flute, viola, harp, and
        percussion, text by Don'o Kim.
1981 Red Sun, Chill Wind, for flute and piano.
1982 Cycles Of Love, for flute, viola, and cello.
1983 Kakan, for flute, marimba and piano.

Theater Pieces

1970 As Far As Crawls The Toad, for five young percus-
        sionists.
1971 The Rose Garden, for mezzo-soprano, chorus, three
        flutes, two guitars, and six percussions.

Solo Instrumentals

1972 Angklung, for piano.
1980 Angklung 2, for violin.
1980 The Book Of The Bells, for piano.

Operas

1978 The Little Mermaid, children's opera in two acts, for
        eleven roles, BATB chorus, seven wind instruments,
        two percussion ensembles and strings, text by Robin
        Lee (English) after Hans Christian Andersen.
1980 The Beginning Of The Day, opera for children in three
        scenes with two interludes, alto solo, SSA chorus,
        dancer, piano, two percussion or orchestral version.

Choral

1975 As I Crossed A Bridge Of Dreams, for three SATB a
        capella.
1979 The Last Of His Tribe, for SSA a capella.

Oratorio

1978 The Death Of Captain Cook, for soprano, tenor and
        baritone soloists, three small choirs, large SATB
        chorus and full orchestra, text by Don'o Kim.

Choral Symphony

Coal River, for orchestra, brass band, large choir
and soloists.

Address of Publisher

Faber Music Ltd, 3 Queen Square, London, WC1N 3AU, England.

Discography

String Quartet I, Oriel String Quartet, ABC Recording RRCS/
126.
As I Crossed The Bridge Of Dreams, EMI OASD 7629.
Angklung, for solo piano, RCA VRL1-0083.
Goldfish Through Summer Rain; Red Sun, Chill Wind; &
Cloudy Mountain, 2 MBSPM Recording, MBS6.

Addresses

ABC Recording Unit, Australian Broadcasting Commission,
Federal Music Department, GPO Box 487, Sydney, NSW
2001, Australia.

EMI, 301 Castlereach Street, Sydney, NSW 2000, Australia.

2MBSPM Recording, 76 Chandos Street, St. Leonards, NSW
2065, Australia.

RCA Records, 1133 Avenue of the Americas, New York, NY
10036.

SYLVIA CADUFF

Orchestral Conductor

Covert discrimination against women in a male-dominated profession is not uncommon. The sacrosanct position of orchestral conductor has a long history of male domination and until recent years it has been male-exclusive.

In 1966 Swiss-born orchestral conductor Sylvia Caduff was the first woman to win first prize in the Dimitri Mitropoulos International Conducting competition in New York and thus became the first woman to officially conduct the New York Philharmonic as an assistant to Maestro Leonard Bernstein. A noted music critic at that time wrote, "Women conductors are as rare as a dinosaur egg."

Her success in this competition is of special interest since at that time the New York Philharmonic, according to Caduff, had no regular women musicians within the membership of the orchestra and the regulations of the Dimitri Mitropoulos Conducting Competition had to be changed to permit her, a woman, to enter. She said, "I have always been the only woman conductor in all of the competitions that I have entered."

In 1977 she accepted the position of general music director with the Orchestra of the City of Solingen in Germany, thus becoming the first European woman to be appointed a general music director. One must admire capacity and talent for Sylvia Caduff paves the road for other women to be accepted as permanent conductors of noted orchestras. It is a hundred times more difficult for a woman to be appointed general music director of an orchestra than a man and Caduff proves that it is possible to attain such a position if one is dedicated, determined and qualified.

SYLVIA CADUFF

Caduff was born in 1938 in Chur, Switzerland near the Alps that are known as the playground of Europe because of the climate and winter sports. Caduff attended Lucerne Conservatory where she studied piano and music theory because she knew even then that she would be a conductor. Her comment, "I knew I would be a conductor not a pianist because the piano didn't give me enough musical colors and possibilities to express what I had in my mind as to what music should be." At the time the young Caduff knew only one woman conductor, a French-Swiss musician from Geneva who had received her diploma from the Paris Conservatory. All the newspapers published articles on her since she was the first woman in Switzerland to reach the status of a professional conductor. Caduff said, "When I read about this conductor I at least knew that a woman could make it on the podium. Everyone thought I was crazy because I was a girl and the male musicians would not want to follow me. They also thought I was not strong enough because conducting was a man's job."

    She was not able to pursue her dream immediately since
her parents insisted that she study "a more female profession" where she would be certain to make a living. She
earned an education diploma as an elementary classroom
teacher. Since there was a shortage of classroom teachers
in her country she was required to spend a period of time
as a teacher; however, as soon as she completed the necessary assignment she devoted all her efforts to establishing
a career as a conductor. Although her parents initially did
not support this choice they eventually became enthused with
her career.

    Following her six months as a classroom teacher Caduff
returned to Lucerne Conservatory to earn her diploma in
music. There is an annual Music Festival in Lucerne and as
a young girl Caduff had the opportunity to hear and see
many of the great professional conductors of the time and
was impressed. While studying for her diploma Herbert von
Karajan came to the conservatory to teach a course. Caduff
considers von Karajan the greatest European conductor and
said, "Normally I would not be allowed to take von Karajan's
course because I did not have a conducting diploma but I
went anyway and one day I asked him what his ideas were on
women conducting. He responded by saying, 'If you are
gifted why not conduct? You should try it and if you are
gifted we can make you an example.' We met the very next
day because he was interested in just what I was capable of
doing as a conductor."

    Herbert von Karajan offered to teach Sylvia Caduff in
Vienna but her parents thought she was too young and they
also wanted her to finish her diploma. When she completed
her schooling she went to Berlin to study with von Karajan
who was then conductor of the Berlin Philharmonic. She
studied with him for three years and recalls that experience
in the following manner:

            He did not tell me what to do but would ask me what
            I thought of certain musical situations, of the or-
            chestra's reaction, was that right, did you wish it
            to be that way? Then do something else. So in
            that way he had an excellent approach. I went to
            all the rehearsals, asked him questions such as why
            he did certain things a particular way, or how you
            do this point or manage a particular program. There

were several other students studying with him at
that time but I was the only woman. When von
Karajan was away we had the opportunity to study
with other guest conductors. It was a good experience.

In 1965 Herbert von Karajan, a venerable legend in
his position as conductor of the Berlin Philharmonic, wrote
the following letter of recommendation for Sylvia Caduff:

Sylvia Caduff has been a student of mine for many
years in Lucerne and Berlin. I recommend with
great pleasure, that her unquestionable talent in the
course of years has developed to one of true master-
ship of the orchestra and artistic interpretation. I
hope very much that her only handicap, namely to
be a woman, will not hinder her in the development
of her career which I wish her from my heart.

Sylvia Caduff continued her study of conducting during
various times under the tutorship of Czech conductor Rafael
Kubelik, Yugoslav conductor Lovro von Matacic and Dutch
conductor Willem van Otterloo. She made her debut with the
Tonhalle Orchestra in Zurich.

Caduff's route to the professional podium was to enter
International Conducting Competitions. According to Sylvia
Caduff most conducting competitions require the contestant
to prepare at least ten different pieces chosen by a committee.
Usually the works cover a time period from Mozart to Stravinsky and the contestants have several months to prepare
the scores.

It was at the Guido Cantelli Conducting Competition in
Novara, Italy when she placed as one of the four finalists,
that two of the judges encouraged her to enter competition in
the United States where they felt certain that women conductors would be judged on their merit as musicians and conductors. At that time both judges felt it would not be possible for a woman conductor to win the competition in Italy
and they told Caduff, "You should not have come to Italy
for here a woman has no chance at all. You should enter
the Dimitri Mitropoulos International Competition."

Heeding the advice of the judges, Caduff entered the

Dimitri Mitropoulos Competition as well as the Nicoline Marro
Competition in Copenhagen. The Swiss government paid for
Caduff's transportation to the United States because it was
an honor for the country to have one of their musicians represented.

In 1966 the Dimitri Mitropoulos Competition had 34
aspiring conductors representing 23 countries. Ms. Caduff
describes the contest as a four-round elimination where each
contestant conducted by number rather than name so there
would be no reference as to nationality. The seven finalists
selected in this season were Theo Alcantarilla of Spain, Walter
Gillessen of Germany, Taijiro Iimori of Japan, Juan Pablo Iz-
quierdo of Chile, Alain Lombard of France, Zdenek Macal of
Czechoslovakia and Sylvia Caduff of Switzerland, indicating
the international scope of the competition.

This competition covered a period of two weeks of performance judged by an unpaid jury of nine musicians, most
of them conductors. One can appreciate the enormous task
of judging this competition if one understands that each contestant conducts fourteen compositions from the classical,
postclassical and contemporary period and the judges must
listen intensely to all of the performances.

To be a finalist in this competition is certainly a prestigious accomplishment for a young conductor but to be named
one of the four winners is considered by some musicians to
be miraculous. The coveted prize in 1966 was $5,000 and an
appointment as assistant conductor of either the New York
Philharmonic or the National Symphony in Washington, for the
1966-67 season.

Sylvia Caduff was a first-place winner, thus becoming
the first woman to ever be awarded this honor. As one music
critic wrote, "In Miss Caduff's case, there was the novelty
of seeing a most attractive, intense young lady on the podium...
Miss Caduff led the orchestra expertly and even passionately."
For the reader's information this author notes that no physical description of any of the male finalists was offered by
the critic.

Caduff was named an assistant to Leonard Bernstein
and the New York Philharmonic. Winthrop Sargeant, writing
for The New Yorker in April 1967, described Sylvia Caduff's

performance on the final evening of the competition when she
conducted David Amram's King Lear and Robert Schumann's
Fourth Symphony. "Her conducting style is very much like
that of Herbert von Karajan--high elbows and gathering--in
movements--which is not surprising, since she studied with
the celebrated Austrian maestro. She gave both works clean
and vigorous readings."

Sylvia Caduff reflects on her experience as an assistant to Leonard Bernstein:

> I was a very controlled conductor when I went to
> New York. I had studied with von Karajan and he
> is a very controlled conductor even though he is
> very expressive.
>   I was maybe too controlled when I won the Dimitri
> Competition and Leonard Bernstein was exactly the
> type of conductor I needed to work with. He made
> me free and gave me the courage to be myself. He
> gave me the support I needed to reach out and find
> the freedom in myself. I learned so much studying
> with him.

The following is a letter of recommendation that Caduff
received from Leonard Bernstein in May 1966 at the conclusion
of her apprenticeship:

> To Whom It May Concern:
>
> This is to certify that Sylvia Caduff was one of the
> three winners of the Dimitri Mitropoulos International
> Conductors Competition in 1966, and most deservedly
> so. She is the only young woman I have ever seen
> conduct with success, that is, to have established a
> real rapport and authoritative control with the or-
> chestra. I feel that she will go far.

In February 1967 Sylvia Caduff and another assistant
conductor were called on to conduct the New York Philharmonic, in scores they had been assigned, when conductor
William Steinberg unexpectedly canceled his appearance because of family illness.

Miles Kastendieck reviewed the concert for the World
Journal Tribune on Feb. 14, 1967 (excerpt):

AT PHILHARMONIC

Two Conductors Meet the Challenge

If Miss Caduff emerged the stronger conductor, the
reason lies in her being more assertive. It goes
deeper perhaps in having a more vibrant personality
and possibly more experience.

At 29 Miss Caduff now has the distinction of being
the first young lady to conduct the Philharmonic officially. Appearing in the children's concerts is
hardly the same category. With her fire, vitality,
and commanding beat, she can have the world at
her feet; indeed, she had the Philharmonic playing
for her in exiciting fashion last night.

Tall, slender, and simply dressed in black, she
took over music, orchestra, and audience in an
amazingly assured way. A long baton extends her
sweeping arm to make her conducting decisive:
there was no mistaking how the music should move.
Once in the third movement she found the orchestra
slow in picking up the tempo but not for long since
it could hardly ignore her insistent beat. Her left
arm is unusually expressive, serving admirably in
coloring a performance.

Given no rehearsal, she still had to mold what
Steinberg had prepared. She did so dynamically,
catching the flavor of the music and neither missing
nor overdoing the dramatic inflections of this romantic score. It was a feat of which she may be proud.

Following her season with the New York Philharmonic
Sylvia Caduff returned to Switzerland where she received
many guest-conducting invitations. She made guest appearances in Germany, Norway, Switzerland, Portugal, Scandina-
via, Yugoslavia, Italy as well as several in the United Kingdom. She made her British debut conducting the Royal Philharmonic Orchestra at the Royal Festival Hall in 1967. This
was an interesting invitation since it had not been too many
years since Sir Thomas Beecham had banned all women from
holding a position in this orchestra. It was the first time in
the history of the orchestra that a woman would conduct a
major concert. As one critic commented, "Beecham would
presumably have been horrified to see his orchestra last night,
then astonished to hear it playing so well."

Eric Mason's review published in the <u>Daily Mail</u> on Dec. 11, 1967 (excerpt):

SYLVIA SCORES 2-FISTED SUCCESS

Sylvia Caduff, a 29-year-old Swiss who has studied with Karajan and Kubelik, shared first prize in an international contest in America last year.   This was her British debut.

She made an immediately businesslike impression.

For the opening chords of Beethoven's <u>Egmont</u> <u>Overture</u>, she took a two-fisted grip on her baton-- a Bernstein characteristic.   There followed a crisp, cogently shaped performance, directed with a clear decisive beat.

The tricky business of conducting a concerto-- Beethoven's <u>Piano Concerto No. 2</u>, with Denis Matthews as soloist--was no problem.

Her reading of Mendelssohn's <u>Italian Symphony</u> was neat, carefully balanced, expressively phrased and pointed, possibly a little deficient in high points, but consistently musical.   The culminating saltarello was unusually delicate.

Then the full orchestra, 84 men and 6 women, went into action in Dukas's <u>The Sorcerer's Appren-</u> <u>tice</u>.   Miss Caduff, vigorously but never histrionic, marshalled her forces with impressive authority.

Few women have successfully invaded this largely masculine preserve.   Miss Caduff is clearly one of them, and we shall be hearing her again.

In 1968 Caduff returned to America to conduct the Orchestra da Camera.   The membership of this orchestra was comprised largely of a group of free-lance New York musicians who chose to have guest conductors rather than a permanent conductor.   The all-Mozart program was given on Feb. 22 at Carnegie Hall.

As music columnist Eric Mason had predicted in his review in 1967 Sylvia Caduff was invited to return to Great Britain in the 1968 concert season to conduct the Royal Philharmonic Orchestra in the first of their Spring Series at the Swiss Cottage Odeon.   The program included Schubert's <u>Fifth</u> <u>Symphony</u>, Berlioz's <u>Beatrice and Benedict Overture</u>, Mozart's <u>Flute and Harp Concerto</u>, and the first two of the three dances from Falla's <u>Three-Cornered Hat Suite</u>.

Letter of recommendation for Sylvia Caduff written by Sir John Barbirolli in October 1969:

> I have had the pleasure of hearing Sylvia Caduff conduct, who I may say, made a very considerable impression upon me.
> Obviously a very fine musician, with a really natural aptitude for conducting, she seemed to be in complete control and capable of expressing her sensitive musicality in full.

Although Sylvia Caduff received a number of impressive invitations to conduct she made a decision in the early 1970s that she needed a career that would be more stable. She accepted an invitation to teach orchestral conducting at the Bern Conservatory, a position she held for four years.

In 1977 Sylvia Caduff was chosen from 12 candidates and appointed general music director with the Orchestra of the City of Solingen, Germany. She was the first woman in Europe to be so honored. In this position she chooses and conducts some 18 to 20 programs per year in addition to special concerts for young people, joining with other orchestras to present larger works, and performing in two televised programs that presented the life and responsibility of general music director, Caduff.

For years the orchestra was supported by national funds as well as ticket subscriptions but at the present time national funding has become extremely limited and the orchestra receives support from the City of Solingen in addition to ticket sales. According to Caduff, "It is a pity that national funding has dried-up since the cultural responsibilities of the group and the needs of the audiences are extensive."

She generally chooses her programs almost a year in advance and although she would like to program more contemporary music the audiences are most conservative in their listening habits. On occasion she does present modern music and the audience has been enthusiastic in their response by discussing their feelings "that new music was nice," they will tell her. "We will attend again if you program it." However, Caduff is certain that she must be extremely careful in her choice of programs and she spends a considerable amount of time before deciding just what works will be appropriate. In

1984 she began her eighth season as general music director,
a clear indication that she is capable of expectations, the high
standard of performance, as well as those mundane tasks that
make the job an artistically respected position in the country.
She is serious and unpretentious.

Caduff still accepts guest-conducting invitations when
her schedule permits. "That conducting is for men is a prejudice that is being cured by her with the second conducting
appearance with the Osnabrucker Symphony Orchestra on
November 26, 1979" according to Manfred Bohmer writing for
the Neue Osnabrucker Zeitung. He praises Sylvia Caduff's
conducting.

A history of resistance to the professional advancement
of women as orchestral conductors is fairly deeply ingrained
and changing only slowly. It is not the musical problems involved in this most responsible job but a psychological fac-
tor, the ability to impose their will and power of suggestion
on the orchestra and board of directors, as well as audiences.
To conduct is to lead and that has traditionally been the sole
responsibility of the male. Consciously or subconsciously
there has been a resistance by members of society to be
dictated to by women. Merit should be based solely on artistic ability, not sex.

Caduff's response to women as orchestral conductors is
as follows:

> To be perfectly honest, and I did not wish to be-
> lieve it for many many years, the acceptance of
> women on the orchestral podium is at least one gener-
> ation away. I thought that when women orchestral
> conductors made music as good as everyone else we
> would be accepted. But this is not so. Some people
> think women are not able to do something special.
> Women conductors have more problems than in
> other professions because a conductor is something
> like a general--the boss as I see it now.
> I never have problems with the orchestral musi-
> cians and the audience likes to attend our concerts.
> They do not come just to see a woman conduct, they
> come to concerts many times.
> Women conductors don't just have to prove they
> are capable of doing the job--they have to prove it

a hundred times over. Even then the men conductors, who have had only a few good reviews, will
be selected to conduct before women.

Sylvia Caduff has reinforced her reputation as something of an orchestral sorceress, her concerts are beautifully programmed and beautifully performed. There is an
expanding and enthusiastic audience for the Orchestra of the
City of Solingen thanks to her musicianship and dedication.
Perhaps she best sums up her career when she says:

> I want to be an orchestral conductor because I love
> the possibilities found in symphonic literature more
> than anything else. I love the different expressions
> found in the music and there is only one possibility
> of interpretation and also a challenge to bring it
> forth through the orchestra to the public.

She is a remarkable woman and there is no question that
her accomplishments are visible and her contributions are
significant. Sylvia Caduff, pioneer European orchestral conductor, had the courage and the conviction to go against the
"odds" of the time. She is young, her credentials are excellent and her career possibilities should be limitless. Her
talent is unmistakable.

Would she choose the same career again if given the opportunity? "Yes, I might get frustrated at times but I would
do it again because I have such a great love for this type of
music."

ANN CARR-BOYD

Composer, Performer, Teacher

In the past 20 years Australian composers have finally re-
ceived recognition in their own country and no longer find it
necessary to attain acceptance abroad, especially in Great
Britain, before their artistic achievements are valued at home.
The country boasts several fine music centers in addition to
the world famous Sydney Opera House; including the Victorian
Arts Centre, the Performing Arts Centre in Brisbane and the
Adelaide Festival Centre. The universities in both New South
Wales and Queensland offer undergraduate degrees in composition. The Australian Broadcasting Corporation has offered
a monthly series of programs which have been broadcast
nationally by ABC Radio 2 titled "Composers of Australia."
There has been a conscious effort to include Australian music
in educational syllabuses along with many other fine efforts
in behalf of the cause.

One of the most active supporters of contemporary
Australian music is composer Ann Carr-Boyd. Her background
of Australian music extends over three generations which is
unusual in a country which will only celebrate its bicentenial
in 1988. Her Bohemian grandfather, a violinist, came to
Australia in 1888 with the Cowen orchestra to appear in centenary celebration concerts in Melbourne. Her father and
uncle were both foundation members of what is now known as
the Sydney Symphony Orchestra.

Ann was born in Sydney in 1938, the daughter of Nor-
bert and Nyora Wentzel. She recalls her childhood:

> It was normal to discuss music at home and I became
> familiar with the work of Beethoven and Wagner at
> a very early age. As a child my brother was the

67

ANN CARR-BOYD   Photo by
Douglass Baglin Pty. Ltd.

musician in the family and I like my mother was the
artist. I loved to draw and paint and received
several awards when I was quite young. But I
wanted to play the piano and I begged my father
who was a teacher, composer and musician to give
me lessons. When I was seven he agreed to lessons
and I really enjoyed it and I've always kept that
interest--I teach piano myself.
     I composed my first piece <u>Running</u> when I was
seven years old and my father wrote it down for me.

When Ann was 9 years old she won first prize in the

Children's Hobbies Exhibition for her portrait of her "Uncle Charles" reading his newspaper. She also received praise for her other entries "Men at Work" and "Shopping." She had been sketching since she was 3 years old and often did illustrations for her young friends including a book written by her classmates. At age 11 she was poster winner of the under 13 colored section of Be Kind To Animals Week Poster Competition. Her entry was displayed with 1,500 posters at the Farmers Exhibitions.

Following graduation from Queenwood School Ann commenced an Arts Degree at Sydney University. She said:

> Here I met one of the truly most loveable and eccentric characters of my life (apart from my Uncle Charles), and this was Professor Donald Peart.
> When he established the music degree at Sydney University in 1948 a rivalry developed between the University and the Conservatorium that continues today. You discover this quickly if you live in Sydney.
> Professor Peart had a tremendous influence on my life in a practical and artistic way. He was the first to awaken me to the existence of early music since I had never had the opportunity to hear any. He was passionately interested in twentieth century music and did a tremendous service to Australian music by opening peoples' ears to the new sounds being written today.
> It was through him that my musical horizons began to widen and he was the one who persuaded me to take the first Bachelor of Music Degree at Sydney University. Previous to that, one could study for an Arts Degree specializing in music.

Carr-Boyd did no serious composing as an undergraduate but did write quite fluently in her final exams for her degree. The degree was modeled after the Oxford program of study and she had to write a large work for double orchestra, a four-part fugue, two-part counterpoint work, Palestrina counterpoint and a song. The requirements were drastically altered the following year and provided a more flexible program of study. When she graduated the newspaper carried the following headline, "Musical History First in New South Wales to Receive Degree of Bachelor of Music." Ann

graduated with first-class honors at a ceremony in the Great
Hall of the University of Sydney on April 27, 1960.

Following graduation she won a Commonwealth Research
Grant under which she devoted three years of work to produce a history of music in Australia. She worked at the
State Archives Department in Sydney, traveled to every Australian state to do original research, and spent countless
hours in various libraries. In 1963 she received her Master
of Arts Degree from the University of Sydney and the title
of her thesis was "The First Hundred Years of European
Music In Australia, 1788-1888." She said, "I didn't realize
that this subject would follow me for the rest of my life. I've
shared that research many times over the years and feel that
it is extremely important and hope someday that my work and
that of many others will be published.

The development of European music in Australia was a
neglected subject and her research has provided the basis
for much of what has been carried out since then. She still
contributes lectures, radio programs, and articles on the
subject. Copies of her work have been catalogued in the
National Library in Canberra, the main libraries in Sydney
and the Hong Kong Arts Centre.

During this same period Carr-Boyd continued her interest in composition and she won the Sydney Moss Scholarship in 1963 which provided for study overseas for graduates
in New South Wales. She chose to go to London, since it
was to her the musical center of the world, where she could
hear more music than anywhere else. She did not pursue a
degree but studied composition with Peter Racine Fricker and
Alexander Goehr and keyboard and harpsichord at the Royal
College of Music. There was ample time for her to compose
and experiment. She recalls writing one piece which she
based on 12-tone technique and found out that it didn't suit
her at all. She didn't think it was a gripping way to write
music although there have been some brilliant exponents of
the process. Her String Quartet was performed at the Royal
College of Music:

> When I heard my music at the first rehearsal I jumped
> out of my seat--it was a tremendous feeling to have
> it come to life. Everything I wrote during this
> time was performed soon after and there was no bias

as to what particular school you were writing in.
It was a very open attitude. This open attitude
has only appeared in Sydney some twenty years
later.

Fricker asked me to enter my Symphony in Three
Movements in a British competition. It was one of
four works performed at the finalists' concert played
by the Royal College of Music orchestra and conducted by Sir Charles Groves.

After Fricker left for America Ann studied privately
with Alexander Goehr. He tore apart every note that she
wrote but it was a fine learning experience for her, even
though she later determined not to use some of his suggestions. During this time she composed a chamber work,
Theme and Variations, which was premiered in London at the
New Music Concerts, in 1965.

Theme and Variations was performed just before the
first of three daughters was born to her and Peter Murray
Carr-Boyd. They remained in England for a couple of years
more before they decided to return to Australia to raise their
family. Ann continued to compose but her time was limited
with the responsibilities of raising three children.

Her first break as a composer in Australia happened
when Peter Richardson asked if he could perform one of the
pieces she had written while in England. He was one of the
main performers in the International Society for Contemporary
Music and was eager to have as much contemporary music as
possible performed in the country. Theme and Variations included a part for harpsichord and was premiered in Sydney
with Robert Goode as harpsichordist. The Richardsons (Peter
and his wife, singer Marilyn Richardson) and Goode were
impressed with Carr-Boyd's music and she was fortunate that
they continued to perform her works since they were three
of the most respected musicians in the country.

In 1972 she wrote Lullaby for Nuck which Robert Goode
premiered; in 1974 Trois Leçons for harpsichord, solo voice
and chimes was commissioned by Robert Goode and premiered
by him with Marilyn Richardson, soprano, and the composer
playing chimes, at the Musica Viva Festival in Geelong, Victoria. This was followed by Three Songs of Love and The
Boomerang Chocolate Cake, a humorous song for soprano and

harpsichord. She received two commissions in 1974 from the
Organ Institute of New South Wales and wrote Couperin for
spoken voice, chamber organ, harpsichord and percussion;
and Patterns for string quartet and pipe organ. The same
year she was commissioned by the Musical Society of Victoria
and wrote Combinations for violin, violoncello and piano and
was also commissioned by the ABC to write a fanfare for the
opening of FM radio.

Ann Carr-Boyd speaks of her music:

> I enjoy exploring every style of music and find great
> benefit in working with performers on a new piece.
> I realize that I have a predilection for certain har-
> monies, rhythms and melodic lines, and that these
> are bound to make themselves evident in one way
> or another.
> I also like the idea of being a composer/improviser/
> performer since it saves the laborious job of com-
> mitting music to paper. Yet I still find much excite-
> ment in working out an idea on paper and having it
> interpreted by other performers.

In 1975 Carr-Boyd's orchestral composition Gold was
commissioned as winner of the prestigious Maggs Award in
Melbourne. It was premiered by the National Training Orchestra conducted by Robert Miller and programmed on their
tour of Asia. Patrick Thomas conducted the piece with the
Queensland Symphony Orchestra at a Music Workshop program
in Brisbane and the ABC recorded it for the national network.

Also in 1975 Robert Goode, one of the most enthusiastic leaders of the harpsichord revival in the country, formed
the chamber music group, The Consort of Sydney which
toured in Australia and overseas for Musica Viva Australia.
Ann Carr-Boyd was resident composer and wrote a number
of chamber works all of which included the harpsichord.
The group programmed Carr-Boyd's Catch 75 and Folk Songs
76 on their eight-week tour of Iran, Czechoslovakia, Bulgaria,
Austria, East Germany, Russia, Poland, Yugoslavia and Li-
thuania. Members of The Consort of Sydney who toured were
Amanda Thane, soprano; Jan Junor, flute; Robert Goode,
harpsichord; Gregory Pikler, guitar; and Marc Bonetti, cello.

Many of the works written by Ann Carr-Boyd in the

past 20 years have been reviewed by Fred Blanks, who has
been the Australian Correspondent of Musical Times (U.K.)
since 1955 and Contributing Music Critic for The Sydney
Morning Herald since 1963. Though professionally an indus-
trial chemist (now retired), he has written and lectured widely
on musical subjects, being particularly interested in the historical and sociological aspects of music. When I met this
amazing man in early 1986 he had attended 6,547 concerts in
the past 40 years and heard 43,982 performances of 16,279
works by 2,260 composers. In addition he has documented
and made a cross-file account of every event. He's a fascinating and brilliant individual whose works should be placed
in the Australian Archives.

The following are brief excerpts from Mr. Blanks' writings on some of the music written by Ann Carr-Boyd: Patterns, 1974, for string quartet and pipe organ, "attractively
textured tonal patterns"; Music for Narjade, 1974, for violoncello, "sonorously grateful and playful"; and Catch 75, 1975,
scored for soprano, flute, guitar, cello, harpsichord, and
aboriginal beating sticks, "the final ripples written by Ann
Carr-Boyd came so to speak, across a billabong in the guise
of an entertaining rather than convincing, Westernization of
Aboriginal sounds."

Music for Sunday was commissioned, with financial assistance from the Music Board of the Australian Council, for
the New South Wales Women in Arts Festival in 1982. According to Carr-Boyd the music was promoted by her associations
and thoughts on the Sydney Opera House itself. Part of the
work reflects the sight of the multitude of people always
strolling around the precincts, an aspect of the building
which its architect, Utzon, was very keen to highlight. Lei-
surely strollers and the lapping waters of Sydney Harbour
are also included in this part. Children embody the many
lively aspects of Opera House activities--children running,
children at concerts, children growing up with the Opera
House. She used these ideas to help work out some of the
tantalizing sounds to be obtained from the combination of
flute, violin and harpsichord. Fred Blanks' review in The
Sydney Morning News, March 11, 1982 on the Midday Music
Recital for ABC and the Sydney Opera House Trust with
music by Carr-Boyd and Bach:

NOT WITH a bang, not with a whimper, but with a

giggle and a romp is how the music brought forward
by the Women and Arts festival ended in the Opera
House Recording Hall on Sunday.

Sydney composer Ann Carr-Boyd wrote Music
For Sunday as a festival commission for the Nuclear
Trio of flautist Christine Draeger, violinist Deborah
Berlin and harpsichordist Romano Crevici, who were
the neat performers.

It is, heaven be praised, a light-hearted charmer
of a piece, designed to entertain. It's two movements
are Promenade and Children; it lapses into jazz and
keyboard twitters but also uses flute flutter-tongue
technique and, in one spot, quarter-tones. It is
uninhibited, witty, as lively as quicksilver. It
ought to become popular.

Ann Carr-Boyd was commissioned in 1982 by The Sydney Mandolins to write Fandango. A feature of the work is
the polyrhythmic effect between 6/8 and 3/4 signatures.
Adrian Hooper, founder and director of the group, included
Fandango on their record, Amcos-HR 001. This is a fascinating recording of mandolins, mandola, guitar, bass and flute/
piccolo.

In 1985 The Canberra Times sponsored a series of four
concerts which offered the works of 13 Australian composers.
The final program in "The Composer Speaks" series of recitals of Australian music was performed in the foyer of the
National Library in Canberra and was devoted to the music
of Ann Carr-Boyd. She was present to introduce the program
which was reviewed by W. L. Hoffmann for The Canberra
Times on Sept. 2, 1985 (excerpt):

> It was an interesting program for two particular
> reasons. Firstly, Ann Carr-Boyd's music has a dia-
> tonic tonal basis which makes it very different in
> sound to much of the other music heard in these
> programs, and it also incorporates popular elements
> as well as being descriptive. Secondly, all three of
> the works played utilized the harpsichord, either as
> a solo instrument or in ensemble, and the harpsi-
> chord is still rarely heard as a transmitter of con-
> temporary music.
>
> These factors made for listening that was easily
> enjoyable. The two works for solo harpsichord--

Suite for Veronique with its references to Bach,
jazz, blues and South American folk song, and the
Lullaby for Nuck which is a descriptive blending of
diverse music elements (Nuck is a Siamese cat)--were
attractive in their lively but unpretentious way.

The harpsichord, with its limited dynamic range
and lack of tonal contrast, throws emphasis on the
music, both in its content and in the playing of it.
Lee Primmer settled down to give crisp, alert and
entertaining performances of both these works. She
then joined with violinist Leonard Dommett and
flautist David Cubbin in the third Carr-Boyd work,
the Music for Sunday for violin, flute and harpsichord, written in 1982 and prompted by the composer's associations with the Sydney Opera House.

It presents a musical picture of people promenad-
ing and children playing around the Opera House on
a Sunday. With its light musical textures and lively
expression, and given an appropriately vital performance, it made a delightful conclusion to the
program.

In 1986 she received congratulations from the Alienor
Harpsichord Compositions Awards that her piece Suite for
Veronique had been chosen as one of the 11 finalists' works.
It was performed by Nicholas Parle at the South Eastern His-
torical Keyboard Society Festival in Washington, D.C. in June
1986.

Ann Carr-Boyd has been an important force in promoting Australian music through her writing, lecturing and broadcasting. She writes:

How many people have noticed that Australian music
content, once a comparative rarity in concerts, is
now an essential part of many programmes, particularly when groups such as The Australia Ensemble, Flederman, Synergy and the newly formed Mag-
pie Musicians are playing?

The enthusiastic audiences who attend concerts
by the smaller ensembles can vouch for the fact that
contemporary music has lost much of its fearsome
image and can be varied, listenable, interesting and
often a great deal of fun.

We haven't fostered enough of our own talent

especially in terms of conductors; we tend to promote the mystique of the overseas conductor and
this must change.

Several years ago Carr-Boyd approached the ABC re-
questing special broadcasts be devoted to Australian compositions. She received their full support, for the monthly
programs. She prepared the script, interviewed composers
and musicians and selected tapes for these special programs.
It was a most successful venture for the composers, musicians
and the listening public.

Carr-Boyd was the Australian representative to the
International Congress on Women in Music in Los Angeles in
1982 and Mexico in 1984. Since 1980 she has been the Honorary Secretary of the Fellowship of Australian Composers and
has, as their representative, presented papers at the Asian
Composers League Conference in Hong Kong in 1981. She
has also prepared papers for the Anzaas Conference in Sydney, the Asian Composers League meeting in Singapore and
the Northern Rivers Chapter of the Australian Musicological
Society in Lismore.

Biographical information on Ann Carr-Boyd appears in
the Encyclopedia of Women Composers, Encyclopedia of Modern Music, International Who's Who in Music, Who's Who of
the Arts in Australia, Who's Who in the World, Who's Who of
Australian Women, The International Book of Honour, and
Biography International Delhi.

Ann Carr-Boyd is a distinguished Australian who has
helped pave the way as a composer, performer, writer, lecturer and broadcaster for the acceptance of 20th-century
Australian music. Her work has brought about change in
the country and she and her colleagues should be proud of
her accomplishments. She has the talent, the capacity and
absolute devotion so necessary to make music a living art.

Selected Compositions of Ann Carr-Boyd

Orchestral

1964   Symphony in Three Movements.
1976   Gold.

1980 Festival.

Vocal

1974 Trois Leçons, for solo voice, harpsichord and chimes.
1975 Three Songs of Love, for solo voice and piano/harpsi-
     chord.
1975 The Boomerang Chocolate Cake, humorous song for
     soprano and harpsichord.
1977 A Composition of Place, SATB choir with piano accompa-
     niment.
1982 A Change of Air, two-part song for primary-school
     children guitar accompaniment and optional piano,
     violin, banjo and percussion.

Vocal/Chamber

1974 Couperin, for spoken voice, chamber organ, harpsi-
     chord and percussion.
1975 Catch 75, for soprano, flute, guitar, cello, harpsichord
     and aboriginal beating sticks.
1976 Folk Songs 76, seven folk songs arranged for soprano,
     flute/recorder, guitar, cello, piano/harpsichord and
     percussion.

Chamber/Instrumental

1974 Patterns, for string quartet and pipe organ.
1974 Fanfare for Aunty in FM, for two trumpets, two pianos,
     snare drum, bass drum and cymbals (AE edition).
1974 Combinations, for violin, violoncello and piano.
1975 Nadir, for violin and harpsichord.
1974 Music for Narjade, for solo violoncello.
1977 Dance for Strings, for primary school violins and piano.
1980 Mandolin Music, for small mandolin group: two first;
     two second; two mandolas; guitars and bass.
1981 Travelling, for massed school recorders and piano with
     optional organ and bongo drums.
1982 Fandango, for small mandolin group.
1982 Music for Sunday, for flute, violin, and harpsichord.
1984 Australian Baroque, for small mandolin group.
1984 Dance Suite, for woodwind quintet.

Keyboard--Piano, Harpsichord, Organ

1962 Six Piano Pictures, for young players (AE edition).
1964 Ten Piano Duets.
1972 Lullaby for Nuck, for harpsichord or piano solo, advanced grade.
1978 Look at the Stars, 14 piano pieces of moderate difficulty (AE edition).
1978 Stars, piano solo, advanced grade.
1978 Woodford Bay, fantasy for solo pipe organ.
1979 Listen!, 17 piano pieces for children, ranging from easy to moderate difficulty. (Hillside Press).
1979 The Bells of Sydney Harbour, festive piece for solo pipe organ.
1982 Suite for Veronique, for solo harpsichord, advanced grade.

Addresses of Publishers

Music Sales Australia, 27 Clarendon Street, Artarmon, Sydney, 2064, Australia.

Hillside Press, 1 McMahons Road, Northwood, Sydney, 2066, Australia.

The Australia Music Centre, P.O. Box 19, Grosvenor Street, Sydney, 2000, Australia.

Discograpy

Australian Songs and Ballads, Larrikin Records, Trois Leçons, 1974, words by Don Marquis; Gregory Martin, baritone; Norma Williams, piano. I And only man is vile. II. The human race. III. Man is so proud.
Sydney Mandolins, Fandango, HR001 Amcos, Mandolin I, Paul Hooper, Joyce Bootsma; Mandolin II, Suze Krawczck, Frona Horback; Mandola, Coralie Tosswell, David Gangemi; guitar, Barbara Hooper, James Allen; bass, Kathleen Wilson; flute/piccolo, Michael Scott.

Addresses

Larrikin Records, Ltd., P.O. Box 162, Paddington, N.S.W.
2021, Australia.

Sydney Mandolins, Adrean Hooper, 21 Kitchener Street, Oat-
ley, N.S.W. 2223, Australia.

GLORIA COATES

Composer, Artist

Numerous reviews appeared throughout Europe in the late 1970s that established Gloria Coates' reputation as a composer on an international level. Dr. Detlef Gojowy's review notes on the Pro Viva Disc, ISPV, 128, West Germany praises Gloria Coates' orchestral work, Music on Open Strings, as the most widely discussed event of the 1978 Warsaw Autumn Festival. He wrote, "Gloria Coates, who was born in Wisconsin, resists categorization into any 'school' of New Music." Wilfried Jahns, music critic for the Saxon News, Dresden, wrote, "With the premiere of Music on Open Strings, the composer Gloria Coates instantly became the talk of the 1978 Warsaw Autumn Festival.

In 1986 the recording of this orchestral work by the Bavarian Radio Symphony Orchestra conducted by Elgar Howarth was a nominee and received honorable mention for the prestigious Serge and Olga Koussevitzky International Record Award, for a recording of an important work by a living composer.

The premiere of Music on Open Strings at the Warsaw Autumn Festival, with Jerzy Maksymiuk conducting the Polish Chamber Orchestra, led to a commission for the 1979 East Berlin Festival, where she became the first non-socialist composer to be performed on this major East European Festival.

The author wishes to thank the following translators of reviews printed in this chapter: Dr. Detlef Gojowy and Professor Roxane Steubing, musicologists from West Germany; Roger Clement, the Swedish Consulate; Dr. Brad Robinson and the South African Consulate.

GLORIA COATES   Photo by
                                 Hilde Zemann

The 1980 performance of <u>Music on Open Strings</u> by the
Bavarian Radio Symphony Orchestra under Elgar Howarth
was the first time an orchestral work by a woman composer
was selected for the Munich Musica Viva concert series.
Founded in 1946 by Karl Amadeus Hartmann, it has been an
important series premiering works by composers such as Karlheinz Stockhausen, Pierre Boulez and Iannis Xenakis.

Gloria Coates was the first woman composer invited to
India. Her <u>Fourth String Quartet</u> was performed by the
Mureca String Quartet in Calcutta and the Bombay String
Quartet in New Delhi. She had radio interviews throughout
India and lectured about her music at the New Delhi Con-
servatory and at the Max-Mueller Bhavans of Calcutta, New
Delhi and Bombay.

Along with Peter Mennin, then president of the Juilliard
School of Music, and Nicolas Slonimsky, she was asked by the

Soviet Composers Union to attend the First International
Festival of New Music in Moscow in 1981.

Born on Oct. 10 during the 1930s Progressive Era,
in Wausau, Wis., she was the middle child of the late state
Senator Roland Kannenberg, innovator and initiator of numerous reforms, and Natalie Zanon, the young Italian coloratura
from the Dolomites who emigrated to the United States in the
1920s.

Reflecting on her childhood Gloria said:

> Since infancy my mother sang to me and from age
> four on I sang solos at political conventions, on
> radio programs, and in church and school assemblies.
> I vividly remember receiving a toy piano for my
> third birthday. One morning my mother awoke and
> played a melody for me which had come to her in
> her sleep. I was very excited and filled with great
> happiness for her, and I began composing on that
> toy piano.
> I received formal piano training at age six from
> a neighborhood piano teacher. When I was ten years
> old I asked her for music by composers I had heard
> both at school and on the radio. She told me I
> would have to wait until I was older and more mature
> to play them. I then used my babysitting money and
> bought sheet music by Massenet, Grieg and Tchaikow-
> sky which were on sale for five or ten cents at the
> local Woolworths Dime Store. I sang and improvised
> in my own private world of music.

At age 12 she began studying voice with Elizabeth
Silverthorn, an active member of the State Federation of
Music Clubs, who recommended a piano teacher, Mary Bandy,
known for her interpretations of Mozart's piano music.

To help structure her improvisations, which had developed into highly emotional clusters and chords, she studied
harmony with the city's most qualified theory teacher, Len-
nard Siem, a graduate of the Peabody Conservatory. Playing for him her newest creation My Heart Yearns he insisted
she modify her clusters, explaining that she had no background to justify what she had written. Thus, arpeggios
and dominant seventh chords harmonized her passionate melody.
Nevertheless, she received a "superior rating" in the National

Federation of Music Clubs Composition Contest (Junior Division) for this piece when she was thirteen years old.

Scholastically in the top one percent of her graduating class from Wausau High School, Gloria Coates received not only the Music Award but also the Best Actress Award, the Helen Farnsworth Mears Art Award, and Quill and Scroll.

She attended Monticello College in Godfrey, Illinois, and was elected president and student conductor of the Monticello College Choir. She acted in Shakespeare's Love's Labours' Lost, published two of her poems, won the college's fencing championship, was elected to the Junior College's Phi Beta Kappa, and Social Activities Chairman of the student body.

In the summer she worked as a waitress in Central City, Colo., and attended daily rehearsals of the Central City Opera House productions of La Bohème and The Marriage of Figaro. The second half of the summer she was a scholarship apprentice at Brookside Playhouse in Petersburg, Pennsylvania, acting the role of "Lizzie" in The Bat, and in Streetcar Named Desire she sang "Summertime" as "the colored Woman." The Altoona Newspaper singled her out: "It was a real pleasure to discover the beautiful singing voice of the actress, Gloria Kannenberg."

Her professional experience that summer led her to the decision to devote her life to the arts. She knew her family's attitude towards an artist's life and their desire for her to learn a more practical profession. She decided not to return to Monticello College.

Gloria remembers:

> This practical attitude towards life was common in my part of the country. I believe it to have been the "pioneer spirit" and the insecurity brought on by the Great Depression in Wisconsin during the thirties.
> In junior high school, we were assigned a paper about a career we would consider. I chose that of an artist and was refused this subject because it was not a profession. I had to decide between art teacher or commercial artist. Three years later in

senior high school we were again required to write
a career paper. This time I chose opera singer or
composer. These were both rejected as career top-
ics and I had to chose between music teacher and
music therapist. I chose the latter which was then
a profession in its infancy.

In truth, my family was interested in the arts.
My great grandfather was a German painter who had
studied with Wilhelm Kaulbach and emigrated to the
United States in 1865. He was always a family hero.
Years later my family also accepted me as an artist.

I do not believe a composer or artist, especially
a woman during the time I was growing up, had
much of a chance without the moral and spiritual
backing of someone acting like a Guru. I was fortunate to have Mrs. Elizabeth Silverthorn, my first
voice teacher, who never gave up encouraging me
and writing to me until her death in 1976. Also,
Alexander Tcherepnin and Otto Luening both encouraged me and never lost contact.

That September Coates moved to Milwaukee, Wis. where
she studied singing with the Norwegian opera singer Nene
Baalstad at the Wisconsin College of Music while working as
a cashier. In October she noticed an announcement in the
Milwaukee Journal, on a lecture, "How a Composer Works" by
Alexander Tcherepnin. Following the lecture Gloria spoke
with Tcherepnin.

After seeing my compositions, he told me I was very
gifted and invited me to study with him at no cost.
But I told him I wanted to be an actress. To this,
he recommended his friend, David Itkin from Chek-
hov's Moscow Arts Theatre, who was then teaching
at DePaul University. Alexander Tcherepnin told
me he would be happy to see my new compositions
and would always be willing to help. I studied with
him privately and later in the summer of 1962 at
the Salzburg Mozarteum. He was my mentor until
he died in 1978.

Coates then moved to Chicago where she worked days
in a book store, attended night school at DePaul University
Theatre School and the Goodman Theatre where David Itkin
taught, and studied with Tcherepnin privately. She took

voice lessons at the Chicago Musical College, and acted with
the Chicago Stage Guild.

Exhausted after a year and a half, she returned to
Wausau to conduct a choir. She enjoyed her youth choir,
sang solos for local events and had her old friends around
her. The job only paid $25 a week, so after five months she
left home again. This time she thought about Minneapolis
and New York, flipped a coin and New York won.

With a reservation at the New York YWCA, and $118
in her pocket from her savings as choir director, she boarded
a train for New York City. While working at various jobs,
she studied acting at Herbert Berghoff's, voice privately,
and eventually art at Cooper Union Art School. She played
the lead in the off-Broadway musical Dacota.

She married (1959-1969) and settled with her husband,
attorney Francis Mitchell Coates Jr. in Baton Rouge, La.
She continued her studies at Louisiana State University,
wrote for the Louisiana State Times as music, art, and drama
critic, and produced and moderated a daily television program.
She composed music for the Baton Rouge Theatre productions
of Thieves Carnival, Everyman, Hamlet, and Saint Joan in
addition to composing a mass, song cycles, and chamber music
which were performed in the Louisiana Festival of New Music.

Sunday Morning Advocate, Baton Rouge, La., March
14, 1965, by Marian Wood (excerpt):

HAMLET

Gloria Coates has composed original music for the
Little Theater production of Hamlet. The music
sometimes precedes scenes, sometimes augments
them, or carries or changes the mood between
scenes. Always it adds to the melodramatic atmosphere of the play.

State Times, Baton Rouge, La., May 8, 1964, by critic
Ann Luck (excerpt):

SAINT JOAN

Among the excellent production devices used for the

play was special music, composed and directed by
Gloria Coates. The composition, sometimes dramatic,
and sometimes liturgic, included the use of organ,
tympani and brass and a boys choir from Sacred
Heart, as well as a men's choir.

College credits from studying in various schools accumulated and she earned bachelor's degrees in voice, art,
composition and theater as well as a master's degree in composition and musicology. Besides Tcherepnin, her composition
teachers were Helen Gunderson and Kenneth Klaus at Louisiana State University and Jack Beeson and Otto Luening at
Columbia. Luening, also a native of Wisconsin, played an
important role in her life, not only in helping her through
times of personal tragedy, but also in giving her courage to
withstand difficulties.

In 1969 Gloria Coates boarded a Greek freighter heading
for Europe with her 5-year-old daughter, Alexandra, a 13-
year-old dachshund called Beatle and 14 boxes and trunks
with articles belonging to all three. (Today her daughter
is a 1986 graduate of Harvard University, a poet and harpist.)
The following is an excerpt from Coates' diary of July 13,
1969, after five days at sea on the Livorno Freighter:

Dear Diary:

I had planned on writing to you sooner, but life
itself stole my hours and the minutes themselves
seemed too precious except for rest--but at last I
feel compelled to write my thoughts and the events
of the past several weeks so that I might never
forget them.
My divorce became final at the end of May--and
to sever unpleasant associations with the past as
well to begin a new section in my life I have decided
to leave the United States for an indefinite period of
time and to experience life first-hand in all its complex and beautiful patterns.

The events that followed brought a focus to her life
and within several years her compositions won international
recognition for their originality and force. Yet, the focus
was not primarily on her own music, but that of her American
contemporaries. Through a music series in Munich, which she

produced and organized without financial remuneration, and radio programs on the West German Radio in Cologne she was able to raise the status of contemporary American music to a new high. She performed and promoted composers from the United States who would have remained unknown on the European continent. The files from both the radio programs and the music series are being transferred to the archives of the Rare Book and Manuscript Library of Butler Library of Columbia University.

In April of 1971, the director of the Munich America House, Mr. Edward Hinker, asked her for suggestions to improve the ongoing German-American Concert Series. She proposed a method of researching American music to include various parts of the country, performing more of the avant-garde music of both Germany and the United States, devised a rotating music library system for the Amerika Haus, a composition contest for young people, and building both the manuscript and record libraries in Munich and Berlin. At that meeting she was unanimously elected to the executive committee of the German-American Contemporary Concert Series.

The concerts were successful and became widely known in Germany. When the value of the dollar plunged in 1973, the funds for the concerts from the Amerika Haus were withdrawn. An application to the Ditson Committee of Columbia University rescued the project and the Munich Ministry of Culture continued their support with the Ditson Fund appropriation. Gloria said:

> By 1974, I was alone with the concert series. Both of my co-directors had resigned. There were from three to five concerts each year, and it took months to organize each one. Volunteers were not to be found who would work without some sort of wage, so my daughter and I usually worked alone. In 1979 the concerts were organized together in the form of a festival.

In 1977 Gloria Coates was asked to review Walter Zimmermann's book on American music, <u>Desert Plants</u>, for Radio Bremen. She said:

After reading the book and finding it extremely

biased, I replied that I could not write a review
without writing a short history about American
music. I was told to go ahead. The review was
translated and read over Radio Bremen. A year
later it was used by Cologne WDR Radio and I was
asked to give musical examples to illustrate the text.
I debated the author on another broadcast. This
led to other programs on that radio station as well
as a co-authorship of a review of the book for the
German musicological magazine Die Musik Forschung.

The radio programs in which she participated the
longest were titled Open House Broadcasts. A composer or
musician was invited to do a program of music of his/her
choice in which light music was intermingled with avant-garde
music. She produced and moderated 28 one-and-one-half-
hour programs. Four of these programs were on women's
music which she divided into chamber, orchestral, electronic,
and vocal music. Other programs included Love Music, Space
Music, Fruit Music, Computer and Electronic Music from
America, Cats and Co., Benjamin Franklin and Co. and Christmas Music.

From 1975 to 1978 she was on the Board of Directors of
the International League of Women Composers, serving as its
foreign representative. Eventually Germany organized its
own league, Frau und Musik. In 1978 Gloria Coates was responsible for bringing Frau und Musik together with the
International League of Women Composers which culminated in
a festival in Bonn, Germany, in 1979.

Since 1978 she has been able to support herself primarily from money she earned through performances, radio
programs and commissions. "I live very simply. I have no
car and no luxuries, but my life is never dull."

The late Dr. Merle Montgomery, president of the
American Music Council, invited Gloria Coates to attend the
World Music Days in Prague, 1977; in Budapest, 1979; Stock-
holm, 1983; and East Berlin, 1985.

In 1981, Ms. Coates received a telegram from the Soviet
Composers Union inviting her to the First International Festival of New Music in Moscow with plane ticket and all expenses
paid. Following a reception in the Kremlin guests were asked

to give speeches. Gloria, speaking on behalf of the United
States, suggested exchanges of musicians, music, and information on musical activities. She said, "Music begins where
words cease to have meaning..."

Her interest in composing ran parallel to her music
series and she found herself with so many commissions that
she never had time to finish them. In 1978 she had 58 commissions, (not all of them paid money), and she was able to
fulfill only a few each year. Her method of composing is
very slow; each work is derived from the previous one and
then expanded into new areas with new forms and colors.
She said:

> As the years went by, my responsibilities as a
> mother, as an organizer of concerts, musicologist,
> and, most of all, as composer increased so that I
> felt like an apple tree with its branches so heavy
> with fruit that they were curved to the ground.
> Gradually, as my daughter left for college and the
> series ended, I had more time to organize my life
> and write larger compositions.

During the 1972 Olympics in Munich she was asked by
the Sinnhoffer Quartet to compose a string quartet for the
opening of an art exhibition. They recorded her String
Quartet No. II for Radio Bremen in 1977, and in 1983 the
Kronos Quartet recorded it for the Stuttgart Radio as well
as a Pro Viva ISPV-128 Record. Her String Quartets, I,
II and III are also included on the recording. In the June
issue of the 1986 Neue Zeitschrift fur Musik, the critic Gisela
Glagla wrote a review of the record (excerpt):

> Gloria Coates' probing of distant sound-color regions
> is executed with tight forms, and a rich tension is
> created by the difference between the openness of
> the material and the strictness with which it is
> presented. This seems to be a characteristic of
> Gloria Coates' personal style which appears in all
> the quartets on the record. For example, the
> second quartet (1972) is based on a canon composed
> of "Klangfarben" motives which are not the usual
> exact parameters that one would expect, but rather
> are long, moving phrases composed of glissandos,
> tremolos on the bridge, and very slow vibratos.

The first quartet is also in one movement, and
its basic structure that of an exact mirror canon.
It grows out of a cello solo which also moves in a
mirror canon. However, while playing with the
other strings, the cello has an independent voice
which move in opposition to them. Already these
two short works possess an expressive quality which
in the fourth quartet (1976-1977) unfolds over three
movements. It reaches its climax in the middle section, an 'Adagio molto con espressione.' In its ges-
ticulative motives, in its expressive power, this
movement has an aura of something out of the past,
as if it wants to evoke the feeling of a movement of
a Schubert quartet.

Gloria Coates' String Quartet No. IV was commissioned
for a concert at SFB (Sender Freie Berlin) Radio in 1978.
In 1982 it was performed in New Delhi, India, by the Bombay String Quartet in the New Delhi College of Music, and in
a concert in the International Center of New Delhi. In the
New Delhi Hindustan Times of Nov. 29, 1982, the critic Saloni
Kaul wrote about the concert (excerpt):

> The evening's highlight was the careful presentation
> of a 1977 string quartet by Gloria Coates, an Ameri-
> can Munich-based composer, in India by invitation.
> The quartet used elements familiar to Indian music--
> finely interlaced glissandi (meend) and controlled
> crescendos of the first, and percussive cross-
> rhythms and rapid tremolos on the heavier strings
> of the cello in the last. The most outstanding move-
> ment was the middle in which the sighing viola wore
> the willow, and the woeful melting brimmed with
> personal emotion.

In Calcutta her fourth quartet was performed by another
Indian quartet, the Mureca Quartet, in a concert at the Calcutta Max Mueller Bhavan. There was also a taped performance on her Music on Open Strings, and Dickinson Songs,
as well as a discussion of her music. The events were taped
for Calcutta Radio.

Her visits to New Delhi as well as Bombay were coupled
with radio interviews in the various cities as well as lectures
and discussions.

Gloria Coates remembers her trip to India:

> My invitation to India was perhaps one of the most
> inspiring periods in my life. I expected the poverty,
> which tugged at my heart, but I did not expect the
> spiritual light in the atmosphere and in the eyes of
> the most poor, and one was aware of the richness of
> their spirit. There were receptions in the German
> and American foreign official's homes as well as in
> homes of Indians. Several women's rights organiza-
> tions had begun, and I was invited to see their work
> and to discuss their problems which were different
> from those of Europe and the United States because
> of the cultural history and political development.

Her chamber-orchestra work, Planets, was commissioned
for the 1975 New Music Days in Hanover, Germany. One of
Germany's two major newspapers singled it out of the festival
in its review written by Detlef Gojowy on Feb. 25, 1975,
Frankfurter Allgemeine Zeitung (excerpt):

> The festival Tage der Neuen Musik in Hanover has
> always been and continues to be the festival that has
> both courage and ability to discover new composers
> who have highly individual and key solutions. At
> the top of the list, I select Gloria Coates. Her
> chamber orchestra work Planets performed under
> the baton of Klaus Bernbacher by the Studio Orches-
> tra of Radio Hanover was in three movements entitled
> "Horizontal," "Diagonal," and "Back and Forth."
> This music was pure, logical and at the same time
> sonorous and sensuous constructivism.

Erich Limmert's review in Melos, March/April, 1975
(excerpt):

> The chamber orchestra work of the American com-
> poser Gloria Coates, Planets, proved not only to be
> a work of solid workmanship and skill, but also it
> was strikingly effective.

A delegation at the Hanover festival from Poland,
headed by Ms. Barbara Dybkovsky, congratulated her on her
composition and invited her to a music seminar in Torun, Poland, the Copernicus City, in the summer of 1975.

In 1975, <u>Planets</u> was selected for a concert in New York's Greenwich House in a competition sponsored by the International League of Women Composers. In 1979 it was performed in three concerts by the Milwaukee Symphony under Kenneth Schermerhorn during the 25th Anniversary Series of the Milwaukee Symphony and recorded for WFMT Radio. <u>Planets</u> was performed in Passau, Germany, as part of the 1981 Bavarian Tonkunstler Festival. An excerpt from a long review which appeared in the <u>Passauer Neue Presse</u> on April 3, 1981, written by Hermann Schmidt, reads:

> There were various degrees of art and quality in the works that were heard this evening, but let me begin the review with the last piece on the program, the one that impressed me the most. That is the piece <u>Planets</u> by the American composer Gloria Coates who has lived some years in Bavaria. Wide stretches of sound point in the direction of G. Ligeti, sudden outbursts, oddities point in the direction of the early and middle Penderecki--and yet it is quite different; it is an individualistic and original musical language which is created by Gloria Coates. The entire composition pulsated through space like a speeding Super Nova. In spite of the wide and forceful stretches of sound areas, the inner order remained recognizable and it was clear that the composer had nothing to do with chaotic playing around with sounds. <u>Planets</u> is a logical and thoroughly organized composition, in which there also was a supra or higher ordering principle which led to constant seeking of new crystallizations of sound color, material and space. This important orchestral work was performed by a small orchestra with thrilling intensity.

The composition that catapulted Gloria Coates to international recognition was <u>Music on Open Strings</u> with its premiere at the Warsaw Autumn Festival in 1978 by the Polish Chamber Orchestra under the baton of Jerzy Maksymiuk. Numerous reviews appeared throughout Europe including the following:

<u>Neue Musikzeitung</u> December/January 1979 by Horst Schwemmer (excerpt):

> The highest points on this year's Warsaw Autumn

Festival were won by a triumvirate. Luciano Berio
with his Coro for orchestra, Gloria Coates, the
American composer living in Munich with the premiere
of her Music on Open Strings, and the grand seig-
neur with his double bass, Fernando Grillo, performing his Itesi.

Gloria Coates talks about the difficulty she had finding
the right musicians to perform this revolutionary work:

> Music on Open Strings had a long waiting period and
> a very difficult birth. The piece was originally a
> commission from Albert Kocis, violinist and director
> of the Rhineland Chamber Orchestra in 1973. I
> finished the work and sent it off to the orchestra in
> Cologne in the spring of 1974. Attending a rehear-
> sal, I realized that their difficulty with the per-
> formance was that they had no conductor. I sug-
> gested a young woman from Poland who had recently
> won a conducting award in Germany, Alicia Monjk,
> to conduct the performance. She was willing to do
> it without honorarium. After much hesitation, the
> orchestra decided to perform it without a conductor.
> I deleted the piece from the program.
>   Years went by, and it stayed in a box unplayed.
> Having almost given up hope that I would ever hear
> it in my lifetime, I sent it off to the Warsaw Autumn
> Festival Committee. It was accepted and scheduled
> on a concert in the Warsaw Philharmonic Hall with
> works by Augustyn Bloch, Akira Matsudaira, Fernando
> Grillo, Stravinsky and Penderecki on September 20,
> 1978.

A review in the Polish musicological magazine Ruch
Muzyczny on Nov. 5, 1978, by the critic Krzysztof Baculewski (excerpt):

> The most interesting, albeit the most controversial
> and certainly the most original composition was that
> of Music on Open Strings by Gloria Coates. This
> four movement work used the colors of open strings
> on the stringed instruments open strings, but also
> retuned (in movements I and II), which later (move-
> ment III) return to their normal tuning for the final
> fourth movement. A characteristic working principle

of this composition is the formation of static chords
(on open strings) as the harmonic foundation for the
expanding harmonic and contrapuntal sections. During the retuning (tuning back) of the instruments
while playing, one noticed a vague, somewhat in-
exactness (it can never be perfectly clear), in not
only the scordatura, but also after the return to
normal tuning. Harmonically, Music on Open Strings
is based on various pentatonic structures and soft
warm colors predominate.

Music on Open Strings was selected by the director of
Musica Viva Munich for performance on Nov. 14, 1980. It
was performed by the Bavarian Radio Symphony Orchestra
under the English conductor Elgar Howarth, the St. Paul
Chamber Orchestra under John McGlaughlin (1982), the New
Amsterdam Orchestra in New York City under Rachel Worby
(1981), the University of Indiana Orchestra under Edmon
Colomer (1983) and the Siegesland Orchestra under Jorge
Rotter (1979). Radio recordings were produced by Radio
Poland, Bavarian Radio, WDR Cologne Radio, and the Min-
meapolis Radio. Additional broadcasts have been in China,
Sweden, Canada, Spain, Portugal, Finland, Belgium, Germany
and the United States. The live performance tape of the Mu-
sica Viva concert with the Bavarian Radio Symphony Orchestra
under Elgar Howarth is on the reverse side of the Kronos
Quartet performance on Pro Viva ISPV 128 Recording.

On July 4, 1982, the conductor Leif Segerstam premiered
her piece Sinfonietta della Notte in Malmo, Sweden. A press
review from Arbetet, Malmo, Sweden, July 6, 1982, written
by Bengt Edlund, reads:

> Far more comprehensible, and music one could savor
> and enjoy was Sinfonietta della Notte by Gloria Coates.
> The three movements present fascinating and unusual
> moods; sometimes seemingly from distant places, and
> often filled with gripping humanity. Gloria Coates
> possesses an original and refined imagination and sen-
> sitivity to sound colors. This is not a mixture of un-
> usual sound effects, but rather a world of sound that
> develops and unfolds purposely toward goald and fixed
> points, and within which the forms are tightly con-
> centrated.

In 1984 the BBC London recorded her work Five Pieces

for Four Wind Players. This piece had been a commission in
1975 by the Southwest German Radio Woodwind Quintet for
the 25th Anniversary of Musique Contemporaine in Geneva,
Switzerland. In 1976 it was performed by the same ensemble
for an Ars Nova Concert of the SWF Baden-Baden in Mainz,
Germany. A review in the Mainzer Allgemeine Zeitung on
Dec. 16, 1976, by the critic Wolf Eberhard von Lewinski (excerpt):

> Exquisitely out of the ordinary, more static and
> pleasing to the ear, almost cantabile, and at times
> euphoniously imploring were the five abstractions by
> Gloria Coates. The first title, "I shall keep singing"
> was chosen as the core or main theme of the music,
> even when it led to dramatic constellations, bitter
> scherzo, and dark, melancholy, song-like passages.
> Balanced in sound and very comprehensible, this
> work successfully achieved the composer's objectives;
> namely: directness, simplicity, and tightly knit
> forms.

Demonstrating another aspect of the creativity of Gloria
Coates' music is a song cycle on poems by Emily Dickinson.
Beginning in 1966 she wrote one or two songs a year for her
own personal expression and by 1985 had 12 songs. The
first five songs were premiered in a recital by Sylvia Anderson and her husband and conductor Matthias Kuntzsch at the
piano, in 1972.

One of the songs from the cycle, "They Dropped like
Flakes," was sung in two international voice contests in Rio
de Janeiro and in Pretoria, South Africa, by the German alto
Cornelia Kallisch, who won first place in both contests. She
was awarded a tour of South Africa and she and her accompanist Siglind Bruhn sang cycles by Moussorgsky, Dvorak,
Ravel, and the Dickinson Cycle of Gloria Coates. The songs
were extremely successful according to the reviews and letters the composer received.

Eastern Province Herald South Africa, Sept. 19, 1985
(excerpt):

> Both Kallisch and Bruhn held the audience in awe
> with the rendering of the morbid Emily Dickinson
> poems set to the music of Gloria Coates. Every

possible emotion from grief to lust was portrayed
here with total conviction again, music which is not
reserved for lesser mortals.

Evening Post Ontvang, South Africa, Sept. 19, 1985
(excerpt):

The duo held their audience riveted with Gloria
Coates' song cycle to poems of Emily Dickinson, con-
veying doom, questioning, passion, and the desperate
fight for breath of a man buried alive.

In 1982, Gloria Coates was the recipient of a Norlin
Foundation Fellowship from the MacDowell Colony in Peter-
borough, New Hampshire, where she spent the autumn working on a piece for orchestra based on texts of Leonardo da
Vinci. She also received a grant from the GEMA Stiftung for
the copying of parts, and the two fragments were premiered
in Bayreuth, Germany, at the International Youth Orchestra
in August 1984, under the direction of Matthias Kuntzsch who
had commissioned the work. The orchestra is composed of
musicians in their 20s from both East and West Europe. The
performance took place in the Stadthalle with a capacity audience. The wild reaction of the audience was one of a split
between "bravos" and "boos." The composer said, "All I
could think as I walked on the stage was, thank you God for
all the bravos!" A review from the Neue Musikzeitung from
the October/November issue, 1984, by Gerhard Rohde (excerpt):

The two fragments from the not-yet-completed hourlong cantata Leonardo proves the composer to have
her own self-willed individualistic intimate connection
to sound colors and structures for the conception,
one must wait for the completed work before reviewing.

In January 1985, a composition Nonett (Halley's Comet)
was recorded by the WDR Cologne Radio. In Italy, from 1979
to 1982, Nonett was performed 38 times in concerts by the ensemble "I Solisti Dauni" under the baton of Domenico Losavio
from the Italian radio RAI.

Another composition that continues to be frequently
performed is Voices of Women in Wartime which she wrote while

working as a tour guide in Dachau Concentration Camp. The
piece pleads for peace and humanity. Although it was composed in 1973, it has been frequently performed at festivals,
and has radio and television recordings in both the United
States and Europe.

In 1983, while Gloria Coates was working on a commission from Ars Nova of Nuremberg for a performance on Musica
Viva, her father died. Her composition entitled Transitions
or Chamber Symphony is related to the composer's struggles
and final acceptance of her father's death. The movements
are "Illumination," "Mystical Plosives" and "Dream Sequence."
The premiere of this work was in the Bavarian Radio Concert
Auditorium on June 23, 1985, under the baton of Werner
Heider. In the Suddeutsche Zeitung of June 25, 1985, Wolfgang Schreiber wrote:

> Transitions is a very personally motivated piece of
> music in three movements that is individually colored.
> It is the altercation and discussion involving a de-
> cisive turning point in her life (death of her father),
> a kind of "lament." However, one must be aware
> that Gloria Coates herself pointed out that she re-
> jects this classification. "Music is free," she said.
> This was the most impressive and penetrating work
> on the program, also in terms of its concise, tense
> transforming of experiences, memories, and dreams
> into musical forms and structures.
>   The frequent use of glissandi in all the instru-
> ments of the ensemble is in agreement with the phe-
> nomenon of the microintervals, and set the title and
> meaning of the music from word to sound: Transi-
> tions. The listener is suddenly thrown into the
> tumbling lines as his musical ground is swept out
> from under his feet and he finds himself moving up
> and down in the artistically twisting and dove-tailing
> of the howling tones of all the instruments. Between
> the first and the second movements a fierce march
> solidifies and meshes them together. This music has
> great depth of feeling, and yet is is a work of great
> artistry, worked out with a secure compositional
> economy of means. [Copyright and permission to
> quote review, Gustav Bosse Verlag GmbH & Co. KG,
> Regensburg, West Germany.]

In the autumn of 1985 her publisher, Sonoton, issued a
recording of Music on Open Strings, and three of her string
quartets performed by the Kronos Quartet. The record was
selected as a record of the month for the Oct. 29, 1985 issue
of the Frankfurter Allgemeine Zeitung. In the magazine Fono
Forum it received special praise, and was reviewed in numerous magazines and newspapers.

Broadcasts and performances of Gloria Coates' music
have been heard in Poland, India, South Africa, People's Republic of China, West Germany, East Germany, Brazil, Sweden,
Spain, Belgium, Mexico, Italy, Switzerland, Canada, Finland,
England and the United States.

She was successful as a painter, winning numerous
prizes and awards. She has exhibited her art in the Munich
Haus der Kunst, in the Erding Artkothek, in the Munich Ara-
bella Haus, and the Munich Amerika Haus. Her work is in
private collections in London, Cologne, Berlin, New York,
Munich, Bonn, Stuttgart, Hamburg, Lake Constance and
Krakau. A photograph of one of her paintings can be seen
on the jacket of her latest Pro Viva recording.

Gloria Coates is an inspiring artist who seeks to convey
through her music a personal expression that reveals her
openness toward life and people. She is a survivor who had
the courage and stamina to find her own way in a creative
world that is so often unkind and unjust. Her works prove
that true creativity can never be stifled.

Selected Compositions of Gloria Coates

Orchestral Works

1974   Music on Open Strings, for full string orchestra, 19
          minutes, Sonoton Verlag publisher.
1974   Planets, for strings, woodwinds, horn, 18 minutes,
          Manuscript publisher.
1976   Chamber Symphony or Transitions, 22 minutes, Manu-
          script publisher.
1982   Sinfonietta della Notte, for full orchestra, 18 minutes,
          Manuscript publisher.
1982   L'Anima della Terra, for large orchestra, soli 4, 11
          minutes, Manuscript publisher.

1984 Symphony No. 3, for large orchestra with chorus, 12
      minutes, Manuscript publisher.
1985 Three Mystical Songs, for chorus and orchestra, 23
      minutes, Manuscript publisher.

Chamber Works

1966 String Quartet No. 1, 5 1/2 minutes, Sonoton Verlag
      publisher.
1972 String Quartet No. 2, 7 1/2 minutes, Sonoton Verlag
      publisher.
1976 String Quartet No. 3, 12 1/2 minutes, Ahn & Simrock
      publisher.
1977 String Quartet No. 4, 12 1/2 minutes, Sonoton Verlag
      publisher.
1966- 12 Songs on Poems of Emily Dickinson, for voice and
85   piano, 18 minutes, Manuscript publisher.
1973 Voices of Women in Wartime, for soprano, 15 minutes,
      piano, percussion, violin, viola and cello, Manuscript
      publisher.
1973 May the Morning Star Rise, for viola and organ, 10
      minutes, Manuscript publisher.
1966 Trio for Three Flutes, 9 minutes, Manuscript publisher.
1971 Spring Morning by Grobholz, for three flutes and tape,
      8 minutes, Manuscript publisher.
1973 Nonett, for violin, viola, cello, bass, flute/piccolo,
      oboe/English horn, bassoon/contra bassoon and horn,
      14 minutes, Manuscript publisher.
1966 Five Pieces for Four Woodwind Players, 12 minutes,
      Ahn & Simrock publisher. Revised 1975.
1976 My Country Tis of Thee, for piano four hands and two
      other instruments, 12 minutes, Manuscript publisher.
1979 Between, 24 minutes, Manuscript publisher.
1980 Valse Triste, 7 minutes, for piano, trombone, clarinet,
      cello, and percussion, Manuscript publisher.
1986 The Meter March, for band, 6 1/2 minutes, Manuscript
      publisher.

Music for Films

1982 Two Artists; One Exhibition, Jaqueline Kaess, director.
1983 Turin; The City on Wheels, Gabriel Heim, director.

Choral Music

1964   Sing Unto the Lord a New Song, SATB, 3 minutes,
         Manuscript publisher.
1964   Missa Brevis, SSA and organ or boys choir, 9 minutes,
         Manuscript publisher.
1979   The Beatitudes, for SATB and organ, 4 minutes, G.
         Schirmer publisher.

Addresses of publishers

Sonoton Verlag, Schleibinger Street, 10, 8 Munich 80, Federal
Republic of Germany.

Manuscript: Gloria Coates, c/o American Music Center Library,
         Room 300, 250 West 54 Street, New York, NY 10019.

Ahn & Simrock, Sonnenstrasse, 19, 8 Munich 2, Federal Republic of Germany.

G. Schirmer, New York/London.

Discography

Bavarian Radio Broadcasting Corp., Munich, West Germany

Tones in Overtones, for piano solo, Hae Kyung Lee, pianist.
Music on Open Strings, performance of Munich Musica Viva
         Bavarian Radio Symphony Orchestra, Elgar Howarth,
         conductor.
Voices of Women in Wartime, Edith Urbancyck, soprano, So-
         prano Chamber Ensemble of Bavarian Radio.
May the Morning Star Rise, Christian Kroll, Organ; Herbert
         Blendinger, viola.
My Country Tis of Thee, for piano four hands and two instru-
         ments, Meinrad Schmidt and Herbert Blendinger, clavier.
Transitions, for chamber orchestra, Ars Nova Ensemble,
         musica Viva Munich performance 1985, Werner Heider,
         conductor.

Polish Radio Broadcasting Corp., Warsaw, Poland

Music on Open Strings, 22 International Festival of Contemporary

Music, 1978 Warsaw, Poland, Polish Chamber Orchestra,
Jerzy Maksymiuk, conducting. (Premier)

West German Radio Broadcasting Corp., WDR Cologne, Germany

Music on Open Strings Siegerland Orchestra, Jorge Rotter,
   conductor.
Voices of Women in Wartime, Constance Navratil, soprano,
   Clementi Trio and percussion, Bonn Festival 1979.
Valse Triste (Valse Macabre), Ensemble West German Radio
   Cologne.
Halley's Comet (Nonett), West German Radio Ensemble Cologne.
Six Movements for String Quartet, String Quartet of Cologne
   Radio.
String Quartet No. 3, Crescent Quartet, Bonn Festival 1979.
Ten Emily Dickinson Songs, Janet Cobb, Mezzo.
Spring Morning at Grobholzes, for three flutes and tape, Karl
   Bernhard Sebon in playback.
Trio for Three Flutes, Karl Bernhard Sebon in playback.

Radio Bremen Broadcasting Corp., Bremen, West Germany

Planets, for chamber orchestra, Studio Orchestra Hanover,
   Klaus Bernbacher, conducting. Tage der Neuen Musik
   1975. (Premier)
String Quartet No. I, Sinnhoffer Quartet, Munich.
String Quartet No. II, Sinnhoffer Quartet, Munich.
String Quartet No. III, Sinnhoffer Quartet, Munich.
String Quartet No. IV, Sinnhoffer Quartet, Munich.

Swiss Romande Radio Broadcasting Corp., Geneva, Switzerland

Five Pieces for Four Wind Players, Southwest German Woodwind Quintet, 25 Anniversary Contemporary Music 1976.
   (Premier)

Southwest German Radio Broadcasting Corp., Baden-Baden, West Germany

Five Pieces for Four Wind Players, Southwest German Woodwind Quartet, Ars Nova Concert 1976; plus extra production.

Sender Freies Berlin (SFB) West Berlin, West Germany

Ecology No. 2 (Between) for tapes and instruments; composer
    plays instruments and reads her poetry.
String Quartet No. 4, Quartet of Sender Freies Radio, tape
    of concert 1977, premier performance.
Twelve Songs after Poems of Emily Dickinson, Cornelia Kal-
    lisch, mezzo soprano, Siglind Bruhn, piano.

North German Radio Broadcasting Corp., Hamburg, West
    Germany

May the Morning Star Rise, Erich Sichermann, viola, Gunther
    Jena, organ, 1979 Scandinavian Festival.

Southwest German Radio Broadcasting Corp., Hamburg, West
    Germany

String Quartet No. I, Kronos Quartet.
String Quartet No. II, Kronos Quartet.
String Quartet No. IV, Kronos Quartet.

British Broadcasting Corp., London, England

Five Pieces for Four Wind Players, Lontano Ensemble, Odaline
    Martinez, conducting.

Nuremberg Radio Broadcasting Corp., Nuremberg, West
    Germany

Anima della Terra (Vita), for solo and orchestra, Bayreuth
    International Youth Orchestra, Matthias Kuntzsch, con-
    ducting.
Symphony No. 3 (Fonte di Rimini), for chorus and orchestra,
    International Youth Orchestra Bayreuth, Matthias
    Kuntzsch, conducting.
Transitions, for chamber orchestra, Ars Nova Ensemble,
    Werner Heider, conducting.

Johannesburg Radio Corp., Johannesburg, South Africa

Ten Poems of Emily Dickinson, Cornelia Kallisch, mezzo; Sig-
    lind Bruhn, piano.

WFMT Chicago Broadcasting Corp.

Planets, for orchestra, Milwaukee Symphony, Kenneth Scher-
    merhorn, conducting.

Minneapolis Radio Braodcasting Corp.

Music on Open Strings, St. Paul Orchestra, John McGlaughlin,
    conducting.

Discography

String Quartets, I, II, III, performed by the Kronos Quartet
    and Music on Open Strings, Bavarian Radio Symphony
    Orchestra, Elgar Howarth, conductor, Musica Viva
    Munich Live Performance, ISPV-128.

Addresses

Pro Viva ISPV-128, Deutsche Austrophon Gmbh, 2480 Diep-
    holz, Federal Republic Germany.

USA Distributor: Theodore Front Musical Literature, Mr.
    Peter Brown, 16122 Cohasset Street, Van Nuys, Ca
    91406.

English Distributor: SLS Distribution, Holly End, Station
    Road, Rayne, Braintree, Essex, England.

SELMA EPSTEIN

Concert Pianist, Teacher

American pianist, Selma Epstein, has been a leading pioneer
of contemporary piano literature for over three decades. She
established her credentials with the more conventional repertoire when she captured national attention with an extraordinary performance at Carnegie Hall at age 15. She has
been honored with international acclaim for her pioneering
efforts, as one of only a few artists, to perform all styles of
contemporary music of all nationalities.

Madame Epstein was born in 1927 in Brooklyn, N.Y. of
an Austrian-Polish mother, Tillie Schneider, and a Russian
father, Samuel Schechtman. Her earliest training on piano,
at the age of 6, was with Stephanie Shehatovich at the Music
School Settlement in New York City.

When Epstein made her debut at Carnegie Hall she received much critical acclaim and recognition for her mastery
of the classical repertoire. Her program included works of
Schumann, Beethoven, Hindemith, Liszt, Scarlatti, Bach and
Chopin. Francis D. Perkins, writing for the New York Herald
Tribune, praised her technical competence, her ability to ex-
hibit a tone of consistent musical quality, as well as her command of dynamic shading. He further wrote, "Her interpretations suggested good taste, musicianship and sympathy with
the works which she offered."

She later studied, on scholarship, with Rosina Lhevinne
where she was her youngest student at the Juilliard School
of Music. Upon graduation she was awarded the D. Hendric
Ezerman Foundation Scholarship in competition at the Philadelphia Conservatory of Music where she studied with Edward
Steuermann. Of Steuermann, Selma says:

SELMA EPSTEIN   Photo by
                                 Joseph Epstein

Studying with Steuermann was a memorable experience. He was an extraordinary musician and an extremely demanding teacher. At the same time he was
a person of warmth and sensitivity.

She also studied with such eminent pedagogues as Karin
Dayas, Isador Philipp, Henry Cowell, Julio Esteban, and Max
Perin. Isador Philipp became interested in Selma's virtuosity
and acted as her teacher and guide until his death. It was
under his direction that she made her debut at Town Hall in
New York in 1950 followed by a second recital in 1951. Max
Rabinowitz, musical director of MGM studios, wrote, "I predict
a sensational career." This prediction written so many years
ago has proven to be correct. Selma Epstein's exceptional
talent as a musician, pianist, and teacher is limitless. She
possesses boundless energy and in her own words considers
herself an "overachiever." One might translate "overachiev-
ing" as an obsession with the world of art that few 20th-
century musicians would dare to venture. She is one of only

a few individuals who can demand of herself a 20-hour day of
practicing, researching and teaching that has continued for
years.

In the beginning of her concert career she was soloist
with Leon Barzin and the National Orchestral Association, a
guest artist in the Young American Artist Series, a guest
artist at the Brooklyn Museum Concert Series and in numerous
recital appearances throughout the United States. It was
when she was playing a number of recitals on college and university campuses that Epstein realized that audiences were
hearing little, if any, of what was being written by composers
of the 20th century. Madame Epstein has always been curious
and restless, qualities she believes artists need in order to
keep producing. "A certain spark is necessary that comes
from within the individual that makes full expression possible,"
according to Epstein.

Alan M. Kriegsman writing for the San Diego Union on
April 12, 1964:

20TH CENTURY PIANO MUSIC IS EXCEPTIONAL

The program alone--an anthology of twentieth century music for piano was enough to make Selma Epstein's recital at San Diego State Thursday evening
an event of exceptional significance. In centuries
past, performances of anything but new or recent
music was unheard of--people only wanted what was
"hot off the press." Nowadays such programs are
as rare as swans, and much to be prized.

The repertoire to which Miss Epstein chose to address herself is, let's face it, not for the lazy either
among performers or the public. In both it demands
the utmost patience, awareness, and care, as well
as a taste for rigor and abstraction. Miss Epstein's
performances possessed these qualities to a remarkable degree, but they also had something else of
even greater importance. She played this music as
if, so to speak, she meant every note of it. The
concert was no mere exercise in intellectual agility,
but a deeply personal encounter, both for the pianist
and her listeners. The program embraced three
groups of pieces, by an older and younger generation of American composers and European masters.

The first group included Carl Ruggles' tonal agglu-
tination entitled Evocation No. 1, six spry vignettes
by Wallingford Riegger, and the intriguing and stag-
geringly original Three Page Sonata of Charles Ives,
written unbelievably in 1905.   The second group consisted of Schoenberg's pithy and poignant Six Little
Pieces op. 19, a sure footed and eloquent Introduction and Song by Paul Hindemith and Alan Berg's
hyperromantic, indelibly Viennese Sonata op. 1.   The
concluding group contained the modest and amiable
Three Improvisations by San Diego State's David
Ward Steinman, two etudes of Benjamin Lees, the intense provocative two movement for piano of Robert
Hall Lewis and finally the fluent Sonata Variations
of Esther Ballou.   As you can see it was a challenging concert, but one that held special remuneration
for the hearer that comes with contact from a living
art.   [Reprinted with permission from The San Diego
Union.]

A veritable apostle of modern music, the following offers
the reader an example of Selma Epstein's adventuresome and
determined effort to program "lost and little known" works
by women composers and black composers.   She reflects:

Quite accidentally I learned that there was an unpublished work, Theme et Variations, by Lili Boulanger (1893-1918).   I made a special trip to the
Bibliotheque Nationale in Paris and found it there.
It took me more than three months to work through
the original manuscript, transcribing it into a play-
able score.   This was an exciting discovery, particularly as even Nadia Boulanger didn't know that
this piano work existed!

During my research into music by black composers
I discovered many superb compositions that have not
been published.   I also discovered there was no anthology of serious classical piano music by black
composers, an oversight which hopefully will change
in the near future.

Epstein continues to play classical pieces which at times
she combines with her pioneering contemporary music efforts
thus projecting her as the touring artist with one of the
largest repertoires.   It demands the utmost patience, awareness,

and care, as well as taste for rigor and abstraction. She is
not arbitrary in her definition of contemporary music; it is
not necessarily tone-row method, or avant-garde, or conservative, or neoromantic. She believes that a composer
should work in the method and the means most congenial to
his/her expressive capacity.

When Epstein first began to present her programs of
contemporary music she was both surprised and pleased with
the results. Her success was due not only to her great skills
as a performing artist but an intuitiveness on her part to
present a seminar prior to the recital. An enlightened audience is a listening audience and Madame Epstein's prerecital
talks make this happen. She is adventuresome and she is
successful in bringing to the listening public the music of living composers rather than continuing to listen to the works
of the dead ones. How refreshing!

In 1965 she made music history, with a herculean effort,
when she played 49 performances in as many days during her
first tour of Australia and the Far East. During this tour
she introduced the music of Ives, Cowell and Crumb among
others. In the Philippines she was hailed as the "Myra Hess
of America," and in New Zealand her pioneering efforts were
compared with those of another pioneer, Harriet Cohen.

The following are two sample programs offered by Selma
Epstein during this tour in which she received plaudits on
every continent where she performed for her deliberate, delicate and irrepressible surge of energy.

PIANOFORTE RECITAL
of works by contemporary American composer

by
SELMA EPSTEIN

Programme

Evocation No. 1   Carl Ruggles (1936)
New and Old   Wallingford Riegger (1947)
   The Augmented Triad
   The Major Second

The Tritone
The Twelve Tones
Twelve Upside Down
Three Page Sonata   Charles Ives
    Allegro moderato
    Andante
    Adagio
    Allegro, march time--Piu mosso

Piano Piece No. 1   George Crumb (1963)
Sonata, Op. 45, No. 1   Alan Stout (1958)
Eclipse   David Burge (1963)

The Willows are New   Chou Wen-chung (1957)
Cianccona dei tempi di guerra   Erich Itor Kahn (1943)

In place of programme notes Miss Epstein
will discuss each work

*   *   *

HOLYWELL MUSIC ROOM

Saturday--May 1, 1965, at 8:15 pm

Contemporary American and Japanese Piano Music

Selma Epstein, pianist
November 11, 1965
Small Hall, Kobe College

PROGRAM

I. American Music of the Past
    To a Water Lily   MacDowell   1905
    Three Page Sonata   Ives   1905

short pause

II. American Music of Today
    New and Old   Riegger   1947
    Piano Piece #1   Crumb   1962
    Experimental Music   Childs   1965

| Eclipse | Burge | 1963 |
| Piano Sonata #1 | Harrison | 1947 |

short pause

III. Japanese Music of Today

Calligraphie	Sato	1957-1960
Hallucination	Tsuji	1965
Spectra	Matsushita	1964

In place of program notes, Mrs. Epstein
will discuss the music.

"Expert Shows How To Play Inside of Piano" was the
headline of a press review from Auckland, New Zealand, in
October 1965. "In a charming informal talk Madame Epstein
gave away many secrets about playing inside the piano." The
article continues by praising the formal part of the program
where she revealed her devotion to modern music with dedicated and virtuoso performances of works by Charles Ives,
Chou Wen-chung, Wallingford Riegger, David Burge, Richard
Moffat and the Japanese composer Keifiro Sato. The pieces
were all brilliantly played.

Upon her return to the United States she was hailed as
a veteran apostle of the modern school and an expert pianist.
One critic wrote: "Although she has power and virtuosity,
her forte is found among the veiled sonorities. She delights
in quiet and meditative passages. She permits the strings to
resonate long before moving to the next notes. The music
is not interrupted." Robin Hopkins, staff writer for the
Wisconsin State Journal, reviewed Epstein's first performance
in the United States, following her history-making tour on
Nov. 24, 1965 (excerpt):

MRS. EPSTEIN SHOWS COMMAND OF MUSIC

Pianist Selma Epstein shared her vast command of
the living breathing spirit of music with Madison
Tuesday night in her lecture-recital on American
music past and present.
Her visit to Madison was the concluding step in

a tour that has taken her to perform in Australia, New Zealand, Okinawa and Japan as well as the United States.

Delicately and deliberately, Mrs. Epstein revealed that she has an irresponsible surge of energy in applying the piano to statements of the best creations of our day's artists.

Mrs. Epstein has so single-mindedly devoted her vast talents and training to her contemporaries, including a generous sample of Japanese composers, that the United States State Department sponsored her tour to strengthen artistic rapport among our Pacific neighbors.

Her performances of Japanese works are a beginning of the development of appreciation among Americans for current Oriental music.

Mrs. Epstein briefly represented the European influence in the form of MacDowell's idyllic To a Wild Rose. She then jumped into the fully American and more modern spirit with Charles Ives' Three Page Sonata.

After that introduction, the present in music held the stage as it does in established performers recitals.

Madame Epstein continued her concertizing with an extensive European tour to Austria, Denmark, Germany, Great Britain, Norway, Sweden, and Switzerland presenting 17 performances. She was the first artist to present an all-American music program at the Royal Danish Conservatory of Music. In Norway she performed under the sponsorship of the Norwegian branch of the ISCM. The highlight was in Oslo where she was met and hosted by Norway's leading composer, Klaus Egge, his wonderful hospitality and thoughtfulness made her stay in Norway one of the highlights of the trip.

Meeting with such eminent composers as Klaus Egge of Norway and Philip Cannon of England gave her wonderful access to a repertoire that is almost totally unknown in the United States or the Far East. She played Egge's beautiful Sonata Pathetica many times, and introduced Philip Cannon's charming Concerto for Piano and Strings op. 2. In addition Cannon has written a delightful series of piano pieces for her, Boutades Bourguignonnes, seven preludes for piano (1982) which she has played worldwide. Thus, her international

tour serves as an exchange medium for both her audiences
and herself.

Following her second tour of Australia, Epstein was in-
vited to teach at the Maitland and Newcastle branches of the
New South Wales conservatorium, where she was the first
American to be appointed to a major teaching post. She was
also the first resident recording artist with the prestigious
Australian Broadcasting Company from 1972-1975.

During her residence in Australia she became interested
in the music of Percy Grainger whose wife, Ella, requested
that she record his piano music, and gave her many of his
unpublished works. Grainger was one of the first native
Australians to achieve worldwide fame as both a composer and
performer.

For the Percy Grainger centenary, Epstein was invited
to record the complete piano works of Percy Grainger and has
recently completed Volume I of this project. (The recording,
RRS-12 in stereo, is available from Richardson Records, 1938
Old Annapolis Blvd., Annapolis, MD 21401.) This is the first
album of Grainger's music to be made by an American artist
in twenty years. The album features both original works and
transcriptions which have never been recorded previously.
Epstein reflects on the great Australian composer's works:

> The music of Percy Grainger is to an unusual degree
> an expression of his feelings and enthusiasm as a
> vital artist. He is a composer who believed in show-
> ing sentiment and emotion which is readily perceived
> in his musical settings of a folk tune or country
> dance. It is a rare occurrence that a classical com-
> poser can appeal equally to the most serious and
> creative minds of his time as well as to popular
> tastes. Such a composer was Percy Aldridge Grain-
> ger.

Madame Epstein is founder and president of the American Grainger Society which promotes the music of Grainger
through a series of International Festivals. Epstein has devoted a considerable amount of her time and energy in pur-
suit of her Grainger "collection" and has accumulated materials
from libraries and individuals in Australia, England, Scotland,
Canada and the United States. In honor of Ella Grainger's

90th birthday, Madame Epstein performed a special all-Grainger recital and is the only touring artist to present such programs. These programs include both original works and transcriptions, many of which she received as gifts from Ella Grainger.

A review of Ella's last birthday concert was written by Marguerite Tjader for The Grainger Journal, Volume 2, Number 2, February 1980:

On June 2, 1979 at White Plains, New York, the dynamic American pianist Selma Epstein gave a recital of Grainger music, balanced with a group of American and Australian compositions which powerfully evoked the verve and drama of Percy Grainger's own style of playing.

A graduate of Juilliard, and concert performer literally all over the world, Selma Epstein has a wide repertoire, but for this concert she chose numbers which enhanced her tribute to Percy Grainger, and to his wife Ella who was celebrating her 90th birthday.

An American Suite, written for her by her son Leslie Epstein, was in the youthful, sprightly style of Grainger, which Selma Epstein seems naturally to follow. This led easily into a group of Grainger compositions: Hornpipe from Handel's Water Music, Now Oh Now, I Needs Must Part, The Leprechaun's Dance, The Immovable Do (with the assistance of Donna Beran--this piece was humorously conceived for a piano with a sticking note!), Hard Hearted Barb'ra Helen and Children's March.

The group of Australian composers next presented would have pleased Grainger. It included premiere performances of Peter Sculthorpe, Larry Sitsky, Dulcie Holland, and Barry Conyngham, young musicians, such as Grainger were always trying to promote. Selma Epstein recently toured the Orient with a cultural program for our State Department, and in Australia found these young talents as they came out to hear Grainger's music which she presented throughout her tour.

Ending with another Grainger group of original compositions and transcriptions Selma Epstein reached the climax of her exciting concert with Grainger's

paraphrase of Tchaikovsky's Waltz of the Flowers.
It was played with tremendous brilliance and power.
I could only recall the playing of Percy himself when
he evoked the Grieg Piano Concerto playing both
piano and orchestra parts--it would seem with more
notes than the piano possesses. Selma Epstein's
great talent can answer any challenge.

Madame Epstein is completely self-trained in art. She
painted many of her pastels, exhibited in her first major art
show, during her overseas concert tours. Her sketch of the
Percy Grainger Museum in Melbourne, Australia was made the
same day that she recorded a piano recital for FM Radio in
Melbourne (and in the same room that the recital was recorded
at the Conservatory of Music of the University of Melbourne).
Her talent as a painter is extraordinary and one must not
miss her exhibitions of beautiful "Landscapes and Flowers"
for they are indeed breathtaking. Check New York newspapers for dates and places where Selma Epstein's art work
can be viewed. Her most recent catalog includes over 30
paintings although not all of them are for sale.

As the recently appointed mid-Atlantic region chairwoman
of the International Congress of Women in Music, Epstein is
now formulating plans for an International Piano Competition,
the first in which the music of women composers will be the
required repertoire rather than the standard repertoire.
During the season 1985-86, in addition to two overseas tours,
she will be soloist in an all concerto program which will include compositions by Florence Price, Grazyna Bacewicz (U.S.
premiere), Nancy Van de Vate (world premiere) and Chopin,
with the newly formed Maryland Woman's Symphony under the
direction of conductor Deborah Freedman. She will also be
performing a unique two concert Polish music series which
will consist of twentieth century Polish women composers including Dziewulska, Bruzdowicz, Matusczak, Bacewicz and an
all Chopin program. Madame Epstein is one of the only regularly touring artists who manages her own tours.

NICOLA LEFANU

Composer

In the words of the American music critic Michael Steinberg:
"Nicola LeFanu is a composer of outstanding gifts of the head
and the heart." One needs only to listen to her music to
agree with Steinberg's comment for LeFanu is an exceptionally
fine composer with an infinite imagination.

Born in 1947 in Essex, England, she is the daughter
of the eminent composer Elizabeth Maconchy and William LeFanu,
a descendant of the Victorian writer Sheridan LeFanu. She
grew up in a home surrounded by music and literature and
loved both of these art forms at an early age. She produced
school plays and studied the piano and later the cello. Although she never studied composition formally with her mother,
she often played musical games with her as a child. Throughout her childhood she wrote plays and composed music for
them. Gradually she came to realize that composition was
central to her, and when she was 15 years old she made a
decision to make a career as a composer.

She studied composition with Jeremy Dale Roberts; then
she entered Oxford University where Egon Wellesz, a composer
and a Schoenberg pupil, was one of her professors. Of this
experience she reflects:

> I chose Oxford because I preferred to follow my own
> path. I wanted to mix with other students of other
> disciplines rather than live in the narrow world of
> a music college, where emphasis is more on per-
> formance.

She pays tribute to what she calls Wellesz's creative approach to history, and also learned an immense amount from
vacation lessons with the English composer Alexander Goehr.

NICOLA LEFANU   Photo by
                            David Lumsdaine

LeFanu graduated from Oxford in 1968 with a bachelor of arts honours degree in music. She then studied for three months in Siena, Italy with Goffredo Petrassi, who taught her the critical importance of listening. After that came a post graduate year at the Royal College of Music.

It was at the Royal College that Nicola won the much coveted Cobbett Prize for her Variations for Oboe Quartet. Her Soliloquy for oboe, composed when she was 17 years old and her first published work, had been played on the Netherlands radio by the Dutch oboist Victor Swillens, who then invited her to write the variations for his Hilversum Oboe Quartet.

She then submitted Variations for Oboe Quartet for a British Broadcasting Corporation competition open to all British composers under the age of 35. Of the 200 entries it received first prize and she was the youngest of the five finalists. The following review appeared in Western Mail, Jan. 15, 1972:

> A young composer who is receiving much attention these days with commissions and the winning of prizes is Nicola LeFanu, daughter of composer Elizabeth Maconchy. Two published works, Soliloquy for Oboe Solo and Variations for Oboe Quartet (Novello), show why. Any work for a solo wind instrument is a risk, the most obvious being monotony. Miss LeFanu cleverly avoids this with a wide variety of invention and also misses the other pitfall of writing a mere study. The quartet shows a similar imaginative approach to instrumental writing coupled with a sure grasp of motivic structure.

In 1969 LeFanu composed Chiaroscuro for pianist Peter Pettinger who premiered the work in London in February 1970. In 1971 she was commissioned by the prestigious Radcliffe Trust to write a quintet. The first performance of Quintet for Clarinet and Strings was performed by Alan Hacker and the Allegri String Quartet in Oxford in October 1971. Her Songs and Sketches for Cellos, an educational work, was commissioned by the Farnham Festival and performed in 1972 by the Kathleen Anderson Cello Ensemble at the festival. During this period she also wrote a dramatic scena But Stars Remaining with words by C. Day Lewis. The

piece was premiered by Jane Manning in London in 1971 and
is recorded by her on the Chandos record, ABR 1017.

Christ Calls Man Home, music for service, scored for
unaccompanied SATB choir, was commissioned by and first
performed at the Cheltenham Festival in 1971. During this
period of time LeFanu also wrote Rondeaux, an 11-minute work
for tenor and horn with text from French medieval love poems.
It was written for Ronald Murdock and John Pigneguy and
premiered by them at the Young Artists and Twentieth Century Music Series promoted by the Park Lane Group at the
Purcell Room on Jan. 8, 1973. Richard Lawrence reviewed
the eight concert series for Music and Musicians, Volume 21,
April 1973 (excerpt):

> Equally absorbing was the first performance of Ron-
> deaux for tenor and horn by Nicola LeFanu, a former
> pupil of Searle. Three medieval love poems are
> preceded and followed by a rondeau of Charles d'
> Orleans. The sense of awe that emerged from the
> second song, "Est-il paradis amie?", was far more
> telling in its rapture than a passionate outburst
> would have been, and the epilogue, "let time pass
> by just as Fortune wills it," was not a resigned Gal-
> lic shrug of the shoulders but an impervious injunc-
> tion to take a positive attitude to living. Murdock
> and Pigneguy were impressive here....

LeFanu's first theatrical piece, Anti World, was composed in 1972 for dancer, soprano, baritone, alto flute, clarinet and percussion with text from Russian sources. As a
young girl she had been enchanted with drama and her plan
in Anti World was to have the actors, dancers and singers
share the dramatic action as equals. Accordingly the composition specifies the dancer's movement and all the stage action.
It was first staged at the Cockpit Theatre, London, NW8.

During the early part of her career LeFanu composed
intensely and was the recipient of numerous commissions. A
prestigious commission from the BBC in 1973 culminated in
The Hidden Landscape, her first major essay in orchestral
writing. LeFanu wrote:

> The Hidden Landscape is my first attempt at a large-
> scale orchestral work, my first bite at an apple which

offers irresistible musical temptation despite the
practical disadvantages of writing for orchestra--
above all, the prohibitive cost of adequate rehearsal time. To compose for so many musicians working
both as individuals and as parts of a whole, intuitively creating a constantly shifting set of relation-
ships--the possibilities are far too rich to turn one's
back on.

The orchestral work was premiered at a Promenade
Concert in the Royal Albert Hall on Aug. 7, 1973 by the BBC
Symphony Orchestra conducted by Norman Del Mar. Included
on the program was Michael Tippett's Concerto for Double
String Orchestra, Benjamin Britten's Variations and Fugue on
a Theme of Purcell and William Walton's Belshazzar's Feast.
LeFanu commented, "A concert of household gods with the
customary female sacrifice."

But the music critics were impressed with LeFanu's The
Hidden Landscape as indicated in the following review by
Keith Potter published in Music and Musicians, Volume 22,
November 1973 (excerpt):

PROMS COMTEMPORARY

The Hidden Landscape by 26-year-old Nicola LeFanu,
played by the BBC Symphony Orchestra under Norman Del Mar on August 7, was not in the same class
as the Musgrave, but it was a confident first stab
at a large-scale orchestra piece by a determined
young lady whose rise to fame has been somewhat
meteoric. She seems particularly interested in non-
musical concepts allied to music, to judge from her
programme notes: several of her works (for example
Anti World of 1972), involve dance and theatrical
elements, including the dramatic conflict of individual
players' personalities and the exploration on connec-
tions between musical and physical gesture.
Her orchestral piece is at once more and less ambitious than some of her earlier, smaller-scale works.
Although in an interesting article in The Listener
LeFanu draws attention to visual and dramatic concepts and her continuing attraction to the English
landscape (in spite of being told at Oxford not to
write minor thirds because they sounded English),

The Hidden Landscape seems more involved with
purely musical development and, in the process,
less original. At the time it is a sizable piece of
musical construction (22 minutes) for large orchestra,
in which she quite obviously has control both of her
material and its presentation in orchestral terms.
Particular groups of instruments are prominent in
each of the two sections (clarinets, flutes and trumpets in the quick first section and cellos, oboes and
bassoons in the slow second section, which is divided
into five verses, continuous expansions of the solo
cello opening). Solo instruments are also used freely,
mainly those in the warmer middle register (alto
flute, horn, alto saxophone, cor anglais and cello);
and texture is integrated with structure in ways
which are easily apparent to the ear, most obviously
the chords at the end of the prologue which precedes the first section. These act as "pillars" to the
structure of the piece as a whole, and return in different guises and on different instruments throughout, eventually reappearing in their original form,
horns now replaced by strings, in the epilogue.

In 1972 Nicola LeFanu won the Gulbenkian Dance Award
to work with the Ballet Rambert. The Last Laugh, for soprano, tape, flute, cor anglais, clarinet, bassoon, trumpet,
percussion, viola and double bass, was first performed by
the troupe at the Young Vic Theatre the following year. In
1973 she was awarded two esteemed grants, the Mendelssohn
Scholarship and a Harkness Award which took her for a year
to the United States, where she studied composition with Earl
Kim at Harvard and Seymour Shifrin at Brandeis. While in
the United States she received a Fromm Foundation commission and wrote the song cycle The Same Day Dawns which
was premiered in Boston by Diana Hoagland and members of
the Boston Symphony Orchestra conducted by LeFanu. This
was her first professional appearance as a conductor, and she
commented later: "I was always grateful to Earl and Seymour
for encouraging me to conduct, because it has led to many
very fruitful occasions when I have had the chance to work
with outstanding players, as well as being invaluable in my
work as a composition teacher."

The Same Day Dawns, for soprano and five players,
flute and alto flute, clarinet and bass-clarinet, violin, cello

and percussion, has as its text works based on Tamil, Chinese
and Japanese poems. One American music critic said, "These
songs, despite a delicacy of color and texture appropriate to
the oriental text, also have the hardness and specificity of
precise craft: They are like a polished butterfly, fashioned
of silver." Michael Steinberg writing for the Boston Globe
on May 11, 1974 was enraptured with the work as indicated
by his review (excerpt):

LEFANU'S SAME DAY DAWNS NEW AND DELICATE

The Same Day Dawns is a cycle of 15 songs--actually
11, because four of the first five are repeated in
reversed order toward the end. The poetic fragments are translated from various Eastern languages,
and they are sung by a soprano with a small instrumental ensemble. The words are words of unendur-
able love, longing, distance, sleeplessness, death;
and the music responds beautifully to their senti-
ments and their sounds.

It is in its poetic sensibility, in its pleasure in
virtuosity, in its delicate marryings of voice to instrument, The Same Day Dawns reminds me of "Pierrot" or better, strikes me as one of a host of works
whose physiognomy and character would not be what
they are without great and seductive model. But
LeFanu's cycle is a lyric, reserved, non-theatrical,
non-parodic piece, and if it has a fault, it is that of
being delicate and soft almost to excess. For about
half a minute, a setting of a poem about a green-
finch lets loose a wonderful and tiny conflagration
of violin harmonics, bells, wire-brushed cymbals,
and flutter-tonguing, and I wished then that the
composer had found--or, in her selection of verses,
had made--occasion to reach for the peppermill at
least one more time.

But Ms. LeFanu, a 26-year-old English composer
living in Cambridge just now, handles the "sensitive"
style surely and imaginatively. There is a giving
into loveliness that is a new development in her always clean and intelligent work, and her "fragments
from a book of songs," as she subtitles The Same
Day Dawns, is a touching utterance by a composer
of exceptional gifts of heart and head.

She herself conducted the premiere, and in Harvey

122 Women Composers

Seigel (violin), Martha Babcock (cello), Paul Fried (flutes), Felix Viscuglia (clarinets), and Frank Epstein (percussion), she had a fine group of players. [Reprinted courtesy of The Boston Globe.]

In April 1975 LeFanu conducted the British premiere of The Same Day Dawns with the American soprano Diana Hoagland and five members of the Dreamtiger Ensemble at the Purcell Room in London. According to one British newspaper review this piece confirmed what many had suspected for some time--"LeFanu is a real composer." Hugo Cole reported in The Guardian on April 29, 1975 the following:

> At one extreme, there is music which begins as abstract pattern; at the other, music which seems to grow from the nature of the sounds themselves. In the latter class, comes Nicola LeFanu's new song cycle The Same Day Dawns centered, surely, on the remarkable voice of Diana Hoagland, an American singer of great sensitivity with serene clarity of tone in upper registers and the ability to sustain an almost instrumental melodic line without losing the colours and inflexions of natural speech.
>
> Nicola LeFanu sets her short poems from Tamil, Chinese and Japanese, as though every sound from the voice and the small accompanying ensemble was truly precious to her. These short atmospheric pieces grow directly from the mood and colour of the words; instruments are used with great discrimination and imagination. It is the most immediately communicative of her works that I have yet heard, flowing spontaneously and freely, so easily that we never feel (as in much contemporary music and in one or two of her own past works) that we are being taught a difficult lesson.

Columbia Falls, commissioned by the Feeney Trust, was first performed in Birmingham by the City of Birmingham Symphony Orchestra, conducted by Louis Fremaux, on Nov. 20, 1975. The London premiere was performed the following day at the Royal Festival Hall. According to LeFanu the piece was inspired by the rolling hills and high moors of Maine's "blueberry barrens" during her previous stay in the United States when she went to a small village in Maine which she found to be a beautiful and inspiring place in one of the

wildest and most lovely of the American states. Although
LeFanu does not feel her music encompasses direct pictorial
representation, the village and its surrounding area made a
deep impression on her. To a certain degree Columbia Falls
expands on LeFanu's musical thinking that began to appear
in The Hidden Landscape when each instrument was accorded
individual attention.

> LeFanu describes the work as a continuous arch
> where the strings, brass and wind instruments are
> on three different planes, inhabiting three completely
> different regions, but moving within their own music
> to the climax where the three planes meet. The
> three groups of instruments are characterized by dif-
> ferent kinds of material: different sorts of melodic
> and rhythmic shapes and contrasting areas of har-
> mony. In the overall control of the form, in par-
> ticular the long-term harmonic structuring, the piece
> marks the maturing of many aspects of LeFanu's lan-
> guage: she refers to it as 'a coming of age', and
> it remains one of her major works, and one of her
> own favorites.

In 1976 LeFanu spent six months in Australia, taking
leave from her post as director of music, St. Paul's Girls
School, to fulfill a commission for a chamber opera from the
New Opera Company. Dawnpath, a chamber opera on American Indian texts, was staged in London in 1977 and in Sussex
in 1978.

In 1977 Nicola LeFanu took up a post as lecturer in
music at Kings College, University of London, and began to
build up a department of postgraduate composition there.
She married the composer David Lumsdaine in 1979, and that
year they were in Sydney again as joint composers-in-residence
at the New South Wales Conservatorium of Music.

In 1979 she was commissioned by the Camden Festival
with funds from the Greater London Arts Association to compose Deva for cellist Christopher Van Kampen which was
premiered by him with the Nash Emsemble, in the Camden
Festival, at Rosslyn Hill Chapel, in London on March 23, 1979.
The piece is scored for solo cello and seven players: flute
and alto flute, clarinet, bassoon, horn, violin, viola and
double bass. The following are LeFanu's program notes:

'Deva', a Hindu word, means 'a good spirit'. It is
particularly used of nature spirits, but it is really
the same word as our 'dea' or 'diva', a goddess.

My Deva is for solo cello with an ensemble of alto
flute, clarinet, bassoon, horn, violin, viola and bass.
It is written for Christopher Van Kampen.

Deva lasts about eighteen minutes. The solo cello
creates a shape which is easy to follow: it is a
gradual descent from the top of its register to the
bottom, moving back towards the centre in the coda.
As the cello line grows it becomes increasingly sono-
rous. The cello is very much alive, always moving
onward, its moments of parenthesis or summary
reinforcing its progress through time.

The ensemble play as a group, rather than as
seven individuals, so their music is simpler, especially in its rhythmic shapes, than that of the soloist. Two principal ensemble ideas emerge, the first
moving in quietly stepping chords, the second fast
and brilliant. These act as refrains, pacing the
gradual descent of the cello. Sometimes they recur
literally and sometimes in transformation.

Thus the overall structure of Deva is created
two ways: by the highly articulated line of the
cello, and by the ensemble refrains which give it
perspective. As a whole, the ensemble music creates
the harmonic context from which the cello melody can
grow: from the soft and distant opening to the
resolution glimpsed near the end. Perhaps I should
turn once more to metaphor and describe the ensemble as the landscape through which the cello passes
like a stream...becoming a river...becoming sea.

When the Nash Ensemble premiered Deva at the Camden
Festival, Hugo Cole reviewed the event for The Guardian on
March 27, 1979 (excerpt):

Nicola LeFanu's Deva, specially commissioned for this
concert, displays solo cello against a chamber-ensemble
background. The composer, not for the first time
suggests a landscape metaphor. The cello, starting
in higher registers, descends and gains in forceful-
ness and definition like a stream becoming river, becoming sea.

The work evolves from very high and very quiet

sounds, cello harmonics carrying no real cello character, so that we sometimes have to look before we
know whether cello, flute or viola is playing (as in
the water meadows near Cirencester, one looks at
the various pools, springs and puddles, wondering
which is really the source of the Thames).
        The soloist only gradually establishes his role as
the central active protagonist, and then retreats
into the middle ground. The process gives the work
clarity and shape for the listener, who knows nothing of its constructional processes. LeFanu's feeling for subtle and refined texture is as strong as
ever. There is also (for me) a new sort of plain-
ness in some of the harmonic writing and an almost
reckless violence in one climactic passage which suggests that she is moving out of the old familiar landscape into new country.

        The frequent references to landscape show how fruitful
a metaphor LeFanu finds it; she writes: "When we look at a
natural landscape, we can delight in a tiny detail (like a
flower at our feet) while taking in the shapes and the mass
of the whole view, near and far. I react in the same way to
the mass of, say, an orchestral piece: My perspective is
constantly shifting, my attention is continually taken by fore-
ground detail but I never lose sight of those distant horizons."

        Metaphors aside, the first ideas for some of LeFanu's
pieces have come when she and her husband are out walking,
whether in her native landscape (East Anglia, in England) or
his (the Australian bush, and in particular the country
around Sydney).

        In 1981 the University of London created a joint teach-
ing post for David Lumsdaine and Nicola LeFanu. Freed from
the constraints of full-time teaching, LeFanu has produced a
spate of works since then, both chamber works, two trios, a
saxophone quartet, the song cycle A Penny for a Song for
soprano and piano and larger pieces--the Variations for Piano
and orchestra and a choral work Stranded on my Heart.

        In progress 1985-86 is a radio opera for voices, The
Story of Mary O'Neill. Of all the works from the 1980s, it
is The Old Woman of Beare (1981) a monodrama for soprano
and 13 instruments, which best reveals the nature of her

work: a dramatic music and text, dense textures and rich harmonics reminiscent of the orchestral works, lyrical writing for the solo soprano, and (not least) an evocation of the wild coasts of Ireland, where her family once lived.

Looking back over her career so far, LeFanu wrote in 1985:

> If I look back and consider my life so far (over twenty years of composing) I would say that the two formative influences in my life are two composers: my mother, Elizabeth Maconchy, and my husband David Lumsdaine. What I owe them is inestimable.
>
> Beyond that I would look back at my education, and remember the years of musical discovery in my late teens--studying with Jeremy Dale Roberts. Friendships begun at Oxford which still continue and then later the inspiration of working with Earl Kim at Harvard. If I was to single out particular events, then I think the premiere performances of Columbia Falls in 1975, and the experience of raising an infant (my son Peter was born in November 1982) would stand out above all else for me. If I had to choose one work to represent me, it would be The Old Woman of Beare. I think it encompasses both the lyric and the dramatic aspect of my work and it could only have been composed by a woman!

When anyone assesses LeFanu's position as an artist one must be impressed with the great originality of the woman and her music. It is probably the strongly dramatic quality of all her writing that makes her music so exhilarating. At this time one cannot predict the full impact that LeFanu's music will have on the 20th and 21st centuries. Time and continual output will eventually determine her place on the rostrum of contemporary composers; however, one can safely predict that she is a leader among young contemporary composers. One must surely admire her talent and capacity for she has made a strong imprint.

Selected Compositions of Nicola LeFanu

Orchestral

1967   Preludio I, 6 minutes.

1973 The Hidden Landscape, 23 minutes.
1975 Columbia Falls, 22 minutes.
1982 Variations for Piano and Orchestra, 15 minutes.

Chamber & Instrumental

1965 Soliloquy, for oboe, 4 minutes.
1968 Variations for Oboe Quartet, 11 minutes.
1969 Chiaroscuro, for piano, 13 minutes.
1979 Deva, for solo cello and seven players: flute and alto
        flute, clarinet, bassoon, horn, violin, viola, double
        bass, 20 minutes.
1984 Stranded on my Heart, for SATB choir, solo tenor,
        and stringed orchestra, 22 minutes.
1984 Quartet for Saxophones, duration 12 minutes.

Vocal & Choral

1968 II Cantico dei Cantici II, for soprano solo, 5 minutes.
1970 But Stars Remaining, for soprano solo, 8 minutes.
1974 The Same Day Dawns, for soprano and five players:
        flute and alto flute, clarinet and bass clarinet, violin,
        cello, percussion, 18 minutes.
1978 For We are the Stars, for sixteen voices SATB, 8 min-
        utes.
1981 Like a Wave of the Sea, for mixed choir and ensemble
        of early instruments, 20 minutes.
1981 The Old Woman of Beare, for soprano (preferably am-
        plified) and thirteen players, 18 minutes.
1981 A Penny for a Song, for soprano and piano, 18 minutes.
1982 Rory's Rounds, 13 rounds for children's voices.

Theatrical

1972 Anti-World, for dancer, with soprano, baritone, alto
        flute, clarinet, percussion, 20 minutes.
1977 Dawnpath, chamber opera for baritone, soprano, male
        dancer, flute and alto flute, clarinet and bass clari-
        net, horn, cello, percussion, 50 minutes.

Addresses of Publishers

Printed Music on Sale.   Other Music available on hire, or on
   sale to special order.

Novello and Company Limited, Fairfield Road, Borough Green,
   Sevenoaks, Kent.

Theodore Presser Company, Presser Place, Bryn Mawr, PA
   19010.

Discography

The Same Day Dawns, Jane Manning (soprano), Kathryn
      Lukas (flute), Ian Mitchel (clarinet, violin and cello),
      James Wood (percussion), conducted by Nicola LeFanu,
      ABR1017.
But Stars Remaining, Jane Manning, soprano, ABR1017.
Deva, for solo cello and seven players, Christopher Van
      Kampen, cello, The Nash Ensemble, ABR1017.

Addresses

Chandos Records Ltd., 41 Charing Cross Road, London, England WC2H ORH.

PRISCILLA McLEAN

Composer, Performer

Priscilla McLean has composed music in virtually all traditional and contemporary media but she is best known for her works that have been electronically generated. She has a vivid imagination, originality, and communicates via her music her humanistic tendencies as an ardent conservationist. She prefers to work with environmental and/or nature sounds in combination with electronics until they merge into what she describes as "imago-abstract sound"--sounds that are suggestive of amny images and ideas. Although the sounds may be programmatic, she does not treat them that way in her compositions, for it is their musical properties which she develops.

Born in 1942 in Fitchburg, Mass., she is the daughter of Conrad and Grace Taylor, manager of gas-heating sales and elementary-school teacher, respectively. Recalling her childhood:

> I began to create as soon as I could read and write. Since my parents could not afford a piano until I was twelve years old, I spent my early years writing poems and short stories.
> I was brought up to believe that all composers were men, and that women, to work at all, should take a temporary position such as nursing or teaching, until they married and had children.
> Following my mother's advice I trained as an elementary school teacher but found after a very short period that I could not keep the musical creative impulse buried forever without severe problems. I came close to a nervous breakdown twice in my early career, and decided at the age of twenty-three,

PRISCILLA McLEAN   Photo by
                                          Bart McLean

to sell everything I owned (which was very little)
and move to Indiana to begin my first formal study
in composition at Indiana University.

Since the age of 16 McLean had been composing in a
void. She had not formally studied for any length of time,
and was therefore able to pursue her own individual tonal
world without the restrictions so often imposed by study.
Perhaps this can be noted as a blessing in disguise, for her
ability to express her musical creative thoughts is unique,
and she is continually intrigued by new sound worlds.

During her undergraduate years at Fitchburg (Mass.)
State College she studied music theory with Dr. Richard Kent,
who was the entire department until her last year there. Although theory was not applicable to the degree she was pur-
suing, it was very important to Priscilla's quest to compose.
She reflects:

> Kent was my first mentor--he told me that I had to
> be tough if I wanted to compose, and that one should
> always keep in mind that in the act of composing,
> one was 'communing with the Greats,' in laboring
> towards the same ends as Bach, Brahms, et al.
> Under his tutelage, I wrote a new school alma
> mater, which is still sung, over two decades later,
> by the entire student body at each commencement,
> and several times during the year. I rode high in
> those days, as I was the only composer, except for
> Dick Kent, in the college!
> This was a time in my musical life that I desper-
> ately needed help, and Dr. Kent provided theoretical
> and aesthetic training. Later I studied counterpoint
> privately with Dr. Hugo Norden (Boston University),
> and learned to play several instruments at Lowell
> (Mass.) University (Bachelor of Music Education,
> 1965) with help towards writing for large ensembles
> by Willis Traphagen, the director of symphonic winds.

Priscilla's move to Indiana University, where she received a master's degree in music (composition) in 1969, proved
to be the most important decision she has ever made in her
life and career. While at the university she studied composition and orchestration with Dr. Thomas Beversdorf, who
helped her to open her ears and hear the inside of music.

She said, "he taught me the nitty gritty nuts and bolts of hearing." She also studied composition with Bernhard Heiden, and met and married Barton McLean (who received his doctorate there in 1972), a scholar and fine composer-musician.

Priscilla Taylor McLean's third commercial recording was a result of her study of orchestration at the university. Variations and Mozaics on a Theme of Stravinsky, a 20-minute work, began as an assignment for class and in 1969 became the basis for the composer's master's thesis in composition. Dissatisfied with the original version, she abandoned it for five years until her husband urged her to take it out of the drawer and revise it for the annual national competition given by Indiana State University, the Indianapolis Symphony in residence, in 1975. As one of the winners of that National Symposium, and the first woman ever chosen, she heard its world premiere by the Indianapolis Orchestra, conducted by Oleg Kovalenko. The performance was met with bravos from the audience. Priscilla relates:

> I was so affected by the response of everyone that I went to hide in the ladies' room, to gain control over myself. There I met several violinists from the orchestra who were wildly enthusiastic. It seems that I couldn't get away from the accolades!

Frederick Black writing for the Terre Haute Star on April 25, 1975:

> Priscilla McLean won a real ovation for her Variations & Mozaics on a Theme of Stravinsky. It was well deserved applause for in addition to most competent writing for orchestra there seemed to be a definite style and purpose for each variation.

The work was recorded by the Louisville Orchestra, Jorge Mester, music director, LS 762 (stereo), and performed by them at Kennedy Center during the Inter-American Music Festival in 1977. The work was later nominated for the Pulitzer Prize.

The eight years that it took for McLean to complete this work may be said to correspond with her own growth as an artist. She explains the various styles that are presented and finds an analogy in Stravinsky:

The theme is derived from an early Russian folk song which Stravinsky set for baritone soloist and three-part women's chorus. Fragments of the Theme are quoted and altered throughout the first three variations, interwoven with much original music, and reaching their most fragmentary character while spinning into completely new material in the "Mozaics" movement. This new movement, composed much later than the variations, uses "the techniques of brief sections and interruption," according to the composer, "using melodic and harmonic motives often directly taken from the original Theme. This movement, inspired by Stravinsky's Agon, is a tribute-parody to the later style of Stravinsky." The original theme is restated and expanded in the fourth and in the final variations.

When Stravinsky wrote Agon, parts of which were written a few years earlier than the rest, the ballet straddled two stylistic periods in his life, the neo-classic and the serial. Yet this work is irrevocably unified, producing an intriguing depth of perception, a multi-dimensional quality of time-sense. When I wrote Mozaics, I was deeply inspired by Bransle Gay, one of the serial movements of Agon, the character of which is evident in Mozaics. So I felt closely aligned with Stravinsky, as parts of my work bridged years, and a change of styles, as his did, and I was focusing, through this orchestral work, on a large life-expanse of Stravinsky: his early years, as in the Theme, and his much later period, as in Mozaics.

Iannis Xenakis' tenure as director of the Electronic Music Studio at Indiana University in the late 1960s was to have a strong influence on both Barton and Priscilla McLean. Xenakis' lectures and recordings were like a "nuclear bomb exploding" to Priscilla which she describes:

Xenakis' music was a new voice entirely, a new way of thinking, a completely different perspective of listening.

Instead of predominately melody and harmony, one concentrates on texture--thick textures, thin textures, and how all instruments together interweave to make a special sound mass.

In other words, it's a new concept of listening,
focusing on (large) structures to (small) structures,
hearing moving shapes. This is the way pieces of
this style, especially in the electronic media, can
best be understood. It had a great influence on me.

Within a short period of time, husband Bart would be
director of an electronic studio at a college which provided
the means for both of them to pursue their love of electronic
music. The McLeans have been a strong team, helping each
other out, listening to each other's music and performing together. Yet, they have maintained their own individual styles.
Priscilla said, "Bart's support and artistry has been truly a
miracle for me."

Since her composition Interplanes, written in 1970, a
polyphonic atonal work for two pianos, her focus has been
directed toward electronic and other unique sound-producing
media. Interplanes was recorded by Robert Hamilton and
Christine Douberteen, pianists on Advance Recordings FGR
19S. Included on the disc are other compositions from Volume
V, Journal of Music Scores, of the American Society of University Composers. McLean describes the work as follows:

Interplanes, for two pianos, is in two movements.
A restless dramatic atmosphere pervades the first
movement, as two strong, divergent personalities
with their own planes of music compete for dominance.
In the second movement the two individuals merge
into one broad, complex atmosphere out of which
melodies, motives, and arpeggios emerge and fade,
moving as from one large integrated instrument.
This work, inspired by Charles Ives' The Unanswered
Question, is a collage of superimposed contrasts.

After graduating from Indiana University, the McLeans
moved to South Bend, Ind., where Bart taught composition,
theory and electronic music at the regional Indiana University
campus, and Priscilla, to pay back heavy student loans,
taught art and music for two years in the public schools.

It was the lowest point in my life. Leaving a highly
charged musical community of which I had played an
active role, to enter the public school world which
kept me so busy that I had to give up composing

for two years, and a society that thought of me as a 'faculty wife,' was a bitter experience.

The situation improved in 1972, when she left the public schools to teach part time in theory at Indiana University, Kokomo, traveling 180 miles round trip. "The South Bend campus had the same opening, but they refused to consider me, due to nepotism rules." In 1974 she left Kokomo to teach piano, theory, and composition at St. Mary's College, until the McLeans' departure in 1976. "Bart's course load was full, and I was the only qualified person to teach electronic music in the community in 1975-76. They still refused to hire me, so I tutored students secretly at night in the studio that year." Embarrassed, the university commissioned her to write Invisible Chariots, a 22-minute three-movement work for stereo or quadraphonic (four channel) tape and messages (chorus, small ensemble, including electronics, and soloists), premiering Messages in 1975, conducted by Michael Esselstrom, and gave her the title Resident Composer for 1975-76.

In 1976 they moved to Austin, Texas, where Barton became the director of the University of Texas Electronic Music Center, and Priscilla, after confronting more nepotism barriers, began devoting her life exclusively to mastering her art as composer, performer and author of many articles and reviews, published in national magazines since 1977.

In 1983 the McLeans decided to leave the university world for several years. Bart resigned, and the composers moved to a 1790 farmhouse in rural Petersburg, N.Y., to live exclusively on their composing and performing and their publishing company, MLC Publications. The setting was chosen for its proximity to cultural centers, but also especially for its wildness, and has had a direct influence on their most recent music (1984-85). "On any given morning, we may be confronted by the sights or sounds of coyotes, a pair of golden eagles, wild turkeys, as well as the more common wild animals one sees on the edge of wilderness," Priscilla relates.

In 1985, having lived this way for two years, an ironic twist of fate occurred. Priscilla McLean was invited to teach for a semester at the University of Hawaii, and was appointed full professor, on the merit of her work as a many-times recorded composer and international performer.

Priscilla McLean over the years has become open to all
sounds as possible compositional material, particularly the
merging of diverse and unusual sound events--both electronic
and concrete--to form even newer sound situations which she
describes as surrealistic. Her first live electronic work,
written in 1972, was Spectra I, scored for percussion and
synthesizer. She premiered the work with the main Indiana
University Percussion Ensemble, conducted by George Gaber.
Following the premiere, conductor Gaber wrote:

> It was in the process of rehearsing and developing
> the new work Spectra I that I came to know the
> composer, her talents and her aesthetic and innova-
> tive uses with synthesizers. It was one of the most
> rewarding musical experiences in my life. The pre-
> miere met with great success.

Night Images, two-channel tape, was realized in the
composer's rapidly developing home studio in 1973 and premiered at the University of Rhode Island. Listeners have an
excellent opportunity to hear this piece and the first movement of Invisible Chariots, with descriptive narration, on an
album entitled: Electronic Music from the Outside In, a two-
record set which includes six works, all with narration, Folkways Recording FPX 60503. Jim Aikin writing for Contemporary Keyboard Magazine on July 1979 (excerpt):

RECORD REVIEW: INVISIBLE CHARIOTS

> Invisible Chariots has lots of banging and scraping
> on piano strings, particularly in the first of its
> three movements, and synthesizer filter sweeps are
> combined with the scraping for a truly hair raising
> effect. At other times the banging is reminiscent of
> a herd of gnomes running across a wooden bridge...
> electronic music has never been exactly dull, but a
> comparison of newer pieces with those put together
> a decade ago reveals that the composers have moved
> beyond the stage of creating etudes..., and are
> now utilizing the language thus developed to fashion
> pieces symphonic in scope. It's good to know that
> this fascinating music is getting onto vinyl, and not
> just blowin' in the wind. [By Jim Aikin, © 1979
> Keyboard Magazine, Cupertino, CA. Reprinted by
> permission.]

Invisible Chariots was composed between 1975-1977 and uses musique concrete and synthesizer to express the imago-abstract in the three movements. The title is from Carl Sandburg's Isle of Patmos and according to McLean refers "to the intuitive creative force that shapes a work, often in direct conflict with one's 'external' judgment which has to be obeisant to the voice within." One critic described the work as "sustained, harmonic atmosphere, with scary effects, and wild nature cries."

Bart and Priscilla McLean, unlike most of their university contemporaries, were able to build a solid reputation as composers and performers, and in 1974 they formed The McLean Mix, a composing and performing duo of both taped and live electro-acoustic music. They have toured extensively throughout Europe and the United states.

The McLean Mix have discovered a deep affinity for surrealism and surrealistic painting, which is evident in their musical works. This surrealistic principle which Priscilla had been developing for several years manifested itself with Dance of Dawn composed in 1974 for electronic tape. When Lawrence Morton of Columbia Records auditioned this tape, he described it as "one of the most dramatic and shimmering pieces of music" he had ever auditioned.

McLean realized this quadraphonic tape in the electronic studio at Indiana University on the Synthi-100 synthesizer. It was premiered in a concert in a two-channel version in September 1974 and in the four-channel version during a concert of The McLean Mix in October 1974.

Dance of Dawn has been recorded on Composers Recordings, Inc. CRI SD 335, American Contemporary Electronic Music, her first commercial recording. It was recently cited in a High Fidelity/Musical America article, "CRI-Surprising Survivor" as one of the top dozen "bouquet of CRI's Best" all-time albums. It was the only electronic album so chosen. McLean has been the recipient of numerous awards, grants and commissions including four MacDowell Colony Fellowships, three National Endowment for the Arts Grants, a Martha Baird Rockefeller Grant, a Meet The Composer Grant, two American Music Center grants, as well as several commissions.

"On the third day of the 'Musik protokolls'"--the Autumn

Festival in Graz, Austria in 1979--"the astonished public had
the choice between a whale-chorus by Priscilla McLean and a
five minute pause by John Cage." (quoted from the writing
of Von Hansjorg Spies, Kleine Zeitung, Austria, on that
country's premiere of McLean's Beneath the Horizon III, for
tuba solo, whale ensemble and tape). This piece was one of
the winners of the 1979 Gaudeamus Festival in Holland and
was given its world premiere in Rotterdam by tuba soloist
Melvyn Poore. It is recorded on Opus One Records No. 96,
The Electro Surrealistic Landscapes of the McLean Mix. An
ardent conservationist, McLean is deeply concerned that these
great mammals be saved from extinction, and as a composer
she has created an extremely captivating piece. McLean's
notes on Beneath the Horizon III:

> Who is to say that the only great music can come
> from humans? As more is learned about our rivals
> in intelligence, the whales, the concept of 'cultural
> superiority' comes under fire. The combining of
> recorded whale songs and composed music for tuba
> in Beneath the Horizon III is an attempt to illustrate
> the likeness of our (humans' and whales') musical
> ideas, and to create a special ethereal environment,
> projecting and blending the haunting qualities, often
> symbolic and sometimes contrasting, of both musics.
>
> For this reason, the whale songs are preserved as
> much as possible. Manipulation, when used, has
> involved lowering the songs by an octave (at times)
> into human singing range, overlaying several songs
> to create 'choirs,' and 'cleaning-up' the sounds from
> the recordings Songs Of The Humpbacked Whale and
> Deep Voices (Capitol Records, ST-620 and ST-11598)
> by eliminating distortions, pops, and sea hiss.
>
> It may surprise the listener to hear conventional
> trills and repetitions, discernible melodies. This
> is the way of the whales' musical minds, and the
> echoey medium of the ocean, not so different from
> the tiny human performing with them.

The following passage has been translated by Maria
Ludlow, a Dutch graduate student at the University of Texas,
from an article written by John Kasander on Sept. 8, 1979,
for a Dutch newspaper:

> CLEANED-UP WHALE SOUNDS MIXED WITH TUBA
> SOUNDS

The English tubist Melvyn Poore, who once before
received attention at a Gaudeamus competition,
presented a curious work by the American Priscilla
McLean, who 'cleansed' whale sounds from existing
recordings in nature; that is, got rid of the by-
sounds, and manipulated the tempos on tape. It
seems that whales produce sounds which timbre-wise
correspond to a tone on a tuba, so that the sounds
of the whale ensemble can be united with those of
the tuba in such a way, that they cannot be told
apart (from one another). Beneath The Horizon III,
sometimes with long howling tones mixed with melodic tuba-passages, delivered an exciting and also
often aesthetically beautiful composition.

The Inner Universe, eight pieces for piano, tape and
electron-microscope slides, was written in 1979-82, and premiered by Priscilla on a McLean Mix concert in Antwerp, Belgium. "Salt Canyons," one of the eight pieces, is recorded
on Opus One Records, No. 96. It was performed and recorded
on a five-foot baby grand piano because of its high partials
on the bass strings when stroked. Her notes on the piece
are as follows:

"Salt Canyons" takes its title from an electron-microscope slide of 'canyons of salt' by well-known photo-
grapher David Scharf. It is the longest piece from
The Inner Universe, a set of eight surrealistic tone
poems for piano, tape, and electron-microscope
slides (all photos can be seen in Scharf's book Mag-
nifications). "Salt Canyons" has a most bizarre
piano part which involves stroking strings with wood
pieces, damping strings with books and towels for
a brittle keyboard percussive effect, using percussion mallets, and generally evoking timbres not associated with a piano. The tape part includes a
steady rich chordal drone, created by bowing bass
string of the piano with a full haired bass bow, the
hairs placed underneath the string and drawn up-
wards. The total sonic effect is one of the large
extended instrument, the music evoking a sense of
the spatial timelessness and peace of desert canyons,
whether cavernous or microscopic.

During a year of three major United States tours,

Priscilla performed The Inner Universe in the 1982 New Music
Festival at California State University in Sacramento. the Mc-
Lean Mix was the major focus of this festival. Their music
is considered less electronic, and more human-oriented, because both McLeans use real sounds as the basis of their
tapes, and they often mix tapes with live performers. William
Glackin writing for The Sacramento Bee on Nov. 7, 1982, had
only praise for Priscilla and Bart McLean's music. A lengthy
article included the following excerpt:

> MORE AMBITIOUS on a larger scale and not unlike
> a concerto in some ways was her The Inner Universe,
> in which she played a "prepared" piano (with towels,
> rubber balls and other objects laid on the strings to
> make them more percussive) against a tape played
> by her husband, while four electron-microscope slides
> (plants, a mosquito wing) were shown on a screen
> at one side of the stage. She played both the
> strings and the keyboard with considerable techni-
> que, in trills and rushing waves of notes, while the
> tape surrounded her with sounds ranging from the
> hums and growls of the 1960s to faint, distorted
> echoes of piano music. The work was atonally and
> violently dissonant, but it was also occasionally
> dramatic and downright pretty.

"The McLean Mix: Inner Tension of the Surrealistic"
is the title of an article prepared by Priscilla and Barton
McLean for AWC (American Women Composers) News, January
1982, Volume III no. 3. The article affords the reader an
in-depth understanding of the McLeans as 20th-century composers and performers. Because of its length, only an excerpt is offered, but the entire article is a must for readers
interested in the inner workings of the creative duo, The
McLean Mix:

> A unique characteristic about the music of the McLean
> Mix is a directed and deeply felt technique of prob-
> ing the listeners' subsonscious through the choice
> of emotionally loaded ideas (primal screams, placid
> landscapes, various emotionally-charged gestures),
> combined with attention to fine detail and large
> structure, as one could also say about the artist
> Salvador Dali's process.
>   To give an idea of how the McLean Mix concertizes,

one program in the spring of 1981 began with Barton's Mysteries from the Ancient Nahuatl, with him performing prepared piano, recorders, and percussion, while Priscilla narrated and sang poetry from the ancient pre-Columbian Nahuatl culture, along with performing on the recorder and percussion. Second on the program was a three-movement "electro-symphonic landscape" for tape called Invisible Chariots--a quadraphonic work by Priscilla, who then premiered four surrealistic tone poems from a set of eight such works for piano, tape, and electron-microscope slides (intriguingly biological in origin) entitled The Inner Universe. Last on the program was Barton's premiere of his Dimensions VIII from Volvox. This program was given in Brussels, Antwerp, Ghent, Hilversum, and at the International Zagreb (Yugoslavia) Muzicki Biennale.

Although we were also educated as performers (as were most composers), it was not until 1974 that we "fell into" a McLean Mix situation with an invitation to give a concert. We soon discovered that we enjoyed personally reaching out to people in a "live" vs. "canned" experience. Soon the response to our duo was far beyond our expectations, and by 1979 we had toured the Midwest, Northeast, and Southwest, performing for diverse audiences.

Since 1983, the McLeans have been composing and touring exclusively, working out of their historic 1790 New York farmhouse. Their hundreds of performances have led them through eight European countries, and throughout the United States, including Hawaii.

From 1982-84, McLean created, after a long absence from the medium, her second mature work for orchestra, coupled this time with electronic tape, entitled A Magic Dwells. The many ensuing years of work with electronic media makes this piece a radically different sonic experience from the Variations & Mozaics. On tape is a bowed piano drone (bass strings) which sounds, most of the time, like gradually changing timbres. Also on tape are groups of sustained live orchestral chords, which are mixed with a trio of voices singing multireligious phrases about the Creation, and processed through an electronic filtering device called a vocoder. When these "choir chords" on tape emerge from the orchestra in performance, the effect is of the instruments suddenly changing character and singing in English. The orchestral part is virtuosic, with a series of overlapping ostinatos building to a climax with the taped phrase "The Tree of Life," "All Colors of the World," "were upon it," from ancient American Wintu Indian creation mythology, and slowly receding to "it was not born; it sees not and is not seen," from Laotzu: The Way of Life.

In 1985 the McLeans were commissioned by Bowling Green (Ohio) University, to create an evening of music entitled In Wilderness is the Preservation of the World for their annual Festival of New Music, during American Music Week, premiered by the McLean Mix and the university chorus, with audience Participation, on Nov. 9, 1985. Priscilla reflects:

> I had begun thinking of a joyous piece celebrating the Alaskan Wilderness Act, with wolves (on tape) howling along with the audience singing amid an uproar of drums and choral Eskimo chants, back in 1980. I wanted to get the audience participating in this celebration of life. However, I realized that a whole evening's worth of music would take me many years to write, as I am a slow, meticulous composer who shapes and reshapes a piece for years.
> Bart had been using bird sounds in his music for years, and has the same devotion to the wilderness that I have, so I asked him to join me in a collaborative effort, each of us creating separate pieces that fit together in a grand gesture of celebration. We were working on these when the commission came through.

In Wilderness is the Preservation of the World (quote from Thoreau in his essay "Wilderness") is one of the most ambitious and dramatic of large environmental works involving tape to be using actual animal, whale, bird, sounds with performers, singing audience, chorus, slides, live participants (a motorcyclist driving through the auditorium and a dog on stage during "O Beautiful Suburbia"), along with strategically placed narrative quotes from Whitman, Thoreau, American Indian writing, and several others. The pieces are

> Invocation, by Priscilla McLean, using soloist, chorus, a combination clarinet and flute instrument played

by the McLeans, along with their playing percussion,
audience singing, and tape: wolves, birds, Eskimo
chant, drums, etc.; Voices of the Water, by Barton
McLean, using water sounds on tape, Barton stroking and striking a mounted amplified bicycle wheel,
and Priscilla improvising mouth sounds; Beneath the
Horizon by Priscilla, with multiple slide projections
of whales and sea choreographed to the tape of
whale and tuba quartet sound; "O Beautiful Suburbia!"
by Priscilla, for audience singing "America the Beautiful" repeatedly as the sonic environment builds in
a cacophonous crescendo of dog barks, bug zappers,
motorcycles, chainsaws, garish TV ads, which dis-
perse finally into a "lost" wilderness of north wind,
wolves and narrations by Thoreau. The last work,
Passages of the Night, by Barton McLean, is a
haunting, introspective musical portrayal using owls,
Texas summer crickets, deep parrot calls, instruments on tape, and concluding thoughtful narration,
ending their tribute to the American wilderness and
concern for its preservation.

Priscilla states, "The joy of composing with these
sounds, and performing them yourself, is that you
are not restricted by a conservative, timid, mercan-
tile society, that you can reach out to that audience
who is still interested, curious, and involved with
new artistic expressions, and give a definitive performance, straight from the horse's mouth.

Priscilla McLean is a member of the American Society of
University Composers, having served on its executive com-
mittee from 1978-82. From 1974-82, she co-directed with
Barton two 13-week radio series, entitled: "Radiofest, New
American Music," sponsored by A.S.U.C. The second series
was awarded a National Endowment Media Arts grant, and
Priscilla became the radio moderator, traveling across country
to interview and feature 35 composers and their music.

She is also a member of the American Women Composers,
Inc., the American Music Center, Composers Forum, and BMI
(Broadcast Music Inc.). As she is involved spiritually as
well as musically with conservation and the environment, she
is also a member of The Sierra Club, The Nature Conser-
vancy, and The Wilderness Society.

Priscilla McLean became a guest contributor to <u>High Fidelity/Musical America</u> magazine, publishing a report of the Zagreb Biennale in October 1981, and has contributed an article on the 1981 International Computer Music Conference held at North Texas State University, published in the February, 1982 issue and an article on "The Albany (N.Y.) Symphony's Daring Path" in the April 1985 issue.

In addition she has had articles published in the following magazines: <u>Notes</u>, March 1978, "Vladimir Ussachevsky and Otto Luening: 1952 Electronic Tape Music: The First Compositions"; <u>Paid my Dues</u> magazine, Volume II, No. 4, summer 1978, "To Make a Universe of Sound"; <u>Perspectives of New Music</u>, Volume 16/1, Fall/Winter 1978, "Fire and Ice: A Query," <u>Perspectives of New Music</u>, Volume 20, Nos. 1 and 2, Fall/Winter 1981, Spring/Summer, 1982, "Thoughts as a (Woman) Composer"; <u>AWC News</u>, January 1982: "The McLean Mix: Inner Tension of the Surrealistic," in collaboration with Bart McLean.

Of the McLeans' life together, they express a remarkable spirit of cooperation and mutual support. Priscilla comments: "Whenever I am writing a work, Bart is my first very critical and discerning audience, and I am his. Thus we each have a stake in the success of the other's work. Our touring together increases this feeling, and has enriched our lives enormously." Bart states: "The spectre of two independent composers with similar tastes but individual approaches and careers living together in harmony and without competition for 18 years is in itself surrealistic!"

Priscilla McLean is emerging as one of America's leading electronic-acoustic composers of the contemporary artistic community. The stimuli triggering her creative process is clearly linked to the healthy relationship she shares with her husband. A continuing body of works over an extended period of time has established The McLean Mix as an Internationally acclaimed duo of electronic-acoustical music. She writes music that moves the listener to new heights of hearing that is absolutely fascinating. To hear her music is to believe that she opens new avenues of listening adventures.

<u>Selected Compositions of Priscilla McLean</u>

<u>MLC Publications</u>

Beneath the Horizon I for tuba quartet and taped whale en-
      semble.
Beneath the Horizon III for tuba solo and taped whale en-
      semble.
Elan! A Dance to All Rising Things from the Earth for flute,
      violin, violincello, piano, percussion.
Fantasies for Adults and Other Children, eight songs for
      soprano and amplified piano, two performers.
Fire and Ice for trombone and piano (2 performers)
The Inner Universe, 8 pieces for piano, tape and slides
Interplanes for two pianos
Messages for soloists, chorus, amplified recorders, percus-
      sion, amplified autoharp
A Magic Dwells for full or chamber orchestra and tape
Ranier Maria Rilke Poems: Three Songs for Voice and Violin
Wilderness for soprano, tape and nine-piece chamber ensemble

ABI/Alexander Broude, Inc (on Rental)

Variations and Mozaics on a Theme of Stravinsky for full or-
      chestra

Elkan-Vogel Co., Inc.

Men and Angels Share (SATB)

Bourne Co., Inc

Holiday for Youth (concert band), In the Spring the Mountains
      Sing (SA, piano)

Silver-Burdett Co.

Three Children's Night Songs (SSA, piano), There Must Be
      a Time (SAB, flute, piano)

Tape compositions or pieces involving the McLean Mix are
only available from the composer on request.

Addresses of Publishers

MCL Publications, R.D. 2, Box 33, Petersburg, NY   12138.

Elkan-Vogel Co. Inc., 1712-16 Sansom Street, Philadelphia,
    PA 19103.

AB1/Alexander Broude, Inc., 575 8th Avenue, New York,
    NY 10018.

Silver-Burdett Co., subsidiary of General Learning, Corpora-
    tion, 250 James Street, Morristown, NJ 07960.

Discography

Invisible Chariots, Folkways Recordings, FTS 33450.
Night Images, Invisible Chariots Mvt I., Folkways recordings
    FPX 60503.
Variations and Mozaics On A Theme Of Stravinsky, Louisville
    Orchestra First Edition Records, LS 762.
Dance of Dawn, Composers Recordings, Inc., CRI SD 335.
Interplanes, Advance Recordings, FGR 19S.
Beneath The Horizon III, "Salt Canyons" from The Inner
    Universe, Opus One Records, No. 96.

Addresses of Record Companies

Folkway Records Service Corp., 632 Broadway, New York,
    NY 10012.

The Louisville Orchestra, 609 West Main Street, Louisville, KY
    40202.

Composers Recordings Inc., 170 West 74th Street, New York,
    NY 10023.

Advance Recordings, 170 West 74th Street, New York, NY 10023.

Opus One Records, Box 604, Greenville, ME   04441.

ELIZABETH MACONCHY

Composer

Elizabeth Maconchy, noted 20th-century English composer of
Irish parentage, was born in Broxbourne, Herts in 1907. She
grew up in a country setting in Ireland and was ill-prepared
to pursue a musical career. There was no radio or phono-
graph in the family home so the only music she heard as a
child was what her father could play on the piano. Her own
limited facility at the keyboard was the accepted musical training for a girl at that period of time. In spite of these ad-
versities she began to write piano music at the age of 6 and
always knew that composing would be the major goal in her
life.

When Maconchy's widowed mother took her to London
at the age of 16 to enroll at the Royal College of Music to
study with Charles Wood she had only heard one symphony
concert, a performance of Carmen, and a piano recital by
Myra Hess. What she lacked in musical credentials she more
than compensated for in determination and she acquired the
necessary skills, at the college where she studied from 1923
to 1929, under the tutorage of Charles Wood and Vaughan
Williams in composition, Kitson in counterpoint and Arthur
Alexander on piano. The example set by Vaughan Williams
had an enduring influence on Maconchy and they became life-
long friends.

At the Royal College of Music she was easily recognized
as one of the ablest composers. Since there were almost equal
numbers of men and women studying at the time it did not
occur to Maconchy that being female might prejudice her
chances of being a recipient of prestigious awards. Although
she did win prizes and scholarships she was denied the much-
coveted Mendelssohn Scholarship. Sir Hugh Allen told her,

ELIZABETH MACONCHY

"if we give you the scholarship, you will only get married
and never write another note." At the time prejudice against
women composers was prevalent so it was especially rewarding
to Elizabeth Maconchy when years later her daughter, Nicola,
won the Mendelssohn Scholarship and early recognition as a
serious composer.

As a composer she continued to search out her own way
and eventually she was awarded a Blumenthal Travelling
Scholarship and went to Prague to study with K. B. Jirak.
It was here that her first major work, Concertino, for piano
and orchestra was premiered by the Prague Philharmonic Orchestra on her 23rd birthday.

In the 1930s there were no commissions and sponsorships
for composers. So at the age of 23 she sent a score to Henry
Wood on speculation and her orchestral suite, The Land, was
premiered at the London Proms. The reviews were excellent
and startling but no commissions or grants were forthcoming.
The publishers were not interested; according to Maconchy,
"they were all men, of course, and tended to think of women
composers being capable of only an odd song or two."

As Sir Hugh Allen had prophesied, Elizabeth Maconchy
married William LeFanu, one of a well-known Irish literary
family, the librarian and bibliographer, and Swift scholar.
The same week in August 1930 her orchestral suite was performed at the Proms.

The plight of the young composer in London in the
1930s was a series of struggles and disappointments. Maconchy said, "no one had given thought to helping a composer
to establish himself--still less herself--or even to learn the
craft of composition by hearing his work performed." In 1931
a group of three students put on a series of concerts to promote young British composers. Elizabeth Lutyens, Anne
Macnaghten and Iris Lemare originated the Macnaghten-Lemare
Concerts. In the first series, women composers were strongly
favored and included works by Lutyens, Imogen Holst and
Maconchy. "It was probably the best thing that ever happened for young composers here, and it was the only thing
that happened for a long time," according to Maconchy.

Still in existence today, the Macnaghten Concert Series
started with performances in a tiny theater in Notting Hill

with a loyal and devoted group of listeners. Maconchy can
recall when Benjamin Britten at the age of 18 had one of his
first public performances in the series.

Interestingly enough, one music critic responded to Maconchy's artistic talent very early in her career when he
wrote in The Listener: "I could wish to go down to posterity
as one who had the uncommon good sense to salute the gifts
of Elizabeth Maconchy." This review by Scott Goddard, five
decades ago, is testament to the brilliant accomplishments of
a gifted composer. Today Elizabeth Maconchy has an extensive output of orchestral, operatic, vocal and chamber music.
According to Maconchy, "a very small germ emerges and my
thoughts develop around and from this germ. The background
of my writing has been string quartets which I began to write
in 1933."

Unfortunately a severe illness disrupted her career in
1932 and she had to leave London to live in the country where
she slowly cured herself of tuberculosis. Other difficult times
were to follow; during the war years she spent much of her
time raising her family. Trying to combine family responsibilities with being a composer might seem impossible but she
said, "It certainly helped to be married to a man sympathetic
to my work. For the thirty years we have lived in Essex,
two thick walls divide his study from the room where I work
at my piano, composing. He maintains a keen interest in everything I write."

The few opportunities for the performance of large-
scale works helped to shape the first 20 years of Maconchy's
creative writing. She concentrated on chamber works and
her series of string quartets numbering 12 is the music for
which she has become best known and in which her characteristic and unmistakable voice can be most easily heard. Maconchy's personal comments:

> The natural way for a composer to express himself
> is not with words but with notes, and in any case
> to describe a musical concept in words is like trying
> to paint a picture of a good smell!
> Writing chamber music has always been my main
> preoccupation. I have found the string quartet
> above all best suited to the expression of the kind
> of music I want to write--music as an impassioned
> argument. And in this medium I have worked mainly

with contrapuntal ideas--that is, a counterpoint of rhythms as well as melodic lines.

Counterpoint wears so many faces: it may be a serene weaving of melodic parts, or it may be a means of harmonic development--the moving horizontal lines coalesce to form new vertical combinations and harmonic progressions--something that has always interested me more than harmony treated merely as color. Or counterpoint may be used to heighten the emotional tension as in Beethoven's dramatic use of it, particularly in his string quartets.

Dramatic and emotional tension is created by means of counterpoint in much the same way as happens in a play. The characters are established as individuals, each with his own differentiated characteristics: the drama then grows from the interplay of these characters--the clash of their ideas and the way in which they react upon each other.

Thus in a string quartet one has the perfect vehicle for dramatic expression of this sort: four characters engaged in statement and comment, passionate argument, digression, restatement, perhaps final agreement--the solution of the problem.

Maconchy's String Quartet No. 1 was premiered at the Macnaghten-Lemare Concert Series in London in 1933. At a subsequent performance in 1957 Colin Mason wrote in the Musical Times V. 98, August (excerpt):

Elizabeth Maconchy's String Quartet No. 1 was written in 1933. It is not very different in style from her more recent music, except perhaps that it is less terse, and that the composer chooses a traditional four-movement form. The thematic material is relatively slight and fragmentary, consisting almost entirely of short motives and figurations, with no sustained melodic line, in a rudimentary harmonic setting. The working out is in accordance with the material--an almost obsessively repetitive, very dynamic and rhythmical hammering away at these motives, with little in the way of melodic or harmonic growth or development. At this deliberately primitive level the music is effective and aurally stimulating.

Maconchy's String Quartet No. 2 was premiered at the
Paris International Society of Contemporary Music in 1937,
String Quartet No. 3 at a B.B.C. contemporary music concert. In 1938 and 1939 performances of her chamber music
were given at Krakow and Warsaw. When String Quartet No.
4 was performed in 1950 one music critic commented, "Miss
Maconchy's new Quartet interests us as a clear offshoot of
Bartok's middle string quartets. It shares its models' par-
tiality for terse musical subjects based on minute intervallic
steps, and also their preoccupation with ingenious rhythmical
transformation."

Her music has always been characterized by an extreme
economy of thematic material. Maconchy's description of her
writing:

> To me music is a sort of impassioned argument, pro-
> pelled by the force of its own inner logic, and by
> virtue of this logic each new idea will derive from
> the original premise and throw new light on the
> whole.
>   The rigid self-discipline which the composer must
> impose on himself must always be directed to the
> fullest expression of the underlying emotion and
> never to its exclusion.
>   This passionately intellectual and intellectually
> passionate musical discourse is what I seek to ex-
> press in my music.

Maconchy's String Quartet No. 5, for which she received
the Edwin Evans Prize, was premiered in 1949 and recorded
by Allegri Quartet on Argo RG329. Music critics praised the
excellence of the writing and the quality of the piece and
Maconchy's allegiance to a poetic romanticism. With String
Quartet No. 6, written in 1950, she sought to avoid "musical
side-tracking." She was successful according to William Wordsworth's review of her String Quartet No. 6 published in Music
and Letters, July 1952 (excerpt):

> ...All four movements are extremely competently
> written, and in the first (Passacaglia) she has
> brought all her ingenuity into play. The 'ground'
> has two main characteristics, side-stepping major
> thirds and sixths, and a short scale-like motive.
> Although these two ideas permeate the movement

they soon become integrated into the fascinating
rhythmic and harmonic patterns.... [Reprinted by
permission of Oxford University Press.]

In 1953 the London County Council competition for a
Coronation Overture had 73 scores considered by the adjudi-
cators, Sir Adrian Boult, Dr. Edmund Rubbra and Gerald
Finzi. The prize of 150 pounds and a performance in the
Royal Festival Hall was won by Elizabeth Maconchy for the
best work submitted, Proud Thames. It was premiered by
the B.B.C. Symphony Orchestra conducted by Sir Malcolm
Sargent and recorded by London Philharmonic Orchestra conducted by Vernon Handley on Lyrita SRCS 57.

Elizabeth Maconchy wrote her first opera, The Sofa,
in 1956/57 with a libretto by Ursula Vaughan Williams. The
work was performed by the New Opera Company in 1959 as
part of its policy to enable the public to hear the work of
contemporary British composers. She adapted her second
opera, The Three Strangers, from a story by Thomas Hardy.
Written between 1958-67 the work was premiered at Bishops
Stortford in 1968. The world premiere of her third opera,
The Departure, was given by the New Opera Company at
Sadler's Wells on Dec. 16, 1962. This half-hour work is
scored for small orchestra and a small off-stage chorus and
has two characters. Julia, a mezzo-soprano, who carries
most of the opera and her husband Mark, a baritone. Elizabeth Maconchy wrote the following for the Composers Forum
(excerpt):

The Opera is a new treatment of the theme of Death
and the Lady--not the traditional expostulation of
the Lady with Death, but the expression of her
struggle to accept death.
The Three One-Act Operas may be performed
separately or as a Triple Bill (as in 1977), and are
scored for the same forces soloists, SATB chorus
and chamber orchestra (14 instruments).
It is in more than one sense a woman's opera.
It seeks to express through music the emotional
history of a woman's life--youth, love, the shared
joy of marriage and children and then death. The
death which she must go to alone. Julia's death
provides the frame for the recapitulation of her life.

On a commission from the "Proms" in 1964 Maconchy
wrote Variazioni Concertante scored for oboe, clarinet, bassoon, horn and string orchestra. The premiere was given
by the B.B.C. Scottish Orchestra conducted by James Lough-
ran. Of the performance one reviewer wrote, "The piece
does precisely what she set out to do. A nondescript sort
of introduction presents the material that can turn into quite
definite and admirably neat variations. Each variation seems
to be determined by the solo instrument that has the lead at
any given moment, and the whole work, is neat, elegant and
civilized."

Elizabeth Maconchy has not held any musical position
and uses all her time to compose and care for her family.
Although she lives in the country her musical life has always
centered on London. She considers her musical style independent of any particular school. She said, "I pursue my
own trend of thought. I was greatly influenced when I discovered Bartok in my student days and he was the most
formative influence in the evolution of my musical style."

On a commission in 1970 from Dorchester Abbey, Maconchy wrote the opera The Jesse Tree with words by Anne
Ridler. This church opera, one hour and 12 minutes long,
is scored for 12 players, chorus, mimes, dancers, actors and
four soloists. Maconchy comments, "the dramatic tension is
as important an ingredient of church opera as of conventional
opera, but it must be achieved in a different way."

Maconchy has been commissioned by numerous festivals
and leading performers throughout the years. Her String
Quartet No. 10 commissioned by the Cheltenham Festival was
premiered in 1972. This quartet is a marvelous example of
her musical creativeness and her love for string quartet writing. She comments on this work:

> My tenth quartet is in one continuous movement, a
> single span, lasting about fifteen minutes, within
> which are contained a number of contrasting sec-
> tions. It is framed by a recurrent lento passage of
> repeated chords. This opens and closes the move-
> ment, and there are further references to it on the
> way. Combined with the opening chords is a brief
> motif in the viola, which dominates the whole quartet
> in one way or another. In the course of the movement

there are three contrasted quick sections deriving
in different ways from the motif, punctuated by
slow, more lyrical passages.
 The tension grows as ideas are combined and a
climax is reached with a restatement of the opening
material, extended and transformed by what has gone
before.
 The quartet ends as quietly as it began.

 Elizabeth Maconchy has always played an active part
in the musical life of her country. She has spent countless
hours over a long period of years in behalf of her fellow
musicians and has won their respect and admiration. She
became the first woman chairman of the Composers' Guild
(1959-1960) an organization founded in 1944 to further the
artistic and professional interest of British composers. The
Society for the Promotion of New Music was founded in London in 1942 to play and discuss the works of young composers.
Maconchy has a long association with this organization, including chairing the executive committee from 1972 to 1975.
Upon the death of Benjamin Britten she was unanimously
elected President of SPNM. "She has worked tirelessly and
selflessly for her fellow-musicians," wrote a critic in 1976,
"and has won their admiration and love in return." Jeremy
Dale Roberts expresses the feeling of many of Elizabeth Maconchy's friends and contemporaries:

> Betty's self is in her music, and I love in her what
> I love in her music: ardour, warmth, energy, gen-
> tle humour, youth--(futile and clumsy to try to list
> all the things that draw so many to her). But I
> cannot forget her practical wisdom, and grace: and
> a certain obstinacy and courage which have put
> spirit into a lot of us when we were low.

 Maconchy's Serenata Concertante, for violin and orchestra, commissioned in 1962 by the Birmingham Feeney
Trust, was programmed by the London Philharmonic Orchestra
conducted by Vernon Handley and introduced a fine young
soloist, Levon Chilingirian. Music critic David Simmons stated,
"The work emerged as an original re-distillation of considerable purpose and point. Maconchy understands the pressing
demands of today whenever such concertante writing is at-
tempted. The exposed writing suggests an element of improvi-
sation, against the groundwork, of a developing thematic
scheme well entrenched in expressive orchestral paint."

In 1975 Elizabeth Maconchy wrote Epyllion (Greek short
epic) for cellist Kenneth Heath and the Academy of St. Martin-
in-the-Fields conducted by Neville Marriner. Scored for 16
strings, the piece received unanimous praise from the press
such as Felix Aprahamian's acute observation, "Hers is a work
both useful and beautiful." The Cheltenham Festival is noted
for its fine programs, and Maconchy's Epyllion was not to be
denied. The Times (London), July 15, 1975, written by
Stephen Walsh, said in part:

> ...In effect, the piece is a cello concertino, conven-
> tially in four movements. The music, almost per-
> fectly balanced in texture throughout its 15 or so
> minutes, draws a clear line between the rhapsodic
> and melancholy sides of the cello's character, and
> the shimmering metallic fabrics of sound available to
> a modern string orchestra, using free aleatoric
> counterpoint and special effects like glissando har-
> monics. In the scherzo, the most instantly attrac-
> tive movement, the cello sings almost idly across a
> rhythmically elaborate mesh of orchestral ostinati.
> But the control of movement is so remarkably assured
> that the irregular rhythm is felt to be purposeful,
> never merely whimsical. [Reprinted by permission
> of Times Newspapers Limited.]

In 1977 the Society for the Promotion of New Music
(with financial assistance from the Arts Council of Great
Britain) paid its own tribute to Elizabeth Maconchy in honor
of her 70th-birthday in a program of her choice. The gala
concert was played at St. John's Smith Square and included
such noted artists as the Gabrieli String Quartet; Thea King,
clarinet; Saltarello Choir; Richard Bernas, conductor; Philip
Langridge, tenor and John Constable, piano. The program
included Maconchy's String Quartet No. 10; Three Donne
Songs for tenor and piano; Nocturnal and Sirens' Song for
chorus; Clarinet Quintet and Beethoven's String Quartet in
F minor, Op. 95. During the same year Elizabeth Maconchy
was made a C.B.E. (Commander of the Order of the British
Empire).

Maconchy's large-scale dramatic cantata, Heloise and
Abelard, (commissioned by the Croydon Philharmonic Society)
was premiered in London in March 1979. Scored for orchestra, SATB chorus and soli (soprano, tenor and bass) with a
text by the composer, was admired by the musical establishment

as well as the critics. One critic praised especially its,
"beautiful and sumptuous score ... seventy-five minutes' worth
of ravishing; luxuriant score...." Heloise and Abelard was
the longest and most ambitious piece written by Maconchy
for orchestra and voices and is a clear indication that her
creative ability is limitless.

Stephen Walsh covered the Cheltenham Music Festival
for the Observer on June 19, 1981 (excerpt):

> Elizabeth Maconchy's Piccola Musica for string trio,
> premiered by the Nash Trio at the Pum Room, showed
> that this fine composer has lost none of her flair
> for lucid and arresting chamber writing.

Piccola Musica was commissioned by the Cheltenham
Music Festival and Maconchy chose to write for violin, viola
and cello. These five short pieces were played by Marcia
Craylord violin, Roger Chase viola and Christopher van Kampen, cello. Another music critic described the trio as "deeply
thoughtful music without a wasted note, showing an impeccable
sense of texture and design."

The Albion Ensemble is a wind quintet founded in 1977.
In 1982 this chamber group premiered Maconchy's Wind Quintet for flute, oboe, clarinet, bassoon and horn. Commissioned
by the Chricklade Arts Festival it was praised as a "suave
and idiomatic new quintet."

During the same season her Pied Beauty and Heaven
Haven were performed at the Proms by the BBC Singers.
Maconchy used as the text poetry of Gerard Manley Hopkins
which she feels "not only suggests but seems to demand music." The work was conducted by John Poole and considered
to be one of the most striking works of the Proms Season.

The Proms commission offered to Elizabeth Maconchy in
1983 was for a large group of strings and she was delighted
with the opportunity to write in this genre. She offered to
return the commission when she became ill and felt she might
never write another note of music but the B.B.C. refused
because they felt confident that she would finish the work.
She did complete it. The world premiere was given at the
Albert Hall some 53 years after her first Proms appearance.
Maconchy speaks of this work:

My Music for Strings is in four movements and plays
about twenty four minutes. It opens quietly with
warm sombre repeated chords placed low in the
strings. The texture then breaks up into individual
lines, and the rest of this fairly extended movement
is contrapuntal in character. The opening chords
recur once on the way and again at the end of the
movement while a solo violin moves over them.

The scherzo is in direct contrast, very lightly
scored, much of it pizzicato. A broad melody in
five-four time breaks in and later combines with the
five-eight pizzicato figures, which then thin out
and end in a wisp of sound. The third movement,
mesto, sad,--opens with a statement for solo viola,
and this lonely melody stamps its character on the
whole movement. A more vigorous passage builds
up, with long interweaving lines, but subsides again,
leaving the solo viola alone at the end.

The finale is an extrovert happy-go-lucky movement, strongly rhythmical. The strings toss little
melodic figures backwards and forwards, stabbing
them with off-beat accents.

The broad five-four tune from the scherzo makes
a brief reappearance, combined with the rhythmic
figures, and leads to an insouciant throw-away ending.

Music for Strings received outstanding reviews in the
New Standard, The Daily Telegraph, The Guardian, as well
as the following excerpt from a review published in The Times
on July 27, 1983, written by Max Harrison:

PROMENADE CONCERT

The first of several works commissioned for the
Proms by the BBC had its world premiere last night
from the BBC Philharmonic Orchestra. Elizabeth
Maconchy's Music for Strings, proved to be a distinguished (and also enjoyable), contribution to a
tradition that goes back, in modern times, to Elgar's Introduction and Allegro. Not that it was ever,
despite its frequently elgiac tone, self-consciously
English.

The first movement, basically moderato, had many
changes of emphasis, and solo lines detached themselves

from time to time. But the textures were usually full, and in the best sense heavy with the weight of meaning. The scherzo was mainly pizzicato and there was a return to intense emotion with the third movement, a mesto.

Here again individual voices were heard yet the ensemble dominated with the same richness as in the opening movement. By now one had realized that it was the music's feeling of spaciousness which made its emotional intensity allowable, its vehicle being a prolific but disciplined invention. This last was most evident in Miss Maconchy's finale, which in some ways proved to be the liveliest and most powerful movement.

The performance, under the BBC Philharmonic's principal conductor, Edward Downes, was admirable and those who want to hear this piece again should tune in to Radio Three on Saturday night. [Reprinted by permission of Times Newspapers Limited.]

Elizabeth Maconchy, one of Britain's foremost 20th-century composers, has written music of true quality. For many years she has quietly worked to build in her music a personal style and never allowed any fashion or modish convention to threaten her integrity. Every aspect of her work displays deep insight and inspiration. Her music is both original and definite. She is an artist who will always remain part of this century's music.

Selected Compositions of Elizabeth Maconchy

Orchestral

1929 The Land, 4 mvts, Lengnick.
1940 Puck Fair, 6 mvts, from the Ballet, Lengnick.
1942 Theme and Variations for Strings, Lengnick.
1950/ Nocturne for Orchestra, Lengnick.
  51
1950 Two dances from 'Puck Fair', 2 mvts, Lengnick.
1953 Overture: Proud Thames, Lengnick.
1953 Symphony for Double String Orchestra, 4 mvts. Lengnick.
1966 An Essex Overture, British & Continental.
1966 Music for Woodwind and Brass, MS.
1968 Three Cloudscapes, MS.

1976   Sinfonietta, Chester.
1980   Little Symphony, MS.

Orchestra with Voices

1963/ Samson and the Gates of Gaza, Chappell, on Chorus &
  64   Orchestra.
1964- The Starlight Night; Peace; May Magnificat, Chester,
  70   high voice and orchestra.
1970   Adriadne, Chester, soprano and orchestra, C. Daylenis.
1978   Heloise et Abelard, dramatic cantata, for soprano,
          tenor, baritone soloists, chorus and orchestra

Orchestra with Solo Instruments

1928   Concertino, for piano and chamber orchestra, Lengnick.
1940   Dialogue, for piano and orchestra, Lengnick.
1956   Double Concerto, for oboe, bassoon and string orches-
          tra, Lengnick.
1950   Concerto, for bassoon and string orchestra, Lengnick.
1962   Serenata Concertante, for violin and orchestra, Oxford
          University Press.
1964/ Variazioni Concertante, MS, in four winds and strings.
  65
1975   Epyllion, Chester, for solo cello and strings.
1979   Romanza, for solo viola and chamber orchestra (10
          instruments), Chester.

Chamber Music

1932   Quintet, for oboe and strings, Oxford University Press.
1933   String Quartet No. 1, Lengnick.
1936   String Quartet No. 2, Lengnick.
1938   String Quartet No. 3, Lengnick.
1942/ String Quartet No. 4, Lengnick.
  43
1944   Divertimento, for cello and piano, Lengnick.
1948   String Quartet No. 5, Lengnick.
1949   A Winter's Tale, soprano and string quartet, MS.
1950   String Quartet No. 6, Lengnick.
1951   Duo, theme and variations for violin and cello, Leng-
          nick.

1955/ String Quartet No. 7, Lengnick.
56
1960 Reflections, Oxford University Press.
1963 Quintet, for clarinet and strings, Oxford University
      Press.
1963 Sonatina, for string quartet, Chappell.
1966 String Quartet No. 8, Faber.
1967 Preludio Fugato and Finale, MS, piano, 4 hands.
1967/ Conversations, MS, clarinet and viola.
68
1968 String Quartet No. 9, Chester.
1970 Music for Double Bass and Piano, York Edition.
1971 String Quartet No. 10, Chester.
1972 Three Bagatelles, Oxford University Press, oboe and
      harpsichord.
1972 Oboe Quartet, MS.
1972 Three Preludes, MS, violin and piano.
1976 String Quartet No. 11, Chester.
1980 Piccola Musica, violin, viola, cello.
1980 Trittico, 2 oboes, bassoon, harpsichord.
1981 My Dark Heart, J.M. Synge, soprano, for flute, oboe,
      horn, violin, viola and cello.
1981 Wind Quintet, for flute, oboe, clarinet, bassoon and
      horn.
1982 Tribute, for inslemare, solo violin, two flutes, two
      oboes, two clarinets and two bassoons.
1982 L'Horloge, text by Baudelaire, soprano, clarinet, piano,
      Chester Music.
1982 Music for Strings, for large body of strings.

Operatic

1956/ The Sofa, Ursula Vaughan Williams, 40 mins., one act,
57   Chester.
1960/ The Departure, Anne Ridler, 30 mins., one act, Ches-
61   ter.
1958/ The Three Strangers, Elizabeth Maconchy after Thomas
67   Hardy, 55 min., one act. Chester.
1967 The Birds, 30 min., one act, Boosey & Hawkes.
1969/ The Jesse Tree, Anne Ridler, Church Opera, one act.
70   MS.
1969 Johnny and the Mohawks, for young children, Elizabeth
      Maconchy, Unison voices, Oxford University Press.
1976 The King of the Golden River, Children's opera, 1 hr.
      32 min., MS, (Libretto Anne Ridler).

Ballet

1940   Puck Fair, 25 min., orchestra or two pianos, MS.

Choral Accompanied

1951   Six Yeats Settings, W.B. Yeats, clarinet, two horns,
           harp, SSA, soprano solo, MS.
1962   Christmas Morning, The Bible and traditional carols,
           piano (or small ensemble of recorders or other wind,
           percussion and piano), women's voices, Ricordi.
1962   The Armado, SATB and piano, Ricordi.
1968/ The Death shall have no Dominion, Dylan Thomas, SATB
  69   (or treble ATB) two horns, three trumpets, three
           trombones, MS.
1973   Fly-by-Nights, seven anonymous poems, treble voices
           and harp, Boosey & Hawkes.
1975   Pied Beauty, Heavenhaven, G.M Hopkins, choir and
           brass, Chester Music.

Choral Unaccompanied

1965   Nocturnal, William Barnes; Edward Thomas; Shelley,
           SATB, Oxford University Press.
1965   Propheta Mendax, Medieval Latin, boys' or women's
           voices in three parts, Faber.
1966   I Sing of a Maiden This Day, Carols, mixed voices (4
           part) high voices (3 part), Faber.
1971   Prayer Before Birth, Louis MacNeice, women's voices
           (4 part), high voices MS.
1974   Sirens' Song, William Browne, SATB, Chester.
1975   Two Epitaphs, Francis Quarles and Anon SSA, Chester.

Solo Voice

1929   Ophelia's Song, Shakespeare, soprano and piano, Ox-
           ford University Press.
1938   The Garland, song cycle Anacreontica, (trans. William
           LeFanu), soprano and piano, MS.
1965/ Hymn to God the Father; Hymn to Christ, The Sunris-
  66   ing, John Donne, tenor and piano, Chester.

1965 Four Shakespeare Songs, 8 min., soprano or tenor and
         piano, MS.
1971 Faustus Christopher Marlowe, tenor and piano, MS.
1974 Three Songs, Bryon; Shelley; Campbell, soprano or
         tenor and harp, Chester.
1977 Sun, Moon and Stars (song cycle), Traherne, soprano
         and piano.

Solo Instrument

1939 A Country Town, 9 short pieces, piano, Hinrichsen.
1957 Variations on a Theme from Vaugham Williams, cello,
         Lengnick.
1962 The Yaffle, Mill Race, piano, Ricordi.
1965/ Sonatina, for harpsichord, Lengnick.
  66
1966 Notebook, for harpsichord, Chester.
1966 Six Pieces, for solo violin, Chester.
1976 Morning, Noon and Night, harp, Chester.

Publishers

Boosey & Hawkes, 295 Regent Street, London W1A 1BR, Eng-
      land

Chappell, 50 New Bond Street, London W1A 1DR, England.

Faber, 3 Queen Square, London WC1, England.

Lengnick, 421a Brighton Road, South Croydon, Surrey CR2
      6YR, England.

Ricordi, The Bury, Church Street, Chesham, Bucks, England.

British & Continental, 64 Dean Street, London W1V 6AU, Eng-
      land.

Chester, 7-9 Eagle Court, London EC1M 5QD, England.

Hinrichsen, 10-12 Baches Street, London N1 6DN, England.

Oxford University Press, 44 Conduit Street, London W1R
      0DE, England.

Yorke Edition, 8 Cecil Road, London W3 0DA, England.

Discography

<u>Overture: Proud Thames</u>, Recorded LPOF, Lyrita SRCS 57.
<u>Ariadne</u>, Recorded, Heather Harper, Raymond Leppard, ECO,
      L'Oiseau-Lyre SOL 331.
<u>String Quartet No. 5</u>, Recorded by Allegri Quartet, ARGO
      RG 329.
<u>String Quartet No. 9</u>
<u>Oboe Quartet</u>, Recorded by Evelyn Barbirolli and Valada Avel-
      ing, on HMV HQS 1298.

Addresses

Lyrita, A.R. Itter, 99 Green Lane, Burnham, Birchs, Eng-
      land.

ARGO, The Decca Record Company Limited, Argo Division,
      115 Fulham Road, London SW3 6RR, England.

L'Oiseau Lyre, Boite Pastale 515, MC98015, Monaco.

HMV HQS, His Master's Voice, 142 Wardown Street, London,
      W, England.

MARY MAGEAU

Harpsichordist

American composer Mary Mageau was born in Milwaukee, Wis.
in 1934. In 1974 she accepted an Australian guest lecture-
ship and later married Kenneth White, a Brisbane architect.
She is now a permanent Australian resident with two sons,
Leigh and Peter.

Her parents, Helen Roestel and Wallace Mageau, moved
the family when Mary was a young child to a small town on
the iron range in Minnesota called Virginia. She has fond
memories of growing up with her brother Thomas and sister
Diane and recalls her mother as a musician par excellence:

> My mother was a fine pianist, teacher and performer.
> I studied piano with her from my early years until
> the time I went to college. We had a great relation-
> ship and it was one of those mother-daughter teams
> that worked very well. I look back and say, 'she's
> the one who made me what I am today.'
> When the time came to continue my studies away
> from home I attended the College of St. Scholastica
> in Duluth, Minnesota. This was a Benedictine Col-
> lege with a fine music department. I later entered
> the Benedictine Order which was devoted to teach-
> ing and nursing but I did not remain.
> It was at DePaul University in Chicago that I
> completed my Bachelor of Music degree. At the end
> of my programme I took an elective course in compo-
> sition from Dr. Leon Stein and realized that writing
> music was what I must do.

Mageau was elated when she heard her first composition performed and she credits Leon Stein for pointing her in

MARY MAGEAU   Photo by
                                Wendy Rozworski

the right direction. She realized that she would need a more
extensive background in composition to pursue a graduate
degree. She completed a preparatory semester of work at
the University of Michigan at Ann Arbor before starting a
master of music degree in composition. Mary Mageau's mentor
of all mentors was Ross Lee Finney. She said:

> Ross Lee Finney was marvelous--what Leon Stein
> started Finney encouraged and nurtured. He never
> pushed a student into a certain style, he tried to
> give direction but always encouraged the student to
> find his/her own voice as a composer. He treated
> you as a professional even when you were a student.

It was the policy at Ann Arbor that student compositions must be heard and assessed. For Mageau this was a
great opportunity for it was the one way she could grow as
a composer. She developed a feeling for different instrumental combinations by composing a variety of chamber works.
She also wrote one orchestral piece because the thesis at Ann
Arbor was a work for full orchestra. Just before her graduation with honors in 1969, the University of Michigan Symphony
Orchestra premiered her work, Variegations for Orchestra.
Although she was pleased with the performance and it helped
to build her confidence, she knew that she would need to
write more tightly as she developed the craft of composing.
At Ann Arbor she also studied privately with Leslie Bassett
who made her more acutely aware of the craft of composing
which she felt was extremely important in her growth as a
composer.

Her work Three Movements for unaccompanied violoncello was awarded performance in the 1968 International Festival of the Arts, Honolulu, in a competition sponsored by the
University of Hawaii. Variegations for Orchestra was awarded
a second prix silver medal in the Gottschalk International
Competition sponsored by the Pan American Association in
1970.

In 1970 Mageau was awarded a further opportunity to
study composition with George Crumb at the internationally
renowned Berkshire Music Center Composer's Fellowship Program at Tanglewood in Lenox, Mass. She relates:

> At Tanglewood we gathered for our composition semi-
> nars in Nathaniel Hawthorne's restored cottage, a
> charming American colonial home where he wrote his
> Tanglewood Tales. George Crumb was the composer
> in residence and he offered many interesting ses-
> sions in which he spoke of his own music's growth
> from his West Virginia folk roots. Dr. Chou Wen-
> chung from Columbia was delightful and spent quite
> some time on ethnic Chinese and Japanese music.
> Gunther Schuller's seminars offered a number of
> interesting approaches to contemporary music. I
> still use his ideas in my own teaching today. A man
> of many roles: administrator, teacher, performer,
> composer and conductor, he above all made Tangle-
> wood and the Fromm Festival exciting.

In 1971 she studied at The Electronic Music Center, Catholic University, Washington, D.C.

Her orchestral work Montage was premiered by the Duluth Symphony Orchestra in Minnesota in 1971 and in 1973 Henry Charles Smith conducted the work with the Minnesota Orchestra. The piece was performed several times while the orchestra was on tour. The Des Moines Symphony Orchestra performed Montage during the 1973 season and Patrick Thomas conducted the same work with The Queensland Symphony Orchestra at the Modern Music Forum Series in Brisbane, Australia in 1976.

In addition to composing Mary Mageau has always been an active performer. As a chamber-music pianist she has appeared in concert recitals in both the United States and Australia. From 1967 to 1969 she was the harpsichordist with the University of Michigan's Collegium Musicum and the Contemporary Directions Ensemble.

During the early 1970s Mageau developed an interest in music of other cultures and began to seriously consider studying for a doctorate in ethnomusicology. To prepare for this study she decided it would be best to establish a home-base in an English-speaking country where she could further pursue her interest in Southeast Asian music. She left Scholastica College where she was an assistant professor of music in 1974 and became guest lecturer at the Kelvin Grove College of Advanced Education in Brisbane, Australia. Speaking of this experience she said:

> I arrived in Australia and fell in love with the country and its people. Since I had a one year's contract with the Kelvin Grove College I didn't intend to stay. Near the end of my first term I met Ken White, a Brisbane architect, who had returned to his home town after seven years of work and postgraduate study in the United Kingdom. We became friends and his family also welcomed me. Plans for our marriage followed and we celebrated a Christmas wedding,--the happiest chapter in my Australian story.

When Mary Mageau looked for a performance outlet in Brisbane she found her studies of continuo harpsichord with

Ellwood Derr at the University of Michigan played an important role. There were many fine harpsichords in Brisbane
that were neglected and not being played. It was a performers' paradise which she enjoyed while continuing to write
pieces for both the harpsichord and piano.

Many of her keyboard pieces had been published by G.
Schirmer and Schmitt, Hall & McCreary before she left the
United States. The American Music Teacher published the
following comments on Mageau's keyboard piece, Forecasts,
in March 1973: "Indeed amazing forecasts!...Would that
there were more similar material available!"

When G. Schirmer, New York, published Mageau's Australia's Animals in 1976 the collection of six piano solos was
reviewed by Margaret Tolson for The Piano Quarterly, winter
edition 1978-79:

> It is a pleasure to meet a new composer of children's
> pieces who has good musical ideas, works them out
> skillfully with varied and appropriate keyboard ac-
> tivity, and puts them right under the fingers of
> young players. These irresistible sound pictures
> (none longer than three lines) introduce us to some
> of the exotic creatures inhabiting a large Australian
> sanctuary. The Sleepy Koala is sometimes upside
> down. Wandering Wombat covers a lot of space on
> a whole tone scale. Both of these non-conformist
> creatures like to change meter. Ponderous Platypus
> swings in low, slow syncopation (chords too) but
> he never moves very far. The Silver Swan, on the
> other hand, is all over the pond, swimming in light
> and shadow in whole tone patterns. Capering Kanga-
> roo and Elegant Emu engage in their respective ac-
> tivities of jumping near and far or running in ever-
> widening patterns disappearing in a glissando.
>   This is a prize set of pieces which offers the
> student a joyous experience while enlarging his
> listening and playing capabilities. Fingering and
> pedal indications are just fine and the free tonal
> palette is a delight.

Mageau's Interaction written in 1969 for solo clarinet
and magnetic tape received its Australian premiere at the
International Society for Contemporary Music in Brisbane.

The performance was reviewed by Kevin Siddell for The Australian on June 12, 1976 (excerpt):

> Mary Mageau's Interaction is a work for clarinet and prepared tape. The clarinet was used to inject a personal element into the work which the composer prepared and synthesised.
>
> As the title suggests, the work offers a series of comments on tape which are reacted to by the clarinet. This is a work based on small gestures of sound. Nevertheless there is an immediate appeal about it. There was spontaneity and yet evident structure. Perhaps it was the compelling nature of the prepared tape which carried over into the performance of the clarinettist.

In 1979 Mageau, Gary Williams, an American who is principal cellist with the Queensland Symphony Orchestra and Adelaide Brown, the English principal flutist with the orchestra, decided to join together for a Baroque Bash which proved to be the stepping stone for an exciting musical venture. When they performed trio sonatas they found that their three different personalities, living three totally different lifestyles, were meant for each other. When they played music it was exciting and beautiful. The next step was a public performance out of which was born the Brisbane Baroque Trio. One such early concert was reviewed by John Villaume for The Courier-Mail on Aug. 20, 1979:

> A FAMILY bereavement prescribed a purely instrumental programme for the Bach Society of Queensland's concert at the Arts Theatre yesterday evening.
>
> Adelaide Brown (flute), Gary Williams (cello) and Mary Mageau (harpsichord) all have a repertory of baroque music wide enough to see them through such an emergency. The modest opening Sonata for Flute and Continuo illustrated the gifts of Jean Baptiste Loeillet, who popularized the transverse flute in 18th century London. Vivaldi's E Minor Sonata for Cello and Harpsichord is sterner stuff, and was accorded its due respect. A sonata for Solo Flute by C.P.E. Bach took us to the borderline of late baroque. For the rest, J.S. Bach's presiding genius took charge in stylish and satisfying accounts of works for various

combinations. And <u>A Telemann Suite for Flute and Harpsichord</u> added to our admiration for players able to rise more than adequately to a sadly unlooked-for occasion.

The members of the Brisbane Baroque Trio enjoy researching and performing music of the 17th and early 18th centuries and since its inception the group has performed a large and varied repertoire. They have recorded for the Australian Broadcasting Commission and Grevillea Records. One of their unique and important contributions has been to commission Queensland composers to write for the Trio thus providing a performance opportunity for 20th-century music to be heard as well as recorded. In a country with a small population and only a few commercial recordings of 20th-century music available to the listening public, their work has been an extremely important contribution to Australia's musical heritage.

In 1980 Mary Mageau was awarded an Australia Council grant to compose a new work for the Brisbane Trio. <u>Sonate Concertate</u> for flute, cello and harpsichord received its world premiere on May 14, 1980 at the national conference of music education lecturers at Queensland University. It was later recorded by the Trio on the Grevillea Label. The following program notes were written by Mageau for the cover of the recording:

> Mary Mageau's <u>Sonate Concertate</u> (in stilo moderno) integrates contemporary rhythms and sonorities into a design which is characteristically Baroque, drawing its germinal idea from the <u>Sonate Concertate</u> of Dario Castello, 1621. This form, developed by the Venetian Castello in a series of chamber works, provided the link between the instrumental canzona and emerging solo concerto through the emphasis placed on concerted virtuoso playing. In the opening Overture, Mary Mageau subtly pokes fun at the pompous French overture form. <u>The Cantilena</u>, an embellished solo song for the flute with a traditional basso continuo style of accompaniment follows. <u>The Galliarde</u>, cast in a Minuet and Trio form with rhythmic groupings of 3's and 5's precedes the Gay, which brings the work to a fast-paced, breathless close.

A second recording by the Brisbane Baroque Trio was released in 1982 and includes the works of two Queensland composers: Mary Mageau's Scarborough Fair and Cinque Partite by Dr. Philip Bracanin of the Queensland University department of music. The quality of the recording is excellent and a must for the library of music lovers. The album was recorded at the Brisbane College of Advanced Education at Kelvin Grove by Rodney Jacobsen who must be credited for his tremendous ability with sound technique.

John Villaume writing for The Courier Mail on July 27, 1982 reviewed one of the many performances by the Trio:

> Sunday afternoon's concert by the Brisbane Baroque Trio at Griffith University clinched this group's claim to its title with some beautifully scaled music from baroque and earlier periods.
> In Handel's Sonata in F, Op. 1, No. 11, Adelaide Brown's treble recorder traced a quiet, carefully judged line above Mary Mageau's matching harpsichord and Gary Williams' deftly touched-in continuo on cello. This was baroque performance-practice at its unobtrusive best.
> Equally acceptable were Mary Mageau's solo performances of harpsichord pieces from an earlier period by Bull, Byrd and our old friend Anon--solid, rather than florid.
> Gary Williams' cello guided Vivaldi's Sonata No. 6 in B flat into a more modern gambit, but was worth hearing for its expressive solo movements.
> Piccolo Victory (Images of Colonial Australia), by Brisbane composer Betty Beath, improves on further acquaintance.
> Sunday's performance benefited by incorporating violinist Harold Wilson's skill on the didgeridoo, an Aboriginal wind instrument, giving the piece much additional point.

The live performances and recordings by the Brisbane Baroque Trio are of great importance to the musicians, composers and audiences in Queensland. Many of the chamber groups in the area perform no contemporary music and it is a sad state of affairs in a country that is trying to establish its own cultural values and encourage music written by Australians. The Brisbane Baroque Trio has been performing and recording for nine years and one can only hope that their fine work will continue, for in a country that is vast and very isolated there is a great need for quality performances and recordings.

George Tintner and the Queensland Theatre Orchestra performed the world premiere of Mary Mageau's Concerto Grosso with Adelaide Brown, flute, Gary Williams, cello and the composer on harpsichord responsible for the solo sections. Music critic John Villaume praised Mageau for the fresh ideas she explored in the work. In addition he wrote for The Courier Mail on Nov. 29, 1986 (excerpt):

> ....the work exhibited a firm grasp of the appropriate style for each instrument, expressed in a harmonic idiom of the early 20th century.

Since 1983 Mageau has been working to promote new music for harpsichord and is planning to record a solo album which will include the music of fellow composers Ann Carr-Boyd, Dale Craig and herself. During the same year she completed two commissions, Pacific Portfolio, written for St. Margaret's College Orchestra and a piano trio.

Asked why she writes music she responded in the following way:

> I have something to say and I must express myself. Since I am not a literary person I speak best through my music. My location in Brisbane has been fortuitous for two reasons. The city is large, its population is just under one million people and there are a variety of performance outlets for a composer. However, Brisbane is also isolated from the mainstream of contemporary music thought. This situation has caused me to explore and find my own individual voice as a composer and not rely on the ideas and idioms of others. My work must have an accessible meaning to performers and audiences alike. These few lines best sum up my philosophy:
>
> > MUSIC--the art of sound in time.
> > For its creation:
> >   a sensitive ear

an intuitive feeling for the wholeness of things
a developed craft
an elegant solution.

In 1985 The Canberra Times, in association with the La-
Trobe University School of Music and the National Library,
sponsored a series of concerts including an anthology of contemporary Australian piano music performed by Larry Sitsky,
composer-pianist. The series titled The Composer Speaks
proved to be one of the most valuable presentations ever
performed in Australia. Mary Mageau's Elite Syncopations
was included in the nine piano pieces by nine Australian
composers performed by Sitsky which is included in an anthology published by LaTrobe University. Music reviewer
W.L. Hoffman considered Mageau's work the maverick of the
program. He wrote, "its cheerful lightheartedness is in distinct contrast to the serious tone of all other works."

Winter's Shadow was written by Mageau in 1984 and is
scored for harpsichord and wind chimes. The work is based
on a Japanese pentatonic scale and derives its program from
haiku. She included this piece in a 1986 recital in which she
performed the works of Dale Craig, Ann Carr-Boyd and
Gertrud Roberts. She has been a pioneer in a country where
until recent years there were perhaps no more then six active composers in all of Queensland. But Mageau feels there
is a hub of world-standard composers living in Australia and
it is extremely important that their works be heard and whenever possible recorded.

The past two decades have produced a conscious effort
on the part of musicians, conductors and composers to make
their music more Australian based. For most of its young
history Australian composers and conductors have had to gain
acceptance overseas, especially in Great Britain, before being
recognized at home. Mary Mageau has been an active contributor, in her adopted country, and has encouraged and
fostered the work of 20th-century Australian musicians. She
is a pioneer with a multifaceted career who has made major
contributions which should be recorded in the history of 20th-
century Australian music.

Selected Compositions of Mary Mageau

Large Ensemble Works

1968 Variegations, symphony orchestra, MS.
1970 Montage, symphony orchestra, MS.
1971 Celebration Music, symphonic band, MS.
1976 Indian Summer, youth orchestra, MS.
1982 Concerto Grosso, for flute, cello, harpsichord, percussion and string orchestra, MS.

Chamber and Solo Instrumental Works

1969 Interaction, for solo clarinet and magnetic tape, MS.
1972 Fantasy Music, for violin and piano, MS.
1973 Forensis, for flute oboe, clarinet, bassoon, percussion I and II, MS.
1976 Contrasts, for solo cello, published by J. Albert & Son, Sydney.
1977 Dialogues, SATB recorder quartet, MS.
1977 Doubles, SATB recorder quartet and percussion, MS.
1979 Statement and Variations, for solo viola, MS.
1979 Dialogues, for clarinet, cello and piano, MS.
1980 Sonate Concertate, for flute, cello and harpsichord, MS.
1986 Doubles, SATB recorder quartet, published by The American Recorder Magazine.

Keyboard Collections

1972- Adventures in Time and Space, Volumes I-V, published
75   by The Schmitt Music Center, Minneapolis, includes 13 graded pieces for solo piano.
1976 Australia's Animals, published by G. Schirmer, New York.
1980 Keyboard Strategies, edited by Melvin Stecher & Norman Horowitz, published by G. Schirmer, New York, includes Clouds for solo piano.
1982 Duet Book, Volume III, published by Allans Music, Melbourne, includes March for piano--four hands.
1986 Elite Syncopations, for contemporary Australian piano, published by LaTrobe University Press, Melbourne.

Keyboard Works

1969 Three Pieces for Organ, for solo organ, published by
         The World Library of Sacred Music, Cincinnati.
1970 Cycles and Series, for solo piano, MS.
1974 Forecasts, for solo piano, published by G. Schirmer,
         New York.
1976 Australia's Animals, for solo piano, published by G.
         Schirmer, New York.
1977 Ragtime, for solo piano, MS.
1978 Cityscapes, for solo piano, MS.
1979 Pacific Ports, for piano--four hands, MS.
1980 Pacific Ports, for piano duet, published by ASMUSC,
         Brisbane.

Choral Works

1967 Mass for our Lady of Victory, for unison and organ,
         published by The Priory Press, Duluth.
1971 A Chime of Windbells, SATB flute and percussion, MS.
1972 Lacrimae, SAT, percussion, MS.
1978 A Community Mass, SATB, congregation and organ, MS.
1981 The Line Always There, SSAA, flute, percussion, piano
         duet, published by ASMUSE, Brisbane.

Addresses

J. Albert & Son, Pty. Ltd., 139 King Street, Sydney, New
   South Wales, 2000, Australia.

G. Schirmer, Inc., 866 Third Avenue, New York, NY 10022.

Schmitt Music Centers, 110 North Fifth Street, Minneapolis,
   MN 55403.

LaTrobe University Press, Bundoora, Melbourne, Victoria,
   Australia 3083.

Allans Music Australia Pty. Ltd., c/o Allans Publishing Pty.
   Ltd., 165-169 Gladstone Street, South Melbourne,
   Victoria, Australia, 3205.

The American Recorder Magazine, 596 Broadway, No. 902,
New York, NY 10012.

World Library of Sacred Music, 2145 Central Parkway, Cin-
cinnati, OH 45214.

Discography

Original Music

Lacrimae, chorus and percussion, The Duluth Minstrels, Sound
80--S80 1995.
Sonate Concertate, flute, cello, harpsichord, The Brisbane
Baroque Trio, Grevillea--GRV 1080.
Contrasts, Gary Williams, cello, Grevillea--GRV1070.
Variations--Scarborough Fair, The Brisbane Baroque Trio,
Grevillea--GRV 1081.
Elite Syncopations, Larry Sitsky, piano, MOVE Records.

Arrangements

Greensleeves To a Ground, The Brisbane Baroque Trio--GRV
1080.
Adagio, Albinoni/Mageau, The Brisbane Baroque Trio--GRV
1082.
La Follia, Corelli/Mageau, The Brisbane Baroque Trio--GRV
1082.

Addresses

The Duluth Minstrels, Scholastica College, Duluth, MN 55811.

Grevillea Records, 26B Wallace Street, Albion, Brisbane,
Queensland, Australia 4010.

MOVE Records, 10 Glen Drive, Eaglemont, Melbourne, Victoria, Australia 3084.

URSULA MAMLOK

Composer

Success is all the more imposing when the artist comes from "extraordinarily" difficult beginnings. Ursula Mamlok was born in Berlin, Germany in 1928 the only child of Dorothy and John Lewis. When the family escaped from Nazi Germany in 1939, it was too late to choose a country, so they went to Ecuador where refugees were still being accepted.

Ursula's uncle was a German "pop" musician and when she was 3 years old she would play all the melodies she had heard him perform on the piano. "I probably played all the tunes in the key of C but I found the right chords and used accompaniment. It was unfortunate that a doctor friend of the family recommended to my parents that I not study piano because I was too nervous and overactive. That was a big mistake, and I was nine before I began piano lessons which is too old, for one aiming to become a concert pianist."

As a youngster she composed as a "game" and thought composing was something every child did. Her first teacher had been a student of Franz Liszt and was well into his 80s when she studied with him. She took some of her own compositions to the first lesson and he agreed to teach her piano and composition. She immediately had to stop composing and learn harmony and counterpoint. He told her he could teach her in three months what it would take years to learn in a conservatory and he did.

Ursula became attached to this teacher, a well-known musicologist and composer, who had changed his Jewish name to Gustav Ernest, and under his tutelage she learned to identify with the great masters of music which she felt was a marvelous experience. She remained with him until they were forced to

URSULA MAMLOK   Photo by
                                 Steven W. Kinigstein

flee Germany. He wanted to take her to Holland and she begged her parents to allow her to go, but they decided otherwise which was fortunate since he was killed by the Nazis.

Ursula and her family escaped to Guayaquil, Ecuador, where no possibility for serious musical studies existed. She was disappointed and hurt because there was no way for her to continue her music until her mother recalled the name of an American musician whom she had met on a train ride to Czechoslovakia several years earlier. Her mother wrote to this person, Harwood Simmons, who happened to be a professor at Columbia University, and he suggested that Ursula apply to Juilliard, Curtis, or the Mannes School of Music. Both Juilliard and Curtis required an audition for acceptance and this was impossible for a refugee living in Ecuador. But Mannes was a small school, interested in what was happening to refugees, and they requested samples of Ursula's compositions. Some months later she had a reply, a full scholarship to study piano and to work with the conductor and composition teacher George Szell at the Mannes School of Music in New York.

Although immigration laws prevented her parents from joining her, she came to the United States alone, a teen-ager, and began her studies. She said, "I was a fanatic, I wanted to study composition and nothing could stop me. At a later date I found sponsors and my parents joined me."

From 1942 to 1945 Ursula Mamlok studied composition with George Szell at the Mannes School. She reflects on those years:

> George Szell was an excellent musician and teacher. He required me to study harmony and counterpoint and write string quartets according to classical techniques. At this point in my life, I disliked most contemporary music, not having been exposed to it sufficiently. Mr. Szell influenced his students, as many teachers still do, to acquire fluency in the idiom of the masters of the 18th and 19th century. He did accept attempts reminiscent of such moderns as Prokofiev, Stravinsky and Shostakovitch, but discouraged those of the atonal school. He did teach me a lot of valuable literature, but I was fortunate

when he went to Cleveland because in essence that
particular period in my life was coming to a close.

During this time Mamlok received several first prizes in
competitions sponsored by the National Federation of Music
Clubs. Awards are important in a young composer's career
and Ursula is appreciative of the recognition she received at
a very young age.

An important turning point in her career occurred in
1944 when she attended the summer institute of music at Black
Mountain College in North Carolina. The institute was held
to celebrate Arnold Schoenberg's 70th birthday. Here, for
the first time, she was exposed to the music of Schoenberg
and Berg by such notable musicians as Ernest Krenek, Roger
Sessions, Edward Steuermann and the Kolisch Quartet. She
recalls:

> I was seventeen, and I couldn't digest all of the
> music I was hearing--I was baffled by the sounds.
> I knew I had to find a way to learn more about this
> music. My parents were factory workers and they
> had no money but I did approach Roger Sessions
> about studying with him, and he was very generous.
> I studied with him for a year until he left for Berke-
> ley. He told me, 'forget all the harmony and counter-
> point--just write what you hear.'

This proved to be a very difficult task for Ursula. A
new world of music was opened to her, and she wanted to
express herself in a contemporary idiom but, having been cut
loose from her traditional moorings, felt ambivalent about her
freedom. Sessions did influence her, but at the time she
was uncertain and destroyed all that she wrote during that
year. She said, "I simply could not connect all the atonal
music that I was working with."

After Sessions left, Ursula studied composition on her
own but eventually realized that if she ever hoped to teach
at the college level she would have to earn her degrees. At
the age of 27 she received a scholarship and attended the
Manhattan School of Music (1955-1958), earning her bachelor's
and master's degrees in a short span of time because of her
previous musical background. Mamlok said:

I went with my Sessionish music to study with Vit-
torio Giannini, and he said, 'You have too many lines
in your music, and you must simplify your style.'
He really didn't help me much, but I did receive my
degrees and wrote a lot of tonal music during that
period. Actually much of the music I wrote at that
time is being played more and more today. Some
composers never change, but I have always been
adventurous, striving to learn all that I can and to
assimilate it into my own style.

Interest in Mamlok's compositions have increased progressively since 1960. She studied with Stefan Wolfe for a
short period of time and wrote one piece: Variations for Solo
Flute which is today her most performed piece of music and
has been recorded twice. Harvey Sollberger premiered Variations for Solo Flute and Mamlok discusses both the piece and
the premiere:

I thought it was amazing that this piece could have
been written by me. I was beginning to write close
to the Schoenberg style, and at first I had mixed
feelings about working with these--to me new--tech-
niques. I began to like this kind of music and I
haven't changed much in style since then. The flute
variations combine classical procedures with the 12-
tone technique--each of the short variations dealing
with specific musical problems all done with the row,
or parts of the row, or abandoning the row altogether. It's a very clear piece.
When it was premiered in 1961 in Carnegie Hall,
New York City, one reviewer labeled it a 'landmark
of difficult twentieth century pieces.' But this is
not true today--many people perform it.

Variations for Solo Flute has been recorded by Katherine
Hoover, Opus One no. 72 and by Samuel Baron on CRI 202.
Hoover, a well-known composer herself, has recorded a brilliant performance of the work. As one critic wrote, "the
work is a landmark in American serialism, long overdue for a
recording of this quality."

Eric Salzman, writing for the New York Herald Tribune
on Dec. 19, 1963 hailed Mamlok's String Quartet as one of the
season's new works that has something to say. The Franklin

String Quartet, Joseph Schor and Ernestine Briesmeister,
violins; Jacob Glick, viola; Donald Anderson, cello; performed
the piece. The review further read (partial):

> The big new piece was a String Quartet by Ursula
> Mamlok, written in 1962 and just recently revised.
> This is music of a great deal of character with a
> strong intense first movement and a scherzo which
> has a remarkable, literal repeat of its main section
> that works just the way such repeats used to work
> in the dear old days. But the most interesting fea-
> ture is the quiet last movement which is literally
> built up out of levels of intensity--of dynamics,
> string color and vibrato and durations; the build-
> up tensions literally explode just before the end.
> [© I.H.T. Corporation. Reprinted by permission.]

The work had been premiered the previous summer at
the Bennington, Vt. Composers Conference at which time Mamlok said, "Composers are not superhumans who rely on the
divine 'inspiration' alone, but like sculptors and painters,
working with clay and colors, they are architects in sound,
who form acoustic pictures out of tones." Bennington College
with its unique summer programs for composers, conductors
and musicians has been admired and respected in the United
States and has fostered the career of many an aspiring artist.
The first conference was organized by Alan Carter, director
of the Vermont Symphony and the music director of Middlebury College. It was fashioned after the internationally known
writers conference held yearly at Middlebury.

Stray Birds, a setting of five aphorisms by Tagore,
also tried out at Bennington, is a chamber work for soprano,
flute and cello, rather than a song cycle in the traditional
sense. Written between August 1963 and Nov. 22, 1963, it
is dedicated to the memory of President Kennedy. One of
Mamlok's most frequently performed compositions, it was premiered by Antonia Lavanne, soprano, Harvey Sollberger, flute,
and Toby Saks, cello in a concert of the Group for Contemporary Music at Columbia University. According to the composer, "the instruments are not supplying mere accompaniment
for the vocal line, but participate, often with great virtuosity,
in expressing the character of the poetry as it suggested itself to me." John Voorhees wrote in the Seattle Post: "This
writing is highly imaginative--highly difficult. The entire

piece has a fragile ethereal quality about it that is almost
mesmerizing."

Stray Birds has been recorded by Phyllis Bryn-Julson,
soprano; Harvey Sollberger, flute; and Fred Sherry, cello;
on Composers Recordings CRI SD 301.

In 1964 Mamlok wrote Concert Piece for Four scored
for flute, oboe, viola, and percussion. She felt that by
writing a fun piece it might help dispel the idea held by
some people that the 12-tone technique is not capable of expressing a light-hearted music. Concert Piece is playful and
in the last movement a boisterously humorous piece. She
explains:

> The last movement is an unusual kind of ostinato
> type variation set, in which the three pitched instru-
> ments are in contest with the percussion. In the
> process of the movement, single notes, then motifs
> are dropped, while the percussion in turn is adding
> material until at the end of the movement it is heard
> alone. A coda of almost theatrical quality brings
> each instrument back once more, uniting them in a
> climax on a trill, then dissolving it all, until the
> viola takes up the beginning, but is abruptly and
> finally stopped by the others.

Anthony Korf, conductor of Parnassus, an internationally known contemporary group noted for commissioning and
performing new music, chose to conduct Mamlok's Concert
Piece for Four early in his career because he enjoyed conducting complicated music. "Today Korf is among the two or
three conductors that form the colorism of modern music, who
later commissioned and recorded Sextet." One critic wrote:

> Ursula Mamlok's Concert Piece for Four--four being
> flute, oboe, viola and percussion--was a twelve-tone
> sort of work with careful, even elegant, charm.

Ursula Mamlok remembers her life very clearly because
somehow it centers around the pieces she has written. There
have been several times during her career when she found
herself at crossroads. She questions:

> Should I continue to write atonal music or return to

earlier tonal music, should I make my music simpler
or should I continue in the same way or make my
music more difficult?

Composing in this century is very difficult--one
must ask oneself whom one is composing for--which
audience is the composer's music to address? Ul-
timately I have to be my own most critical audience.
If convinced that the composition 'works' for me I
know that the attentive listener will respond to the
work.

When I was a student of Stefan Wolfe I found his
music too complex. Yet, today I see that he as well
as Ralph Shapey, with whom I later studied, were
most important influences on me. From Shapey I
learned to work with rhythmic structures allowing
for a more interesting textural surface than that of
my earlier, more symmetrical music. In addition he
became my mentor by providing first performance
opportunities for the music I was writing.

In 1967 Mamlok wrote Haiku Settings for soprano and
flute. The five movements used the following: I) So cold
are the waves the rocking gull can scarcely fold itself to
sleep (Basho); II) When a nightingale sang out the sparrow
flew off to a further tree (Jurin); III) A leaf is falling alas
another and another falls (Rasetsu); IV) A tree frog softly
begins to trill as raindrops spatter the new leaves (Rogetsu);
V) How cool the green hay smells carried in through the
farmgate at sunshine. The work has been recorded on Grenadilla Records GS-1015 by Sue Ann Kahn, flute, and Lucy
Shelton, soprano. The three examples of contemporary pieces
heard on this disc are excellent. One reviewer wrote of the
recording, "Haiku Settings are brief, angular pieces of a
frankly descriptive, almost programmatic nature. Mamlok's
music never intrudes on the distilled essence of the poetry,
but rather enhances it considerably, especially as sung by
Miss Shelton." The following are notes by Ursula Mamlok on
Haiku Settings:

> The piece may be listened to on various levels. The
> structural design is most likely of interest mainly
> to composers. More important for the listener is to
> note the connection between the music and the poetry.
>
> In these settings much attention has been paid to
> the content of each poem. In a way the songs may

be heard as a kind of mood painting, quite similar
to the treatment of much vocal music of the past.

The chill of icy waves is expressed here by asym-
metrical angular shapes in the flute line, set against
the repeated motion of the interval of a minor third
in the vocal line, depicting the rocking gull.

Larger intervals and longer note values were
chosen for the line 'When a nightingale sang out,'
contrasted by the short notes in the following phrase
'the sparrow flew off,' etc. The heavier timbre of
the alto flute contributes to the melancholy mood of
the third song in addition to the fact that there is
a minimum of intervallic motion.

As a complete contrast, song four (played as fast
as possible) displays large skips in the instrumental
writing, the vocal line consisting of only two notes
which come closer to each other gradually until merging in a trill on the 'trill.'

The last song, 'How cool the green hay smells,'
is free from the concise rhythmic shapes which were
more suitable for the preceding texts. Here all is
at rest and a feeling of relaxation is accomplished
by slow moving, unaccented lines, the voice and
alto flute rather complementing than contrasting each
other.

When soprano Lee Dougherty and her husband, Tony
Pagano, flutist performed the five Haiku Settings Maritza
Morgan wrote in The Chautauquan Daily on July 9, 1970 (ex-
cerpt):

In all of them, the flute and the human voice managed
to sound like a rocking gull, a nightingale and a
sparrow, a leaf, a trill of a tree frog and the spatter
of rain and the broad, clean fragrance of green hay.
Most unusual sounds were asked of the voice and
flute, and they were delivered.

Donal Henahan of the New York Times spoke of the
"excellent" Haiku Settings at Lee Dougherty's Tully Hall Debut in 1972.

Ursula Mamlok's only electronic composition, Sonar Trajectory, rested on her shelf until April 1984. It was composed
in 1966 when she worked at the Columbia-Princeton Electronic

Studio for the first and--so far--only time. Had not a col-
league-composer Gordon Mumma, who admired her Trio Panta
Rhei at a performance at Bowling Green State University dur-
ing October 1983, asked her for an electronic piece for his
"April in Santa Cruz, Calif. Festival' the piece may never
have seen the light of day. Here are two reviews about
Sonar Trajectory. The first excerpt was written by Phillip
Collins of the Santa Cruz Sentinel, April 22, 1984:

> Mamlok's Sonar Trajectory (1966) received its maiden
> voyage after intermission and fared handsomely. Its
> sound quality was the finest of the evening and made
> animated use of the stereo format. The nature of
> the music revealed an acoustic composer at heart,
> characterized by clear pitch schemes and familiar
> phraseology.

The second review in City on a Hill is by David Gingold (excerpt):

> He introduced the world premiere of Sonar Trajec-
> tory, a spatially-exciting 1966 electronic piece by
> the chamber music composer Ursula Mamlok, also
> created at the Electronic Music Center in New York.
> This composition toyed with the perceptions of the
> audience as it created three dimensional sound im-
> ages through masterful use of stereo recording.

Mamlok wrote five Capriccios for Piano and Oboe in
1968. When performed by the Ensemble Contemporana the
same year they were written, a reviewer praised them not
only for their variety of effects and wide range of dynamics
but found them to be more interesting than other compositions
for the same instruments on the program. The composer offers extensive program notes for the piece which should be
of interest not only to the performers but other composers as
well.

> No. 1   Of interest: canonic treatment of patterns
>   4s against 5s. These patterns are obtained
>   by adding a sixteenth beat to each dura-
>   tion, until a quarter-note results, then sub-
>   tracting a sixteenth, until a final sixteenth
>   is reached, thus creating a mirror shaped
>   phrase. Pitchwise, this piece is built on

repeated dyads within a 12-tone set structure. Three different timbres of the pitch
B-flat are played on the piano: 1) normal,
2) stopped secco and 3) stopped with
pedal.

No. 2   Other aspects of the rhythmic treatment re-
lating to No. 1 are heard. Repeated tones
here have the function of assembling cluster
formations which systematically grow by the
addition of one pitch per cluster, creating
a crescendo in the piano, over which the
oboe spins its seemingly improvisatory line.
Two set forms go on simultaneously.

No. 3   Rhythmically the interplay of 4 against 5
patterns and rapid dynamic contrasts are
giving an edgy feeling to this piece. 3 set
forms operate simultaneously. After the
mid point, a pianissimo climax is reached,
and the piece appears in retrograde form,
while the instruments exchange their parts.

No. 4   Derives its cocky character by the unexpec-
tedness of a sixteenth beat played sfz, which
follows patterns of triplets against 4s. Each
phrase gradually diminishes by one quarter
note, until one quarter plus one sixteenth is
reached, at which point this system dissi-
pates. The form giving extra sfffz chords
now appear following a variety of patterns
and are later heard as piercing single at-
tacks of the oboe which climaxes by trilling
on its g# key. The last phrase of No. 4
sets the mood by anticipating the motivic
idea for No. 5.

No. 5   Uses the same pitch material of all previous
pieces. It is the most expansive piece,
lasting over three minutes. Certain pitches
are singled out to be treated as "prepared
piano" sounds. The interest here rests with
the intervallic repetition, and the adding and
subtracting of pitches, making a sound grow
from tone to tone cluster. Wide ranges are
used in both instruments, but the effect is
not one of jaggedness but, rather, of sustained lyricism.

Variations and Interludes for four percussion was written in 1971. It was premiered with Paul Price, conductor, at
the Library Museum for Performing Arts in December of the
same year. The work, which consists of five movements
separated by four interludes, was also performed by the New
Jersey Percussion Ensemble conducted by Raymond DesRoches.
The score is well-marked and easily read. Equipment needed
to perform this work includes:

Player I; xylophone, 23 inch timpani, piccolo snare drum, 4
bongos, small concert tom-tom, 5 temple blocks, 3 woodblocks, one crotale (A^b), triangle, 3 suspended cymbals.
Player II; glockenspiel, 25 inch timpani, snare drum, 4
bongos, concert tom-tom, 3 woodblocks, triangle, 3
suspended cowbells.
Player III; vibraphone, 28 inch timpani, snare drum, 4 bongos, concert tom-tom, 3 woodblocks, triangle, 3 suspended cowbells.
Player IV; marimba, chime, 32 inch timpani, field drum, 4
bongos, concert tom-tom, 5 temple blocks, 3 woodblocks,
triangle, 3 suspended cymbals.

Kurt Prihoda of the magazine Das Orchester (Germany) wrote
in April 1980:

This piece, from the year 1971, enriches the not
exactly overflowing solo literature for percussion
with seven minutes of remarkable compositional
clarity: five movements, separated by four short
intervals--the opening a slow, rumbling crescendo
roll; accelerando, principally in triplet rhythme is
the second variation; as fast as possible, an explo-
sive, sharply accentuated 16th note passage is the
third--after this climax the piece returns in exact
retrogression back to arrive at the beginning in a
full arch. Uncomplicated listenable rhythms and
clear composition allow the piece to be followed well.
Just such close supervision demands the greatest
virtuosity of the performers. The instrumentation
is rich, so that the arrangements of the instruments,
(only two breathing pauses are permitted in the
otherwise "attaca" flow of the piece), calls for close
attention. In the sonority picture the headed, mallet
instruments (i.e. drums) dominate, whereas in the

interludes it is sustained. The overall sound varies
from dark to clear, and naturally back again in ac-
cord with the structure of the composition. A perhaps forthcoming remonstrance on the formal aca-
demicism would elicit the retort that the use of over
60 percussion instruments with the customary parameters (such as melody) does not so easily indicate
the character of the contrapuntal discipline, indeed
this must be considered as a benefit to the listener's
understanding. In any case, we are dealing with a
commendable enrichment of the repertoire for percussion ensemble.

Mamlok has received two grants from The National Endowment for the Arts, a grant from the C.U.N.Y. Faculty
Research Foundation, many commissions, an award from the
American Academy and Institute of Arts and Letters, and two
Martha Baird Rockefeller Recording Grants. Her music continues to have numerous performances in the United States
and Europe by such organizations as the Group for Contemporary Music, I.S.C.M., Music in Our Time, the Berkshire
Music Festival at Tanglewood, the Da Capo Chamber Players,
the New Music Consort and Parnassus.

Sextet written in 1977 was commissioned by Parnassus
and is scored for flute, piccolo, clarinet, bass clarinet, violin,
bass and piano. The 14-minute piece has three sections, with
fluctuating tension, very calm, light and airy. Richard
Swift reviewed Sextet for Music Library Association Magazine,
Notes in June 1984:

> Ursula Mamlok's Sextet was commissioned by Parnas-
> sus, the ensemble that gave the first performance
> in 1977 and recorded it for Composers Recordings
> (SD 480). It is a polished, substantial work, whose
> sure and imaginative instrumental sonorities shape
> its assured structures.
>   The pitch material for the Sextet is drawn from
> an ordered set (0- 11- 2- 7- 3- 6- 1- 10- 9- 5- 4- 8) by vari-
> ous permutational processes. As counterpart to the
> pitch and interval realm various temporal and dura-
> tional devices are used to project both large-scale
> motion and surface impulses.
>   The first movement begins with scattered trill-
> like figures and motivic abruptions that are derived

from a permutation of the basic set. These elusive,
fleeting figures soon settle down into fluid thematic
contours that present basic set forms, and which
realize implications of the fragmented utterances of
the opening. This middle section is marked by
tempo fluctuations making for an increasing taut-
ness of rhythm to prepare for the return of the
opening. The movement concludes with a brief co-
detta which recalls the middle section in its presentation of basic forms providing a link to the slow
movement.

The large-scale relations of the section of the
slow movement are the inverse of those in the first
movement. It begins with the ordered set in a
serene, solo instrumental texture that shapes a long
melody from overlappings of instrumental colors and
pitches. This soon becomes densely polyphonic,
quickly dying away as a faster music emerges. The
middle section is built upon another permutation of
the basic set. The piano plays irregularly spaced,
lightly articulated chords, as the other instruments
engage in colloquy. Arch-like, the dense polyphonic
section returns first, and the movement concludes
with the opening music. This time, the melodic con-
tour is more richly colored and, as the piece ends,
the piano recalls the middle section.

"Light and airy" is the marking for the last movement. The set permutation used here emphasizes
major and minor thirds and triad-like contours and
harmonies. The motives and tunes in this playful
rondo bubble up joyously, with occasional contrasts
of cooler and calmer passages, as tempos shift in
speed.

Art, as Vladimir Nabokov was fond of saying, is
"divine play." It is the pleasures of the ludic, with
the interplay of wit and tenderness, of comedy and
seriousness, that charges this music with implicative
richness. The Sextet deserves many performances
and rehearings.

Each year the American Academy and Institute of Arts
and Letters makes cash awards and CRI recording to outstanding composers. In 1981 Ursula Mamlok was so honored.
The award was presented to Ursula by Milton Babbitt along
with the following citation:

To Ursula Mamlok, born in Berlin, Germany in 1928,
who has created an elegantly crafted, eloquently
expressive body of chamber music, which, while making no effort to be timely, is as distinctively of its
own time as it is distinguished by its persuasive
claims to musical permanence.

The American Academy and Institute of Arts and Letters
Composers Award Record CRI SD 480 includes Mamlok's Sextet
played by Parnassus, conducted by Anthony Korf.   Additional funding was provided by the Martha Baird Rockefeller
Fund and the Alice M. Ditson Fund.   Don C. Seiber wrote a
lengthy review of the recording for Fanfare in December
1983 Volume 7, No. 2 and praised the piece highly: "Mamlok
writes idiomatically, even graciously, for her instruments.
Thematic materials are in themselves alluring and her treatment of them is skilled, assured, and inspired, her style
could be called controlled expressionism."   Seiber feels that
Mamlok's music is not yet appreciated as it should be and
highly recommends the disc which he says "will bring pleasure
into the home."

Mamlok's When Summer Sang, written in 1979-1980 and
commissioned by the Da Capo Players, is also included on
CRI SD 480.   One reviewer of the recording wrote, "Mamlok
is a master of moods."   She began to work on the piece after
a severe illness, while she was spending the summer in the
country enjoying the serenity of nature.   She said, "the
sounds that I heard were mainly those of dogs, birds and
children--is reflected in the music of When Summer Sang."
The Da Capo Players, Patricia Spencer, flutist, Laura Flax,
clarinetist, Joel Lester, violinist, Andre Emelianoff, cellist,
and Joan Tower, pianist premiered the piece in April 1980.
The composer speaks:

> The quintet consists of two short, interconnected
> movements, the first of which begins with a soft,
> slow duo for flute and violin, followed by six trios
> for various combinations of the instruments.   The
> piano, which is present throughout, plays music that
> is independent of the other two instruments.   Now
> and then a piano string is stopped and struck re-
> peatedly, suggesting the insistent knocking of an
> early-morning woodpecker.   The structure of this
> movement is like a set of phrases or stanzas; the

motives of the initial melodic lines are rotated so
that new melodies arise in each trio. The tempo
speeds up gradually, then slows down, leading into
a second duo which is related to the opening. Joyful, homophonic music, followed by a transformed
reminder of the opening section, creates a bridge to
the second movement, a rondo in which there is almost constant interplay among all five instruments.
Especially noteworthy in the recapitulation of the
rondo is the transformed reappearance of the opening duo from the first movement, the theme now
floating airily in the clarinet part.

The recording has received fantastic reviews, and
rightly so; both the Da Capo Players and Parnassus are excellent ensembles with each musician an expert virtuoso when
required to play a particular part. Mamlok's sense of orchestration and texture in writing for solo instruments as
well as her ability to communicate deeply and movingly is
obvious. One will listen repeatedly to this recording; it is
excellent.

Mamlok is not the type of composer who enjoys success
because she is always concerned with what she is writing at
the moment. As she sees it, "my music is lyrical, friendly,
objective, and joyful. I never plan that a piece should have
a certain emotion, whatever happens just comes out naturally."
She has great respect for Milton Babbitt as well as for his
music. Although she never studied with him, she has spent
considerable time listening to his works. She said, "Babbitt
is a wonderful composer and a kind and understanding person. He appreciates other composers, and helps them. Although he has never been my teacher, he has helped me a
great deal. This is important in a composer's life."

Ursula believes that children should have excellent
music to study and perform. She wrote her first children's
pieces at age 16 and still continues to write in this medium.
She understands the problems of new music notation and
recently wrote piano pieces that will offer children an opportunity to play cluster chords and use other techniques that
are akin to 20th-century music. She said, "children like
something new, and we need music that is accessible to them.
I find great joy in writing for children." Mamlok's educational works are listed at the end of the chapter.

She has taught composition at New York University, City University of New York and is presently on the faculty of the Manhattan School of Music. Mamlok thoroughly enjoys teaching and explains her approach with composition students in the following manner:

> I do not force students into any style--I don't say, 'because I compose this way you must too.' I look at the compositions my students are writing and see where they are. If they need new techniques I give them that. If students want to write tonal music, that's fine. I have to be able to help them with the best possible technique. Whether one writes in a tonal or atonal language, one must have control, and I help the students to develop the craft of composing. I enjoy these students because they are aiming toward professionalism.

Ursula and Dwight Mamlok have been married since 1949. She feels that his emotional support of her writing has been extremely important. In addition he has been her testing person from the day they were married. "He's very imaginative and more critical of my work than many of the musicians who perform it. If he doesn't like what I have written then I am almost sure something is wrong." Mamlok said.

Amid growing applause for her music Ursula Mamlok has developed a style of writing that is remarkably appealing to both the performer and the listener. Interest in her works has increased progressively since 1960. The acclaim she has received is richly deserved because her music is more memorable and more moving than much of the music written in this century.

Selected Compositions of Ursula Mamlok

Chamber Music

1951 Daybreak, Text: Longfellow (P.D.) for soprano and piano or mezzo and piano.
1955 Woodwind Quintet, for flute, oboe, clarinet, horn and bassoon.
1957 Sonatina For Two Clarinets.

1957 German Songs, for medium voice & string orchestra.
1958 Songs, for soprano and piano.
1962 String Quartet.
1962 Designs For Violin & Piano.
1963 Stray Birds, for soprano, flute and violin.
1963 Composition For Seven Players, for trumpet, clarinet,
         bass clarinet, violin, cello, CB, percussion (xylo,
         3 tom-toms, woodblock, cymbal).
1964 Concert Piece For Four, for flute, oboe, viola and per-
         cussion.
1965 Music For Viola & Harp.
1965 Capriccios For Oboe And Piano, published by C. F.
         Peters.
1967 Movements, for flute/alto flute, bass, percussion (wood,
         metal and temple block vibes, bongo drum).
1967 Haiku Settings, for soprano and flute.
1969 Sintra, for alto flute and cello.
1971 Variations & Interludes, for percussion quartet, pub-
         lished by C. F. Peters.
1975 Divertimento, for flute (alto flute and piccolo), cello,
         2 percussion.
1976 Concerto, for oboe and orchestra.
1977 Temporal Interrelations, for flute, oboe, violin, and
         cello.
1977 Sextet, for flute, piccolo, clarinet, bass clarinet, violin,
         published by C. F. Peters.
1978 Festive Sounds, for Woodwind Quintet, published by
         C. F. Peters
1980 When Summer Sang, for flute, clarinet, violin, cello
         and piano, published by C. F. Peters.
1980 Panta Rhei, for piano, published by C. F. Peters.

Solo

1947 Scherzo, for piano solo
1952 Piano Piece.
1961 Variation For Solo Flute.
1962 Composition For Solo Cello.
1964 Sculpture I, for pianoforte solo.
1968 Polyphony For Solo Clarinet.
1972. Polyphony II, for solo English horn.

Orchestral

1950   Concerto For String Orchestra.
1956   Grasshoppers, 6 Humoresques.
1976   Concerto, for oboe and orchestra.

Choral

1958   Psalm I, SATB and soli w/piano.
1968   Mosaics, SATB, piano for rehearsal.

Educational

1943   Children's Suite, for two pianos.
1944   Suite For Children For Orchestra.
1944   Suite For Two Pianos, published by Elkan-Vogel.
1945   Children's Pieces, for piano solo.
1946   Children's Suite No. 2, for two pianos.
1947   Children's Suite, for 1 piano, 4-hands, published by
         Elkan-Vogel.
1953   Suite For Children, for piano solo.
1955   1 Duet For Piano, 4-hands.
1955   1 Solo For Piano Beginners, published by Theodore
         Presser.
1956   Bells, for piano, 4-hands, published by Theodore
         Presser.
1956   Grasshoppers, 6 Humoresques, for piano.
1956   Fanfare Brass Quintet, for horn, 2 trumpets, trombone
         & tuba.
1959   Sonatina, for 2 clarinets.
1959   Divertimento, for young players.
1983   Cycle, 6 pieces for piano, 5 finger position.
1984   Four Recital Pieces, for children or adults.

Tape

1966   Sonar Trajectory.

Addresses of Publishers

C. F. Peters, 373 Park Ave., South, New York, NY 10016.

American Composer Edition, 170 West 74th Street, New York,
    NY 10023.

Theodore Presser Co., Bryn Mawr, PA 19010.

Elkan-Vogel, 1712-16 Sansom Street, Philadelphia, PA 19103.

Discography

Variation for Solo Flute, Samuel Baron, CRI 212.
Variation for Solo Flute, Katherine Hoover, flute, Opus OHE
    721.
Sextet, performed by PARNASSUS, CRI SD 480.
When Summer Sang, Da Capo Chamber Players, CRI SD 480.
Stray Birds, Phyllis Bryn-Julson, soprano, with Harvey Soll-
        berger, flute, Fred Sherry, cello, CRI SD 301.
Haiku Settings, five movements, Sue Ann Kahn, flute, Lucy
        Shelton, soprano, GRENADILLA Record, GS-1015.

Addresses

Opus One, P.O. Box 604, Greenville, ME 04441.

Composer Recordings, Inc., 170 West 74th Street, New York,
    NY 10023.

Grenadilla Enterprises, Inc., or Unisphere Record Corp.,
    142-25 Pershing Crescent, Kew Gardens, NY 11435.

PRIAULX RAINIER

Composer, Performer, Teacher

In her musical career Dr. Priaulx Rainier has unswervingly
dedicated herself to a personal vision rather than to a public
acclaim. Her compositions reveal an original first-class musical personality. Over the past five decades Rainier has
written numerous compositions that are among the most liter-
ate and distinguished of this century. Works range from her
String Quartet (1939), Quanta for oboe and string trio (1962),
to Concertante For Two Winds for solo oboe and clarinet and
orchestra (1981).

Rainier explains her writing in the following manner:

> My music is very different from other contemporary
> composers it has been said. I have had no interest
> in different styles or techniques--work only with the
> imaginative drive encompassing the piece in mind--
> its textures, colours, spacial juxtapositions and con-
> trasts. In the end one hopes these work into a
> meaningful whole which is the ultimate object of the
> struggle.

She was born in 1903 at Howick, Natal, South Africa,
the third of four daughters, of English-Huguenot parents,
Ellen Howard and William Gregory Rainier. Her childhood was
spent in the remote part of South Africa on the border of
Zululand where she could hear the music of the indigenous
people along with the sounds of the birds, wild animals, as
well as sounds from across great open spaces. From her
cradle and later as a child, she listened from under the grand
family piano and so learned the great repertoire of classical
piano music from hearing her sisters practice. She said,
"These sounds have remained with me throughout my entire
life."

PRIAULX RAINIER   Photo by
                         Pamela Ridz

Rainier was impassioned by the sound of the violin which she began to study as a youngster, walking six miles for her lessons. At the age of 10 she entered the South African College of Music Cape Zaon where she was strongly influenced by the principal, W. H. Bell who stressed the importance of studying and playing the great string quartet literature. It was only natural with her background and talent that she received the Cape University of South Africa, Overseas Scholarship in 1920 and as the result went to London, England to

study violin under Rowsby Woof at the Royal Academy of
Music. Following graduation Rainier settled permanently in
London, earning her living as a violinist and teacher. Her
compositions date from as early as 1923, although little of
that period is available. Later she was encouraged by Sir
Arnold Bax who was interested in her work. Then she was
awarded an anonymous grant in 1935 enabling her to con-
centrate on composing. In 1937 she went to Paris to study
for a short period of time with Nadia Boulanger. Reflecting
on that important period of her life she said:

> I studied with Nadia Boulanger in Paris before the
> outbreak of the war. I took my String Quartet to
> her and I think she was impressed although she
> never directly said so.
> I was very shy about thinking of myself as a
> composer. I had had no formal composition lessons
> when I wrote my quartet. It was based on my ex-
> perience as a performer and from my background of
> playing quartets from an early age; I had not dis-
> cussed the meaning of music at all, so that my les-
> sons with Nadia were really conversations and dis-
> cussions about music. I did not actually write any
> compositions under her, or during this period of
> time.
> Nadia asked me to write down the ideas that
> came into my head the first thing every morning.
> She said, "you are so jammed with ideas that it be-
> comes a problem and you must sift and sort them.
> All your ideas are of value and you must learn to
> release them." I found the experience fascinating
> and most helpful, to be able to discuss in this way.
> I needed to talk about music. At that time I didn't
> even know a composer, with the exception of Arnold
> Bax.

Priaulx Rainier's String Quartet in four movements,
allegro molto serioso, vivace leggiero grazioso, andante tran-
quillo, and presto spiritoso was first performed by the Gertler
Quartet in London on July 12, 1939. Because of the war the
work remained in limbo for several years. Then a performance at the National Gallery Concerts drew attention to the
work. A recording was made under the auspices of the
British Council, by the Amadeus String Quartet on the Decca
Label. At that time one music critic wrote, "she speaks with

a voice more individual than that of most of the composers working in Britain today."

On Feb. 18, 1940, William Glock wrote the following review of the String Quartet for The Observer:

> ...I may as well begin by saying that Miss Rainier comes from South Africa, that she studied for a short while with Nadia Boulanger, but is otherwise self-taught, has had long experience as the leader of a string quartet, and had already written three excellent songs which anticipate the quartet in certain details of rhythm and harmony. The quartet itself has two contrasted qualities, both of which can be understood from Miss Rainier's history; side by side with a most adventurous use of the instruments is an integrity and bareness that insists on saying everything exactly, without a hint of nostalgia or sentimentality or "sublimity," all of which can so easily ruin the directness and precision which make a work authentic. There are weak passages here and there; yet one never loses the impression that Miss Rainier is using tones as a good poet uses words: They are the actual sensuous image of her emotional experience, and one does not notice the technique because every relationship seems to spring directly from an imagination working at pressure.
>
> Even so, there are outward signs of this authentic quality. For example, the harmonies in the first and third movements are too tense to be there for their own sakes, too consistent not to represent a deep-seated individual preference. They are, in fact, nineteenth-century harmonies with precisely those notes missing which would give them nineteenth-century implications as well. The first movement is built upon a contrast between free and fluid rhythms and solid tragic blocks of harmony--the simplest common chords placed so starkly one after the other that they seem to be new inventions.
>
> Quite unlike this and the closely related slow movement are the Scherzo, which trembles with delicacy but yet is far from being just an etude or a set piece; and the Finale, which, I think, is perhaps the most remarkable movement of all. On first hearing, it seems to be a little encyclopedia of technical wonders; yet this surface excitement no longer

imposes itself when heard again. Instead, the harmonics, the glissandi, and the extraordinary slidings
"sul ponticello" seem to belong naturally to the bold,
masterly vision which engulfs them all.

I do not know whether Miss Rainier rounds off
the work as meaningfully as she might have done,
or whether, indeed, music can fulfull the function
she seems to ask of it in this finale. The parallel it
suggests is that of an author who, having devoted
three-quarters of his book to a profound criticism
of life, then gives us his credentials, as it were:
his background. With Miss Rainier the background
is Africa, and whatever conclusion one may reach
over this haunting, barbaric movement, it has countless touches that leave no doubt as to the talent
that created it. I cannot recommend this work too
strongly to enterprising string quartets. It is emotionally satisfying, technically challenging, certain
and precise in all its calculations; and I think audiences all over the country would enjoy it as much as
those at Fyvie Hall and the National Gallery....

The quartet has retained its popularity for over four
decades with numerous performances in many countries. Doris
Humphrey, pioneer choreographer with Jose Limon's famous
New York company, used the quartet for a ballet, Night
Spell, included in their 1957 Sadler's Wells season. In 1983
the piece was recorded by the Alard Quartet for Leonarda
Productions. This is certainly a tribute to the composer,
especially when one realizes that many of the musicians of
the time considered it much too difficult to perform when it
was first published. Rainier is a composer who deserves careful study; her quartet may well be considered one of the
twentieth century's masterpieces.

During this same period she wrote Three Greek Epigrams
for soprano or tenor and piano. The text was from the Greek
of Anyte of Tegea, translated by Richard Aldington. It was
premiered in London in 1939 by Sophie Wyss and Hans Gell-
horn, just before the outbreak of World War II.

During the War many fine musicians tried to keep music
alive by giving concerts and performances wherever and whenever possible. Rainier credits Benjamin Britten, Michael Tippett, Peter Pears as well as Boosey and Hawkes, music

publishers, for their special work during a period of time
that was so difficult for the world. Her Sonata for Viola and
Piano was premiered at the National Gallery Concerts during
this time, and although it received an excellent review in The
Observer it remained dormant for the duration of the War.
Robert Sabin included the work in High Fidelity/Musical
America under New Music Reviews in February 1953, credit-
ing Rainier with "combining to a remarkable degree contrapuntal tension, harmonic color, and rhythmic interest."

In 1943 Priaulx Rainier was appointed professor of
composition at the Royal Academy of Music, a post she held
until 1961. In 1952 she was elected a Fellow of the Royal
Academy. Good composers are few and far between. During
her teaching career she had a few students who were talented
and capable possibly of attaining recognition as composers but
through necessity, perhaps, chose a teaching career instead.
She said, "One must sacrifice if you are to compose. You
can't expect to have a so-called normal life like other people;
you must expect to spend a tremendous amount of time alone.
There are only a few talented people willing to make such a
personal sacrifice."

Just before the end of World War II Rainier's Suite for
clarinet and piano was premiered at the London Contemporary
Music Center, Cowdray Hall in a program sponsored by Boosey
and Hawkes. The performing artists were Stephen Waters
and Anthony Hopkins. Written in five movements, the piece
shows "considerable inventive power and resourcefulness."
In her piano writing she concentrates mainly on the percussive
possibilities of the instrument," according to a review published in Musical Opinion. Recognition was slim in the early
part of Rainier's career and it was not until 18 years later
that she received the plaudits that she so richly deserves
when The Times printed, "Suite brought the house down--
it's the precursor of all the new piano writing."

Priaulx Rainier's Requiem for solo, tenor and chorus
was first performed by Peter Pears with the Purcell Singers,
conducted by Imogen Holst, at the Victoria and Albert Museum
on April 15, 1956. The text had been written specially for
Rainier by David Gascoyne when they were in Paris in 1937.
Rainier said, "We often had lunch together. David wanted
to write a poem with words suitable for singing. He produced
his great poem Requiem which was a prophetic requiem,

preparing for the holocaust about to descend upon us. Paris was filled with writers who at that time were deeply concerned with the happenings surrounding the events to come.

"Peter Pears knew I had David's Text of the Requiem. After the War he asked me to prepare it for performance." This was Rainier's first large choral work and she spent considerable time and effort in preparing the manuscripts, considering the words and their vocal possibilities and traumatic content. As with her instrumental works she again produced an unconventional as well as beautiful composition. The critics who reviewed the performance had mixed reactions to the work, but Colin Mason writing for The Manchester Guardian, on April 17, 1956 responded in the following manner:

> ...Rhythm was always been the dominating element
> in her music, to which melody, harmony and counter-
> point have played second, third, and fourth fiddle,
> in that order. In writing for chorus she has had
> to promote them, and it is no doubt the training of
> them for this promotion that has taken her so long.
> The result justifies and rewards her patience.
> Melody now predominates. Her fragmentary instru-
> mental melodic figures are replaced by a sustained
> arioso line on which the tenor carries the main part
> of the text. With it goes a more developed counter-
> point, not such as would find its way into any text-
> book either as strict or free, but a simultaneous and
> overlapping movement of free often rather florid and
> coherently, if sometimes tenously related, melodic
> lines. The harmony is still very rudimentary and
> there is no harmonic development in any traditional
> sense. But an unaccompanied choir cannot sing long
> in tune without a certain amount of familiar harmony
> to get its bearings by, so the composer intermit-
> tently leads the music, with most striking but natural
> and convincing effect, to a common cause.
> With these means she had produced a genuinely
> extended musical structure that absorbs the atten-
> tion throughout. With numerous telling effects of
> word-painting it makes a most beautiful and original
> work. It is also, as might be guessed, a very dif-
> ficult one, so difficult that it taxed and occasionally
> overtaxed even such a highly trained group as Imogen
> Holst's Purcell Singers, who sang it last night. But

with a musically secure soloist in Peter Pears to
lead them and help them to hold the pitch, as he
did in a wonderfully sure and expressive performance,
they quickly recovered and brought it off with a
success of musical effect and a quality of sound that
proved the composer's judgment in the medium equal
to the unconventionality and daring of her style.
She has made an important addition to modern choral
music which will bear being heard as many times as
singers can be found to sing it.

Priaulx Rainier's commitment to teaching during her
tenure at the Royal Academy of Music made it difficult for
her to find sufficient time to compose, and she had very few
performances of her works during this period, but she was
indeed fortunate to have among her supporters Michael Tippett
and William Glock. She said, "I was never discouraged. Composing has never been an easy process for me; it takes me a
long time to find the right beginning for a work and that
has always been so. I don't necessarily start a work at the
beginning because I haven't always decided exactly what it
should be. I need to work the material over in my mind and
on paper before I can formulate the beginning." Perhaps
this process can be attributed to the fact the Rainier has no
allegiance to any particular school of thought or training.
Her style is uniquely her own and permits no labeling or
reference to other composer's works. As she stated, "My
music seems entirely different from other composers." This
statement alone helps to explain why some music critics were
almost hostile to her work during the earlier part of her
career; they could not neatly package and describe her music.

Priaulx Rainier was commissioned by the London Philharmonic Society to celebrate Sir Adrian Boult's 10 years of
directorship. She wrote Dance Concerto Phala-Phala, a 15-
minute work premiered by the London Philharmonic Orchestra
on Jan. 17, 1961, conducted by Sir Adrian Boult at the Royal
Philharmonic Hall. The piece was unconventional, much like
a dance mosaic, with continually changing sequences of rhythmic patterns. Of course the critics were hostile to the new-
ness of the piece but they in no way deterred the talented
Rainier.

Finally, after years of writing and struggling for acceptance as a composer, she began to receive a growing

number of commissions from the British Broadcasting Corporation as well as such outstanding performers as Yehudi Menuhin
and Peter Pears. The turning point in her career as a composer came with her retirement in 1961 from the Royal Academy
of Music. She could now devote all her energy to what she
loved to do most, compose.

She was commissioned by the B.B.C. in 1961 to write
a chamber piece for their Invitation Concert the following
season. Thus emerged Quanta, a 12-minute piece for oboe
and string trio, which proved to be a key work, with Rainier
feeling she had reached a new level of writing, and the critics
hesitated. The premiere was superbly performed by Janet
Craxton and the Oromonte Trio who later recorded the piece
with Rainier's String Trio (1965) on Argo 606. Excerpt from
Max Loppert's review of a later performance in The Financial
Times of Dec. 5, 1972:

> ...The opening work, Quanta for oboe and string
> trio immediately fixed Rainier's individuality in one's
> mind: The nervy asymmetric ties of music that leap
> about and snap off, the shiny, sharply iridescent
> sonorities, constantly changing in texture, the fine
> craftsmanship that balances these little cells of ac-
> tivity in a form perfectly shaped and controlled, with
> not a bar mismanaged or out of place. Quanta, the
> Shorter Oxford Dictionary, tells those feebly ignor-
> ant non-physicists among us, are "discreet units
> among us, are discreet unit quantities of energy,
> proportional to the frequency of radiation, emitted
> from or absorbed by an atom." One need have no
> technical comprehension of this definition whatever
> to see its fitness of usage in relation to this music...

Rainier's music continued to be performed more frequently and in 1967 the British Broadcasting Company's Invitation Concerts broadcast four of her compositions in one
program. Two of the works were world premieres and according to music critic Anthony Payne, "there was not a
single bar that did not attest to technical mastery and a
gritty independence of mind." Included on that program
were two of her unaccompanied works: Cycle for Declamation with text from Devotions by John Donne, originally commissioned by Peter Pears, who performed it at the Aldeburgh Festival; Suite for Cello premiered by Joan Dickson;

String Trio premiered by the Oromonte String Trio; and
Quanta. During the same year Rainier began to write her
longest and largest piece for orchestra, Aequora Lunae, a
30-minute work commissioned by the British Broadcasting Corporation. It was premiered by the BBC Symphony Orchestra
conducted by Norman Del Mar, at the Cheltenham Festival in
July 1967. The work is a suite of seven movements, each
named after one of the seas of the moon. The work was
highly praised by both the listening audience and critics because of her individual perception of orchestral color and
sonority. Again an indication of Priaulx Rainier's original
and forceful musical personality.

On a 1970 commission by Peter Pears for the Aldeburgh
Festival, Rainier wrote The Bee Oracles for tenor or baritone
solo, flute, oboe, violin, cello and harpsichord. The first
broadcast and the first public performance was given by
Peter Pears, Patricia Lynden, Janet Craxton, Perry Hart,
Olga Hegedus and Alan Harverson. The text by Edith Sit-
well was derived from an ancient Indian text. The elements
of Earth, Water, Fire, Air, Sun and Thunder are presented
after an opening incantation which is later used as a refrain.
According to Timothy Baxter writing for The Royal Academy
of Music Magazine, No. 231, Spring 1983, "Because of its
subject-matter, one is very conscious of the buzzing sounds
in wind and strings, with stinging sounds in the harpsichord."
He felt it was one of her most attractive and approachable
works.

The Promenade Concerts, known as the Proms, trace
their history back to 1938 when the first concert was organized by a group of leading London musicians. When Queens
Hall was bombed in 1941 the concerts were moved to the
Royal Albert Hall. At this time the series of programs became officially known as the Henry Wood Promenade Concerts
in honor of Henry J. Wood, conductor and director of the
series from 1895 to 1941. According to Priaulx Rainier much
credit must be given to William Glock, BBC Controller of
Music from 1959-1972, for broadening the base of the programs and including contemporary music. Today the Proms
are regarded as London's summer music festival. (Note to
music lovers; prior to each concert, tickets are sold on a
first-come basis, and are available for about one pound.
Tickets that will permit the listener to sit on the floor or
stand in the arena in front of the performing groups. If you

are willing to stand you can get within 6 feet of the conductor.)

An interesting and informative aspect of these concerts
are the pre-Prom talks presented by the composers and musicians. Rainier has discussed her music on several occasions
during these talks. The talks are considered essential for
many listeners who enjoy contemporary music.

In 1973 Rainier's Ploermel, written for a B.B.C. commission, was premiered at the Royal Albert Hall during the
Proms season, by the London Sinfonietta conducted by Elgar
Howarth. She based her idea for the piece during a holiday
that she spent in the French town, and so named the piece
in honor of the town, Ploermel. She said, "It was a beautiful morning and I walked into an old grey-stone church just
as the sun was rising. I saw through the stained-glass win-
dow 'shots' of light that were brilliant in color and the bells
were tolling and that to me was the key to the composition."
Scored for winds and percussion, she chose and extended the
percussion section as a special feature of the piece. Instruments included handbells, antique cymbals, sonagli with high
and low pitch gongs, xylophone and marimba. The result
was an extraordinary outpouring of sound that was heard
both as a passionate rage as well as an exhilarating stimulation for one's hearing palette, a remarkable and exciting
combination of timbres. One reviewer commented, "Ploermel
consists of substantial blocks of sound from which the 'melodic' material emerges. There were memorable moments in this
dense tapestry, for tuba, cor anglais, and percussion."

During the same year the B.B.C. broadcast six Retro-
spective Concerts of some of her chamber music to celebrate
the occasion of her 70th birthday. Rainier was most appreciative of the performances and noted, "All of my major chamber
pieces were presented and they were marvelously played."
Included on the program were: Requiem; Organ Gloriana;
The Bee Oracles; String Quartet; Pastoral Triptych; Duo:
Vision and Prayer and Two Primordial Canticles.

Although Priaulx Rainier was impassioned by the sound
of the violin as a child, spent a considerable part of her life
studying, performing and teaching the instrument, it was not
until she was 74 years old that she completed her first violin
concerto on a commission from Yehudi Menuhin. Due Canti

e Finale, a 23-minute piece for solo violin and orchestra, was
premiered by Yehudi Menuhin and the Royal Philharmonic Orchestra conducted by Sir Charles Groves, at the Edinburgh
International Festival on Sept. 8, 1977. Rainier described
the piece at a pre-Proms talk, "It is a duel between the solo
violin, with its lyrical and decorative writing, and the orchestra, which is more fragmented and incisive. These incisive moments punctuate the solo line but never impinge upon
it."

Mr. Yehudi Menuhin, Honorable Knight of the British
Empire, paid tribute to composer Priaulx Rainier in the following published message in honor of her 80th birthday:

> In Priaulx Rainier, we have a musical imagination at
> work of a colour and variety scarcely to be believed.
> It was incidentally Diana, my own great lady, who,
> with her infallible instinct, first marked Priaulx
> Rainier as my composer.
> From the materials of nature--the scherzo for the
> concerto she wrote for me is a veritable ornitholo-
> gical aviary--to the sounds of Africa and Africans,
> to Indians and last, but not least, to a very solid,
> European grounding, to giving structure and form
> to such rich and varied sources, from the first I
> was intensely fascinated by this great and sweet
> lady.
> I love her and all her work and congratulate her
> on reaching 80 years, so young and generous in
> heart, so lively in mind and so precious to us.

In 1981 she wrote her successful Concertante For Two
Winds for solo oboe, clarinet and orchestra. The music was
specifically designed for Janet Craxton and Thea King. The
totally unexpected and tragic death of the oboe soloist, Janet
Craxton, 10 days prior to the premiere was shocking, but
the program by the B.B.C. Scottish Orchestra conducted by
Sir Charles Groves was performed at a B.B.C. Promenade
Concert with Neil Black replacing the talented Craxton and
Thea King performing the clarinet solo. The piece was dedicated to Miss Craxton's memory. The Times Saturday Review
written by Paul Griffiths, Aug. 9, 1981:

CONCERTANTE FOR TWO WINDS AND ORCHESTRA

Double concertos for woodwind instruments are not

exactly thick on the ground, and it is easy to see
why. The gentle woodwinds always have to be helped
if they are to stand out as soloists, and the problems of balance are not halved but doubled when
there are two principals to be considered, to be allowed to stand out as individuals and as a pair.
But Priaulx Rainier is a composer who has always
thrived on challenges, and in the Concertante for
oboe, clarinet and orchestra, introduced at last
night's Prom at the Albert Hall, she has boldly
wrested success from the continuous danger and
tension in her chosen medium.

A work with this scoring might well have been a
gentle meandering pastorale. Rainier's, however, is
made of sterner stuff. The opening at once an-
nounces the seriousness and abstractness of her
concerns, with a dynamic assertion of crucial motifs
in the orchestra: the composer's own description of
this ensemble as a chamber orchestra is misleading,
for it is a sizable band, and its material particularly
in the first and last of the five movements, is often
brilliant and trenchant.

As for the soloists, they lead the way in steering
the music to ponder longer lines and a more sustained kind of discourse. There are a few more
eruptive moments, when they sound vaguely like
birds escaped from a score of Messiaen's but generally
they engage in smooth colloquies around the work's
germinal themes. And usually, rather surprisingly,
the oboe is felt to dominate and to lead, though that
may be because we were all thinking last night of
the late Janet Craxton, intended soloist in this performance, which was dedicated to her memory.

Neil Black, though no doubt saddened to be replacing his lamented colleague, plays the part with
fine alertness and vitality, and Thea King enjoyed
showing off the clarinet's softer and mellower nature.
Accompanying or rather providing more parallel
threads of ebullience and drama, the BBC Scottish
Symphony Orchestra amply proved their necessity.
[Reprinted by permission of Times Newspapers
Limited.]

In June 1982 the University of Cape Town honored
Priaulx Rainier with a doctorate in music (honoris causa) for

her contributions to the field of music. She said, "I went
back to Cape Town to receive the degree. The ceremony
was marvelous, and they did a beautiful concert of my works
in the evening. I had trained at this school from the age of
10 years to 16. I was pleased that I had drawn sufficient
attention to warrant the honor."

In 1983 the Worshipful Company of Musicians, a guild
that dates back to 1500 A.D., initiated Rainier as the first
woman Liveryman of the Company, an honor never before
bestowed on a woman. Rainier recalls,

> Many years ago I received a Collard Fellowship from
> this Guild which provided me with three hundred
> pounds per year for three years, which was a con-
> siderable sum of money in those days, and it allowed
> me to give up some of my teaching and devote more
> time to composing. Every year the Worshipful Com-
> pany of Musicians have a Ladies Night and a grand
> dinner in one of the marvelous Guild halls in the
> City of London. I was asked if I would answer the
> toast to the guests at the dinner. I accepted but
> was somewhat afraid to drink the superb wines
> served, since I had to speak! I was the guest of
> honor on that night. After my speech, the Master
> rose in his magnificent robes and announced that I
> had been unanimously elected the first Liverywoman
> of the Worshipful Company, and a Freeman of the
> city of London. One of the privileges granted by
> the city to its Freeman is to be drunk and disorderly
> without police interference.

Dr. Priaulx Rainier has made an important addition to
contemporary music. The listener becomes acutely aware of
a distinguished and creative mind, for she is self-disciplined
and rigorously independent of every fashion or influence. Sir
Michael Tippett, Companion of Honour, accurately describes
Rainier and her extraordinary accomplishments in the following letter he wrote of her in January 1983:

> Priaulx Rainier's life has been one of austere dedica-
> tion, resulting in a sizeable list of compositions of
> exceptional quality and integrity. I have watched
> this list grow and observed her commitment and un-
> hurried zeal ever since we first met--through William

Glock and his first wife--in the early part of the
war.
   Latterly, Priaulx has received considerable critical acclaim and public recognition for her work, at
home and abroad. It is all very much deserved, and
I am delighted, here, to offer greetings to someone
I cherish as a friend and colleague and whom I know
is widely respected as a composer and teacher.

   Priaulx Rainier's success and the worldwide attention
that is beginning to be hers are the result of absolute creative integrity.

Selected Compositions of Priaulx Rainier

1960- Dance Concerto Phala-Phala, 15 minutes, for orchestra
  61   8.2.3.2.2.2.2.1--timp., perc. (s. dr., cym., trgle.)--
          hp. cel. (ad lib.)--strings.
1964   Concerto for Cello and Orchestra, 21 minutes, 2.2.2.
          2.2.1.0--temp., perc. (xyl., 3 steel plates, campan-
          ella, trgle., cym., gran cassa)--strings, piano re-
          duction Ed. 10913.
1966- Aequoro Lunae, for orchestra, 30 minutes, 3.3.3.2.2.
  67   2.2.1--timp., perc. (marimba, campanella, gran
          cassa, xyl., 2 cym., ant., cym., 2 tam-tam, 3 steel
          plates., tamb., cast., 2 trgle., military drum)--
          strings.
1976- Due Canti E Finale, 23 minutes, for solo violin and or-
  77   chestra, 3.3.2.2--2.2.0.1--timp., perc. (gran cassa,
          marib., crotales, trgle., cyms., gong, bells, bon-
          gos)--strings, study score Ed. 12132.
1977- Concertante for Two Winds, 18 minutes, for solo oboe,
  80   clarinet and orchestra, 2.1.0.2--2.2.2.0--timp.,
          perc. (marimb., xyl., 2 trgle., cym., susp. cym.,
          gong, bells)--strings, study score Ed. 12082.

Music for String Orchestra

1947   Sinfonia da Camera, 21 minutes.

Music for Wind Instruments

1943   Suite, 16 minutes, Ed. 10409.

1958- Pastoral Triptych, 9 minutes, for solo oboe, Ed.
  59   10636.
1957 Six Pieces, 18 minutes, for five wind instruments,
          flute, oboe, clarinet, horn, bassoon, miniature score
          Ed. 10740.

Vocal Works

1937 Three Greek Epigrams, 6 minutes, for soprano or tenor
          and piano, Ed. 10181.
1947 Dance of the Rain, 10 minutes, for tenor or soprano
          and guitar, Ed. 10902.
1948 Ubunzima, 4 minutes, for tenor or soprano and guitar,
          Zulu text Ed. 11064.
1953 Cycle for Declamation, 9 minutes, for tenor or soprano
          Ed. 10299.
1969 The Bee Oracles, 18 minutes, for tenor or baritone
          solo, flute, oboe, violin, cello and harpsichord, ma-
          terial on hire.

Chamber Music

1939 String Quartet, 16 minutes, miniature score Ed. 10210;
          parts Ed. 10250.
1945 Sonata, 10 minutes, for viola and piano, Ed. 10410.
1947 Trio, 15 minutes, for violin, cello and piano.
1961 Quanta, 12 minutes, for oboe and string trio.
  62
1963- Suite, 10 minutes, for solo cello or viola, dyeline copies
  65   for sale.
1965- String Trio, 15 minutes.
  66
1980- Grand Duo, for cello and piano, dyeline copies for
  82   sale.

Keyboard

1949 Barbaric Dance Suite, 12 minutes, for piano Ed. 10394.
1955 Five Keyboard Pieces, 10 minutes, for piano, dyeline
          copies for sale.
1972 Organ Gloriana, 13 minutes, for organ, dyeline copies
          available for sale.
1971 Quinque, 12 minutes, for harpsichord, dyeline copies

available for sale.
1973 Primordial Canticles, 15 minutes, for organ.

Addresses of Publishers

Schott, 48 Great Marlborough Street, London, England WIV
   2BN.

Dr. Priaulx Rainier, 75 Ladbroke Grove, London, W11 2PD,
   England.

Discography

String Quartet, recorded by the Amadeus String Quartet,
   Decca (out of print).
String Quartet, recorded by the Alard Quartet, Leonarda
   Productions.
Quanta, recorded by the London Oboe Quartet, ARGO ZRG
   660.
String Trio, recorded by Perry Hart, Brian Hawkins, and
   Kenneth Heat, ARGO ZRG 660.
Cycle for Declamation, recorded by Peter Pears, Argo ZRG
   5418.

Addresses of Recording Companies

Decca Company, Argo Division, 115 Fulham Road, London,
   SW3 6RR, England.

Leonarda Productions, Inc., P.O. Box 124, Radio City Station, New York, NY 10019.

Argo Company, 115 Fulham Road, London, SW3 6RR, England.

SHULAMIT RAN

Composer, Pianist

Shulamit Ran, the brilliant young Israeli composer-pianist,
made her debut on the concert stage on Tel Aviv at the age
of 12. Her first orchestral work was premiered two years
later and while still a teenager she performed her own composition, Capriccio for piano and orchestra, with Leonard
Bernstein and the New York Philharmonic in a televised
Young People's Concert. Concert Piece written in 1971 was
premiered by the Israel Philharmonic with Zubin Mehta conducting and composer-pianist Ran as soloist.

Unlike most of her contemporaries, Ran composed before
she began the study of piano at age 8. Although, as a child,
she did not really understand what she was composing, she
did feel it was perfectly normal. She explains:

> Any poems or rhymes I studied in school, I would
> sing. I was absolutely certain that the melody was
> part of the words I was reading. I couldn't under-
> stand how someone else looking at the same words
> couldn't hear the melody I was hearing. I would
> always sing the melody the same way and as far as
> I was concerned the melody was right there for any-
> one to read. So composing was a very natural pro-
> cess to me--like speaking and eating.

Shulamit Ran was born in Tel Aviv, Israel, in 1949,
the daughter of Zvi A. and Berta Ran. When her parents
provided piano lessons for her around the age of 8, they did
not have any expectations for her and they were not "stage
parents." Ran said, "It was really by chance that I happened
to go with my parents to visit some friends who had a piano.
I spent the next few hours playing and enjoying myself and

215

SHULAMIT RAN   Photo by
                                   Michael P. Weinstein

I thought the piano was the most wonderful toy that I had ever encountered and I had to have one just like it."

Her first piano lessons were with a local teacher who wrote down the melodies she was playing and sent them to the radio station in Israel. They were played and sung by a children's choir which was a wonderful experience for the gifted Ran. This was the first time that she realized her music was something that lived apart from her and had its own unique existence. This teacher proved to be a good educator and within a year suggested that she study with some other person who would be better able to develop her talent. Ran was very grateful that he recognized her needs and she studied composition with Alexander U. Boscovitz and piano with his wife, Miriam Boscovitz. Later she concurrently became a composition student of Paul Ben Haim and studied piano with Emma Golochov.

Each summer the Jerusalem Academy sponsored courses by prominent teachers and Nadia Reisenberg gave a series of master classes. Shulamit was given the opportunity to audition for Reisenberg when she was 14 years old, and this famous teacher made arrangements for the talented young girl to receive a full scholarship to the Mannes College of Music in New York.

Since it was not feasible for her to live in New York alone, and thinking the scholarship would be for one year, Shulamit's mother accompanied her to the United States. A year later her father joined them and both parents remained in New York until Shulamit finished her degree. They were uniquely devoted and supportive of their daughter's career.

Shortly after Shulamit Ran arrived in the United States she applied to audition for Maestro Bernstein for the Young People's Concert. She chose to perform her own composition, Capriccio for piano and orchestra, as an audition number. This was the first time she had written for piano and orchestra with the intention that she would perform the piano part herself. Since all who auditioned appeared with an accompanist, she transcribed the orchestral part for second piano. A good friend and fellow pianist from Nadia Reisenberg's studio, Christine Berl, played the orchestral part. When they went on stage at Avery Fisher Hall (then Philharmonic Hall), the maestro asked what she was going to perform. Her answer:

I told him my own <u>Capriccio</u> for piano and orchestra and then asked if he would like to look at the
full-score. And he said, "Oh, a score!" and I'll
never forget the tone of his voice--I'm sure he
thought the whole thing was hilarious and that it
certainly couldn't be anything serious since I was
just a young girl at the time. I suppose that being
a female child augumented his apprehension about
the seriousness of what he was about to hear.
There was something mocking and almost sarcastic
in his voice when he said, "Oh, a score!"

But I must say that he responded just as honestly
and directly when I finished as he did before, except this time his reaction was totally different and
exceptionally heart-warming. He jumped to his feet,
applauded and said, "Bravo! Bravo!" I will never
forget that moment.

<u>Capriccio</u> was scheduled for performance on Nov. 2,
1963. When Ran come out of rehearsal the bells all over the
city were tolling--President John F. Kennedy had been as-
sassinated. The concert was rescheduled for Nov. 30, 1963.

Shulamit had an agreement with Mannes College that
she would finish her high-school education before she would
be granted a college degree. Difficult as it was to complete,
via correspondence study, she did earn her high-school diploma shortly before she graduated from Mannes College.

Ran completed a double major in piano and composition
at Mannes College of Music. She studied piano with Nadia
Reisenberg and composition with Norman Dello Joio both of
whom Ran praises highly as teachers. She relates her experiences studying with Nadia Reisenberg and later privately
with Dorothy Taubman in New York:

Nadia Reisenberg was a very kind and gracious
teacher who was responsible for my coming to the
United States to study. I studied piano with her
for many years. She was, of course, an exceptionally fine pianist and I recall how she would always
sit at the other piano during my lesson, illustrating
things with the greatest ease and polish. She was
wonderful to me both as a teacher and as a person.
There were so many times and ways in which she
helped me.

Dorothy Taubman is not associated with any school which is not surprising since she has such a maverick approach that she would be more natural in private study. I studied with her for several years, in fact, whenever I go to New York and am in practicing condition (since I now devote myself to composition) I make a point of seeing Mrs. Taubman and playing for her. She is an incredible piano teacher, inventor and true creator. She is unique because of her understanding of human physiology and motion and how it works. Everyone can benefit enormously. Teaching an instrument is by nature an oral art, it can't be captured either on paper or on disc. It worries me as to how this will continue beyond her because certainly what she has to offer should remain. What she does is as much an art as composing or performing--she is nothing short of tremendous.

Following graduation from the Mannes College of Music, Shulamit Ran devoted most of her energy to her career as a concert pianist. Although she continued to compose, her time was limited because of an extensive concert schedule including tours in the United States, Europe, Israel and Canada. Howard Klein, writing for the New York Times on April 24, 1967, reviewed her recital at Carnegie Hall and said in part:

Miss Ran is a bundle of talent. In addition to playing two demanding standard works, the slight pianist also played two of her own: a bright, three-movement eight-minute piece simply called Piano Music and the first performance of her Quartet for Flute, Clarinet, Cello and Piano.

The quartet, a 13-minute work of quick invention, jaunty rhythms and professional workmanship, had hints of Prokofiev and Stravinsky in its dissonances and asymmetries. Like the piano pieces, it was full of fragmentary ideas cleverly worked out. Miss Ran was a deft and musical pianist.

In July 1967 an original score, The Laughing Man (Pantomime), by Ran was performed on the Columbia Broadcasting System's national television network and in October of the same year she was guest soloist with the Kol Israel Orchestra, performing her own Symphonic Poem, for piano and orchestra.

Press reviews for her 1968 season included praise from music
critics in Vienna, England, Switzerland among others. After
her performance at Brahmssaal, Vienna, in a demanding program of works by Schoenberg, Hindemith, Bartok, Sydeman,
Berg and her own music the critics raved. "The strong
talent is easily recognizable, one must talk about her as a
true discovery," reported the Vienna Die Presse. From the
Vienna Express, "A musical phenomenon! She plays magnifi-
cently, it carries one away."

As part of Ran's 1970 concert season, she performed a
recital at the Diligentia in The Hague in Holland. Her program included three pieces from the Vingt Regards sur l'en-
fant Jesus by Messiaen, Schumann's Kreisleriana, Sonata op.
1 by Berg and Beethoven's Sonata op.101. Headline in the
Die Telegraaf read, "Shulamit Ran--Great Talent."

Highlight of composer-pianist Ran's 1971 season was her
performance with the Israel Philharmonic Orchestra conducted
by Zubin Mehta. In addition to performing Ravel's Piano
Concerto in G major her own work, Concert Piece for Piano
and Orchestra was featured. When Ran auditioned for Mehta
he was extremely positive and enthusiastic about her composition and promised that he would program it as soon as possible. She said:

> Zubin Mehta is an extremely busy conductor and I
> won't hide the fact that although I looked forward to
> the whole experience with the greatest anticipation
> and excitement, I also asked myself, will he really
> take my work seriously and give it the attention it
> needs? Well, when I arrived at the first rehearsal,
> in Tel Aviv, Maestro Mehta immediately presented me
> with questions which indicated that he had not only
> thoroughly mastered the score but, in fact, had the
> 14-minute long piece practically memorized. I had
> used some non-standard notational devices and the
> Israel Philharmonic--a first rate orchestra but also
> a group of highly individualistic persons at times
> unruly and occasionally resistant to new sounds with
> unfamiliar notation--at first took the whole thing
> less than seriously. But as the rehearsals progres-
> sed and under Mehta's firm guidance, the music as
> I had envisioned it started to emerge and attitudes
> changed. The skepticism turned into warm, enthusi-

astic collaboration. I remember one player coming over after the dress rehearsal and saying, "You just wait! Tonight this is going to hit the audience with the force of a blast!"

I had been warned ahead of time not to be too disappointed if many of the Philharmonic's concert goers, reputed to be somewhat conservative, would turn back their tickets. Not only did this not happen, but by the third concert seats had to be added and people filled the aisles. For me this was one of the most thrilling moments of my life, especially because it took place in Israel, my home.

From the Jerusalem Post, July 18, 1971 by Benjamin Bai-Am (partial):

ISRAEL PHILHARMONIC ORCHESTRA IN FINE FETTLE

Tense rehearsals in feverish preparation for the pending Israel Festival, and the ambitious five-week tour of Europe have not impaired the orchestra's form. On the contrary, this last programme of the season proved to be one of the best. It was refreshingly interesting, featured new works and had a splendid young composer-pianist, playing a provocative piece of her own as soloist. Mr. Mehta reached new heights of accomplishments; he simply swept his audience away with him....

Shulamit Ran's Concert Piece was a cruel awakening from Webern's magical dream-world. Her music is harsh, angular and uncompromising. The music jumps continuously and nervously from one idea to another, with however, many imaginative episodes and intriguing passages. It is all said with sinewy, defiant sounds and a tremendous amount of dynamic and rhythmic energy. But I failed to hear or feel the basic unifying idea, idiom or approach, underlying the many, 'events and occurrences' (the phrase is taken from the programme notes). However, on a second listening on the following night, it seemed to make sense as a whole, in spite of its fragmentary texture. The constant strong physical impetus gives further coherence.

This piece was followed by Miss Ran's marvelous presentation of Ravel's Concerto. Content and

expression were rich, with a real abundance of imagination and invention. Under her fingertips, the
music flows uninterrupted and gives delight with
every new phrase, chord, and melody. She is
bursting with temperament, and vitality and her
technique is excellent and her tone warm.

Ran enjoyed her career as a performer and traveling
gains its own momentum but she realized that it was not con-
ducive for composing. Performing had its deep artistic re-
wards for Ran, yet she knew that she was denying that which
was the most important motivating force in her life, composing.
She said:

> I became progressively more bothered by the feeling
> that a change of priorities had to take place. Then
> a stroke of luck, completely unplanned: a Turnabout
> recording of Tableau by George Rochberg made its
> way, unknown to me, to Ralph Shapey, professor
> of composition at the University of Chicago. On
> the other side of this recording was my composition
> O, the Chimneys. Shapey flipped the record over
> and listened to my piece. He had never heard my
> name before and I had heard only one work of his
> at a New York concert years earlier.
>
> It so happened that the music department of the
> University of Chicago was looking for a composer to
> fill an opening. They somehow traced me down and
> wrote a letter inviting me to apply for the job; this
> was followed by many telephone calls.
>
> I was interviewed and consequently was offered
> the job. I now spend my time composing and of
> course teaching.
>
> There may well be other periods in my life when
> I again would do more performing but for now I am
> happy doing what I do. Economically, one does not
> go into composition with the idea of supporting a
> living. So certainly there must be another outlet.
> Teaching is an option, so is performing, sometimes.
> However, I never did think of performing as an
> economic solution; it was for me an artistic goal,
> a challenge of the highest order, live music making.
> It was something I wanted and needed to do and the
> active involvement with the great works of the past
> as well as present had, as far as I'm concerned,
> only the most positive impact on my composing.

In 1972 Shulamit Ran received a recording-publication grant from the Ford Foundation for her piece O, The Chimneys, scored for female voice, flute, clarinet, bass clarinet, cello, piano, percussion and tape sequence. She based the text on a setting of poems by Nelly Sachs, the German-Jewish Nobel Prize winner who wrote about the Holocaust. According to Ran her choice of instruments was based on the smallest grouping that would also give her the widest range of instrumental and expressive color. The work was premiered in New York where Ran was a performer in the Art Series for Young Artists at the Metropolitan Museum. The piece was then recorded by Vox-Turnabout and published by Carl Fischer. Several years later the piece received its West Coast premiere at a Holocaust Memorial Concert at the Arnold Schoenberg Institute by members of the Brostoff Jewish Arts Ensemble. Of this performance Donna Perlmutter of the Los Angeles Herald Examiner wrote, "A work of uncompromising brilliance ... the score reflects the devastating pain of its obscure, highly personal text, so stark yet full of import."

Ran joined the faculty of the University of Chicago in 1973 and is currently associate professor of composition. She reflects on her experiences at the University of Chicago:

> Without a doubt Ralph Shapey has had a special place in my life during the past ten years as a colleague, friend, and teacher. People would automatically assume that the "natural order of things" was that I was first his student and consequently joined the faculty of the University of Chicago as his colleague. In fact the reverse is true. I joined the faculty in 1973. After about three years, during which time a number of my works received performances, also by Shapey himself, I observed his work with some of the composition students. I became intrigued and interested in his approach as a teacher, having already had the greatest admiration for him as a composer.
> I decided to study composition with him and avail myself of its benefits. For about five minutes I contemplated the possible awkwardness of studying under the circumstances. (What will the students, his and mine, say?) Fortunately, this issue did not bother me for long. The way I see it, learning does not end with the earning of a degree or with

obtaining a job. On the contrary I consider it a
privilege to have a Ralph Shapey or a Dorothy Taubman as part of my life. Why should I not enrich
myself with what they are able to give?

Ran received a Fromm Music Foundation Commission in
1975 when she wrote Ensembles for 17. The work was premiered in Chicago by the Contemporary Chamber Players conducted by Ralph Shapey. High Fidelity/Musical America, July
1975 published a review by Karen Monson (partial):

> Shulamit Ran's Ensembles for 17, ... Ralph Shapey
> led the world premiere of the powerful work commis-
> sioned by the Fromm Foundation especially for this
> annual event. Then, after accepting the capacity
> audience's temperate ovation, the conductor turned
> around and led Ensembles straight through again.
> Shapey made his noble decision to repeat on the
> basis of the music itself. Ensembles for 17 both
> merits and needs this kind of double exposure.
>   During the first time through the eighteen-minute
> work, Miss Ran's use of dramatic timbre and gesture
> was particularly striking.... She ingeniously em-
> ploys the vivid coloristic resources of Ensembles'
> sixteen instruments and soprano (here, Elsa Charls-
> ton) to give the music both variety and a strong
> feeling of determination. The force of this determina-
> tion became clearer during the second performance,
> which pointed up the intimate connection between
> words (the final lines from Shakespeare's Othello).
> Miss Ran presents her text piecemeal through En-
> sembles' two movements and sometimes is as involved
> with syllabic sounds as she is with meaning. But
> the voice and instruments work together to disclose
> the wizened resignation of Othello's words, and the
> mood is carried as deftly by the winds, strings,
> piano, and percussions as by the voice itself.
>   Miss Ran's opus and Tison Street's brilliant
> String Quartet combined on this program to suggest
> that today's young composers are more comfortable
> with their musical heritage than were their fin de
> siecle colleagues.

When the work was later performed at the Festival of
Contemporary Music at Tanglewood one New York critic wrote,

"It was one of the more arresting pieces introduced." It is
of interest to note that Shulamit Ran was a student at Tanglewood shortly after she arrived in the United States and studied
with Aaron Copland and Lucas Foss. Several years later she
returned to Tanglewood as a respected and talented young
composer.

For over three decades the Fromm Foundation has been
the most important commissioning force of new music in America.
Excerpts from a report written by Mr. Paul Fromm on the
work of the Fromm Foundation include:

> Our primary objective over these years has been to
> bridge the gap that exists between contemporary
> composers and society.... Our insistence on main-
> taining organizational flexibility has enabled us to
> reach out to composers, and to act in a variety of
> ways on behalf of individual artists without encroach-
> ing on their artistic independence.
> The central purpose of the Fromm Music Founda-
> tion has been to restore to the composer his rightful
> position at the center of musical life. Rather than
> subsidizing institutions, or supporting other, even
> more anonymous aspects of culture, the Fromm
> Foundation has chosen to focus its programs on in-
> dividual artists, individual works and individual
> musical situations.

Shulamit Ran has great respect and admiration for Mr.
Paul Fromm and for the Fromm Foundation. She pays homage
by saying, "A few more Paul Fromms and the entire new music scene would be drastically different. Even he alone has
made a profound difference. He has always been encouraging and supportive of my work and we have a very fruitful
and joyous relationship."

In 1977, Shulamit Ran received one of the then two
commissions given by the Marion Bard Corbett Memorial Fund
of Contemporary Concerts, an organization that is one of
Chicago's main importers of avant-garde music. She wrote
Double Vision for Two Quintets and Piano, published by
Theodore Presser. The work is scored for woodwind quintet
with two clarinets and brass quintet with two trumpets and
piano. Premiered by the Contemporary Chamber Players conducted by Ralph Shapey at the University of Chicago, it was

later performed under the auspices of Contemporary Concerts,
Inc. and Ran was the pianist at both performances. Karen
Monson reviewed the work for High Fidelity/Musical America
in May 1977 (short excerpt):

> ... Miss Ran has pitted a woodwind quintet against
> a brass quintet in a battle mediated by the piano.
> The war ends in a stalemate, with the two sides pro-
> ducing loud, clashing walls of sound. But during
> the vivid skirmish, which divides into six small or
> three large sections, each contingent has its time on
> top, and even the piano takes time out from running
> messages between winds and brass to play a virtuoso
> cadenza.
>   The mid-section of Double Vision slows from fan-
> fares and quick routs to a freely tonal chorale spread
> among all the participants, indicating that the forces
> can at least lay down their arms to rest together for
> a while. The passage is indicative of Miss Ran's
> feel for drama and directness, like much of her
> recent work. Double Vision grows out of formal
> plans inspired by the instrumentation, but it never
> loses touch with emotional values and becomes, at
> times, almost picturesque.

A performance of Double Vision For Two Quintets and
Piano, three years later by the same group brought accolades
to Ms. Ran from the Chicago Sun Times' writer Robert C.
Marsh who said, "She has a fine-tuned ear. Color, timbre,
and texture are carefully explored. She writes beautifully
for brass, but her taste, her mastery of her craft, mark
every bar. Most of all she is imaginative. You sense her
musical roots, but they support a fully developed artistic
intellect."

Ran attributes part of her success as a composer-pianist
to growing up in Israel for in that country there is a real
sense of involvement in music. Young people are helped with
scholarships as well as study. Music is not the possession
of the rich, it is not a social commodity, the person in the
street is interested. Ran was fortunate for there were always
people encouraging her and always someone who believed in
what she was doing. There was never a time when she had
reason to complain of disinterest and she knew that was a
unique position.

Ran explains, "The notion that I was a woman composer never bothered anyone in Israel, that was never an issue. I was a young person and that was what seemed unique, the fact that I was female was not questioned."

In 1977 Ran was a recipient of a Guggenheim Fellowship in composition. It permitted her to have a whole year 1977-78 to do what she wanted most, to compose.

Radio station WFMT commissioned Ms. Ran in 1978 to write for their special series, Twentieth Century Art Song. There were nine song cycles commissioned for the event which included premieres by Ran, Lukas Foss, Ivan Tcherepnin, Barbara Kolb, Charles Wuorien, Richard Wernick, Philip Glass, Hugo Weisgall and Paul Chihara.

Each program included a conversation with the composer as well as a premiere of the work. Ran wrote Apprehensions for voice, clarinet and piano, set to poetry by Sylvia Plath. When the piece was performed at a later date by the New York New Music Ensemble at Carnegie Recital Hall, John Rockwell wrote in the New York Times, Jan. 31, 1981:

> Ran takes the Plath poem and treats it like an opera libretto. Each of the four stanzas becomes an act in a monodrama that recalls Schoenberg's Erwartung in lurid intensity. [Copyright © 1981 by The New York Times Company. Reprinted by permission.]

On Feb. 9, 1981 John von Rhein wrote in the Chicago Tribune:

> Working within an idiom that seems to derive partly from Expressionist esthetic of Alban Berg and beyond, partly from her own fiercely original creative sensibility, Ran draws you into the bleak, pained, uneasy imagery of the Plath poetry in a way that makes you feel at once assaulted, ennobled and spiritually cleansed. [Reprinted by permission of John von Rhein, music critic of the Chicago Tribune.]

When Ran writes she puts herself into the work; she does not always have a preconceived compositional design. She said: "Form and content are for me, inseparable. I get to know and understand the material I use in each piece and their potentialities only as I work. So the form crystallizes

in my mind during the process, not before. Of course that
does not mean that I do not at times begin with a certain idea
which may be a formal one which I wish to realize in sound.
I plan many things in my mind but I often do some detail
work at the piano." In the past few years most of her works
have been written on commission, although she also composes
other pieces; it's nice to put the two together.

Shulamit Ran has always been inspired to write music
of the highest caliber. She reflects on her career and those
changes that have occurred over a period of time:

> There have been various changes in the way I look
> at what I compose although in some ways I also re-
> main the same. There is a line that goes through
> my music that I believe to be me. People who know
> my music tell me that they can recognize elements
> of what they consider my style in music I wrote ten
> to fifteen years ago.
> Of course I have changed the way I approach a
> composition, what I do and how I do it. Maybe
> evolution is a more appropriate term. For instance,
> my concept of economy in the use of materials has
> changed, because I now have a different under-
> standing of what it means. Ten or fifteen years
> ago I would have thought of economy as limiting in
> a negative sense. Something which would curtail
> my imagination and, therefore, not something with
> which to be overly preoccupied. Now I take economy
> to mean a way of tapping my imagination to its full-
> est. It is not difficult to keep jumping from one
> idea to the next. At least, I do not recall ever hav-
> ing been short on ideas. But the real challenge is
> to take your chosen material and keep finding more
> and more ways to use it, making it appear fresh
> yet "right" each time, allowing it to grow and ex-
> pand.
> I've always been interested in the transformation
> of materials, a continuous line. In some way one
> thing becomes something else but it is also that
> which it was first.
> As my work changes I find myself having to forge
> new tools to accommodate the changes. It is a never-
> ending process, always intriguing and totally involv-
> ing. I can't think of anything else I'd rather do.
> My best work is always the next one to be written.

In 1980 the five members of the Da Capo Players commissioned six composers to write for the celebration of their
10th anniversary. The quintet requested that the composers
somehow work into their pieces the idea of Da Capo, a musical term directing the performer to repeat some of the music
previously played and in most cases directed the performer
to start from the beginning. Commissioned along with Shulamit Ran were Joseph Schwantner, Charles Wuorinen, George
Perle, Philip Glass and Joan Tower, the group's pianist and
founder. Ran wrote Private Game which was reviewed by
Robert Commanday on Feb. 7, 1982 in the San Francisco
Chronicle. He wrote of the piece, "It is so interestingly
varied, makes such full use of the clarinet and cello you
think you're hearing more instruments than that. Ran's
ideas are distinctive, basically three of them in sections which
are repeated in an order which is her private and attractive
game." Private Game is included on the CRI SD 411 record
titled, The Da Capo Players Celebrate Their Tenth Anniversary.

In 1983 in honor of Paul Fromm's 75th birthday and
three decades of support for American Music by the Fromm
Foundation, a special concert was held in Chicago. The
music department of the University of Chicago commissioned
six composers to write for this special event including Peter
Lieberson, John Harbison, Earl Kim, Fred Lerdahl, George
Perle and Richard Wernick. Ran's music as well as Ralph
Shapey, who also conducted the Contemporary Chamber Players in the concert, was also programmed. Mr. Fromm has
long been held in esteem for his financial and vocal support
of composers, the Contemporary Music Festival at Tanglewood
and other areas of the United States.

Shulamit Ran wrote A Prayer, scored for winds and
percussion, which was later performed at Tanglewood as well
as the Whitney Museum's Composers Showcase in New York.
Andrew Porter writing for The New Yorker, March 21, 1983,
listed Ran as one of the two Chicago composers (the other
being Shapey) who had been prominent in New York that
season. On A Prayer he wrote, "Ran's piece, for horn,
clarinet, bass clarinet, bassoon and timpani, is beautiful: a
stretch of affecting wordless song." Another leading New
York critic called the piece, "highly contrapuntal music,
generally gentle in nature but rising to ominous climax."

In the 1983 season New Yorkers had the opportunity
to hear Private Game, A Prayer, Excursions and Verticals.
Of Verticals Andrew Porter wrote in the March 21, 1983, issue
of The New Yorker (excerpt):

> Schulamit Ran's Verticals (1983)--a grand, passion-
> ate, Lisztian composition, rhapsodic and shapely,
> seventeen minutes long--had its premiere. [Reprinted
> by permission; © 1983 Andrew Porter. Originally
> in The New Yorker.]

When Excursions was performed by the Contemporary
Players in Mandel Hall on University of Chicago Campus conducted by Ralph Shapey the program was reviewed by John
von Rhein for the Chicago Tribune on April 15, 1985 (excerpt):

> Shulamit Ran is essentially a passionate Romantic
> working in an atonal idiom. Every measure of her
> Excursions (1980), for violin, cello and piano, is
> charged with dramatic intensity. Within the usual
> piano trio configuration Ran achieves an unusual
> textural variety, contrasting her materials always to
> vivid expressive effect. The sweeping, cadenza-
> like solos reflect a Romantic sense of virtuosity on
> a grand scale. Forceful, compelling, beautifully
> wrought music. Here is a new piece one would very
> much like to encounter again. [Reprinted by per-
> mission of John von Rhein, music critic of the Chicago
> Tribune.]

Ran has special praise for the musicians who perform
her music and comments on concerts in general:

> In my existence as a composer, no one makes as
> much of a difference as does the performer who
> plays my music, putting into it his/her soul, mind,
> and technique. I create, but it takes the performer
> to bring my creation to life. For me, the act of
> putting it all together for the first time--preparing
> a piece with the performers for its first performance--
> is one of the most powerful and rewarding experi-
> ences in my life. And I have been fortunate to
> have some fine performers play my music.
>   There certainly are not enough opportunities for
> the average listener to be exposed to modern music

in this country, and there is far too little financial
support for the creation and presentation of new
music. I would accuse the ones who could do the
most for doing the least. The large successful orchestras, the jet-setting, globe-trotting soloists,
precisely those who have the audiences listening with
rapt attention to their every sound, could do an
enormous service by programming a 20th-century
work amidst their Liszts or Tchaikovskys or whatever. But they are too busy worrying about their
careers to make the necessary investment of time
and effort to learn a new work, or else they tell
themselves that they will lose their audiences if
they program modern music. Of course this is
nonesense: the audience may leave the hall but
the audience will return; it has always been so.

I think we are living for the first time in a
period where modern music, the music of the day,
is not the main fare of the concert stage. Haydn's
and Beethoven's music was played during their life-
time. We slump into a museum age where the concert stage becomes a place to support and enshrine
the past.

I certainly don't think we should break away from
the past, that would be ludicrous; but at the same
time, this attitude that only the great music of the
past should be kept alive is deadly to 20th-century
composers. Modern music is best served when it is
surrounded by other music of other periods and not
put into seclusion such as "an evening of modern
music."

When a fine pianist plays my music as he/she
would play Beethoven--that is when it sounds best.
It ceases to sound like "modern music" and becomes
simply "music."

Ran has received numerous grants, awards and commissions including: a Ford Foundation Grant; The Martha
Baird Rockefeller Fund Grant; American-Israel Cultural Foundation Grant; a Fromm Music Foundation Commission; National
Endowment for the Arts Grant; Guggenheim Fellowship; WFMT
Commissions; Illinois Arts Council; several Meet the Composer
grants; and a commission from Chamber Music America.

Considering her relative youth, Shulamit Ran is an

unusually prolific and successful composer having received
honors and international acclaim. An artist with tremendous
energy, she is filled with ideas, interests and talents. Her
contributions can be evaluated and separated according to
purely qualitative aspects.

Selected Compositions of Shulamit Ran

Orchestra

1963   Capriccio, piano and orchestra.
1967   Symphonic Poem, piano and orchestra.
1970   Concert Piece, piano and orchestra. T. Presser.

Chamber

1968   See vocal
1969   O, The Chimneys, voice ensemble and tape. Carl
            Fischer.
1972   Three Fantasy Pieces, cello and piano. Carl Fischer.
1975   Ensembles for Seventeen. T. Presser.
1977   Double Visions for Two Quintets and Piano. T. Presser.
1978   Apprehensions, voice, clarinet, piano. Israeli Music
            Institute, Boosey, Hawkes.
1979   Private Game, clarinet and cello. T. Presser.
1980   Excursions, for violin, cello, piano. T. Presser.
1982   A Prayer, clarinet, bass clarinet, bassoon, horn, tim-
            pani. T. Presser.
1984   String Quartet
1985   Amichai Songs, mezzo soprano, oboe/English horn,
            viola da gamba, harpsichord.
1985   Adonai Malach, cantor, horn, piccolo, oboe, clarinet.

Piano

1967   Short Piano Pieces, seven pieces, Israeli Music Insti-
            tute. Boosey & Hawkes.
1967   Sonata No. 2. Israeli Music Institute. Boosey & Hawkes.
1968   Structures
1970   Ten Childrens Scenes, 4 hands. C. Fischer.
1977   Hyperbolae, Israeli Music Inst. Boosey & Hawkes.
1982   Sonata Waltzer
1982   Verticals

Vocal

1968 Seven Japanese Love Poems. Israeli Music Institute.
1969 O, The Chimneys. C. Fischer.
1972 Hatzvi Israel Eulogy, voice and ensemble. C. Fischer.
1975 Ensembles for 17. T. Presser.
1978 Apprehensions. Israeli Music Institute.
1980 Fanfare, five voices. T. Presser.

Tape

1973 O, the Chimneys, soprano, instruments, tape. C.
      Fischer.
      Fanfare for two multitracked sopranos.

Solo (other than piano)

1975 Sonata brevis, for harpsichord. T. Presser.
1978 For An Actor, monologue for clarinet. T. Presser.
1980 Fantasy Variations, for cello. T. Presser. Revised
      1984.

Addresses of Publishers

Theodore Presser Company, Bryn Mawr, PA 19010.

Carl Fischer, Inc., 56-62 Cooper Square, New York, NY
      10003.

Israel Music Institute is represented in U.S.A. by Boosey
      and Hawkes, Inc., 30 West 57th Street, New York, NY
      10019.

Discography

Private Games, The Da Capo Players Celebrate Their Tenth
      Anniversary. CRI SD 411.
O, the Chimneys. Vox-Turnabout TVS 34492. Out of Print.
Apprehensions. CRI 509.
For an Actor: Monologue for Clarinet. Mark Educational
      Recordings.

Addresses

Composers Recordings, Inc., 170 West 74th Street, New York,
NY 10023.

Vox-Turnabout, The Moss Music Group Inc., 211 E. 43
Street, New York, NY 10017.

Mark Educational Recordings Inc., 10815 Bodine Road, Clar-
ence, NY 14031.

RUTH SCHONTHAL

Pianist, Teacher

Ruth Schonthal is a very underrated composer judging by
the quality and the expressive appeal of her music, the
variety, and the generally high standard of her output. To
quote her:

> I am never without music going through my head.
> I think about it constantly. Writing music is central
> to my life and as such obsessive. As the music
> floats through my head, I dig for the "ultimate ver-
> sion," shaping, reshaping, developing phrases,
> harmonies, shapes and textures sometimes hundreds
> of times until I have found the "absolute right"
> way. This I do on paper at the piano, and away
> from it in my head. My ideal is to write music for
> people who love music. Although this proved to be,
> for most of my composing life, an unfashionable ob-
> jective. I want my music to be well-crafted, beauti-
> ful and expressing the full range of human emotions.
> Through my own background I feel a special kin-
> ship to the European, especially the German and
> Viennese musical tradition, and often use this as
> the foundation of my own musical creativity. This
> I expand by fusing the old with the new, using
> contemporary techniques and expressing contemporary
> sensitivities, shaped by my own individual concerns,
> esthetic and temperament.

Born in Hamburg, Germany, in 1924 of Viennese parents, Ruth Schonthal improvised at the piano and composed
her first composition, a waltz, in Vienna at the age of 6. On
the basis of this composition she was accepted as the youngest student at the well-known Stern Conservatory in Berlin.

RUTH SCHONTHAL   Photo by
                                 P. Seebel

Her studies included piano lessons twice a week and every
Saturday morning classes in theory, ear-training and dicta-
tion. In addition to going to the Conservatory, she took
private classes in composition and attended a course on the
analysis of Beethoven's piano sonatas and other works with
a Mr. Etthoven in Berlin from 1932-36.

Reflecting on the experience she says:

> Mr. Etthoven had a marvelous way of explaining what
> Beethoven did with his musical ideas. For me this
> proved to be an excellent foundation. Much of what
> I know about the developing of musical material and
> achieving variety and cohesion can be traced back
> to this early immersion into musical, analytical think-
> ing, and awareness. Thus I like to say that my
> greatest teacher was Beethoven introduced to me at
> an early age by Mr. Etthoven.

Schonthal and her parents fled Nazi Germany in 1938
and made their way to Stockholm, Sweden to start a new life.
Her father took her to an audition at the Royal Academy of
Music where she performed not only the traditional repertoire
but also played her own compositions, and she was immediately
given a piano scholarship. The Academy provided many opportunities for the gifted young composer to perform. She
continued her composition with private studies with the Swedish composer Ingemar Liljefors, and it was while studying
with him that she wrote at the age of 13, her first work to
be published, Sonatina in A. She performed the work's premiere at the Moscow Conservatory. Schonthal said, "even
today Sonatina is quite a fine piece and I am not ashamed of
it."

Just three months prior to her graduation from the
academy as a pianist the family decided it would be best to
leave Sweden. In retrospect, the family would have been
safe in the country but the times were uncertain and her
father was concerned that the Nazis might try to conquer
Sweden as they had Denmark. The family wanted to go to
the United States but their visas did not arrive soon enough.
A Mexican visa was available if the family prepaid their travel
tickets and invested money in the country, and that was the
route they took for their escape.

Ms. Schonthal had a letter of recommendation from Ingemar Liljefors which proved to be an important document; in part it read:

> From the beginning Miss Schonthal has manifested an amazing and extraordinarily great talent for composition, which she developed, during two years she studied with me, to a maturity quite unusual for her age.
> Her generous and productive source of inspiration combined with her deep sense for musical form and style promises all the best for the future.
>
> I appeal to whom it may concern to give Miss Schonthal every support she may need for further studies of composition.

Schonthal's father sent a copy of her Sonatina to Leopold Stokowski, who was then in Mexico, and he replied that the work showed a definite talent which should be developed with further study.

A few months after she arrived in Mexico, Schonthal received a full scholarship to study composition with Manuel M. Ponce. She became his favorite student and he made certain that she was included in the musical circle of Mexico City. Her talents as a composer-pianist were soon recognized and at the age of 17 her Concerto for Piano and Orchestra was premiered by the Mexican University Symphony Orchestra, receiving much praise by the critics. Schonthal played many successful concerts, often playing her own compositions, at the Palacio De Bellas Artes.

When she finished her studies with Manuel M. Ponce he wrote:

> In my opinion Ruth Schonthal possesses, besides profound technical knowledge, an artistic temperament of first class quality and a genial intuition for composition which has enabled her to create works of most different styles in spite of her being so young.

In 1946 the Mexican Government invited a giant of contemporary music, Paul Hindemith, to present a series of

concerts conducting his own music. Ruth Schonthal attended
all his rehearsals and concerts and acted as his interpreter
since she spoke not only German but Spanish as well. At a
private audition, after listening to the composer performing
the second movement of her Piano Concerto and sing and
play several of her songs, he invited her to study composition with him at Yale, offering a full scholarship. He had
been very impressed with her talent, melodic gift and compositional accomplishments, but felt that her "basslines" could
be made more interesting.

Schonthal was warmly welcomed at Yale. She said,
"Many seemed in awe that Hindemith had so highly recommended me. Actually many students were intimidated by
him." Because of the great changeover of compositional technique, she did not write anything of quality in her first year
at Yale.

In 1948 Schonthal received her bachelor of music degree
from Yale. She comments on her study with Hindemith:

> Hindemith has often been accused of teaching his
> students to write and sound like he did. He was
> very methodical and in order to teach the craft of
> composition, he felt one had to approach each musi-
> cal element separately. To this he added his esthe-
> tic judgment. Every student did the same exercises
> and thus it was unavoidable that the music produced
> sounded imitative.
> When I was writing my Sonata during a semester
> break, I used to joke that I was writing my "Hinde-
> mith Sonata." In spite of all this, I owe a great
> deal to Hindemith's teaching and I learned much
> about harmonic control and contrapuntal skills.

In 1949 the New York Music critics confirmed Hindemith's evaluation of Schonthal's musical ability in one of her
many Town Hall performances. In a program of mainly her
own works a critic wrote, "She has unusual talent, and much
more will be heard from her." The review from the New York
Herald Tribune of March 3, 1949, read:

RUTH SCHONTHAL AT TIMES HALL

Ruth Schonthal, a young composer-pianist, made her

New York debut in both capacities yesterday afternoon in the Times Hall in a program which, except
for piano works by Paul Hindemith and the late
Manuel Ponce, was devoted to her own music. This
included several piano compositions, eight Songs
with German Texts by Rainer Maria Rilke, and two
set to German adaptations of Chinese Texts.

At 23, Miss Schonthal has a varied background
of studies begun in Germany, continued in Sweden
and later in Mexico, and recently continued at Yale
University on a scholarship offered by Mr. Hindemith. What the reviewer had opportunity to hear
gave an impression of talent and inventiveness,
while also of a style which has not integrated its
influences. German romanticism was marked in the
skillfully written and melodically persuasive Rilke
songs and also in Miss Schonthal's six preludes for
piano, which proved instrumentally idiomatic: her
recently composed Sonata in E flat, judging by its
first movement, was in a more contemporary idiom,
which suggested the influence of Hindemith.

Miss Anderson sang the songs with German texts
acceptably, and added one with a Spanish text, presumably composed during Miss Schonthal's residence
in Mexico. As a pianist, both in the solos and, the
accompaniments, Miss Schonthal displayed ability and
interpretative conviction. [© T.H.T. Corporation.
Reprinted by permission.]

After graduating from Yale, Schonthal realized that she
must redirect her compositional thoughts, and outlined 10
points in which she would disassociate herself from Hindemith's style. She redirected her melodic talent, her melodies
became "more natural" (without constant artificial tonal and
chromatic digressions) and she found a variety of esthetic
and technical components to develop her stylistic preferences.

I wanted my music to express different things, and
I was a very different person and of different
temperament and sensitivity than Hindemith whom
and whose music I much admire.

Although Hindemith did not practice what he
preached, he exhorted us: "It matters not how
much your music is played so long as on your death-
bed you feel you have two or three compositions
that you are proud of."

This advice she followed mistakenly for too many years before she discovered the fallacy. Apart from the fact that this state of affairs produces much unhealthy self-pity and bitterness, it is extremely important to explore one's own sense and that can be an important inspirational force.

The following review appeared many years after Schonthal made her decision to revamp her compositional style and write only in a medium that could be her personal expression. Written by Raymond Ericson for the New York Times on April 13, 1964--it is well-worth reading:

WORKS BY RUTH SCHONTHAL

Ruth Schonthal, who has studied in Europe, Mexico and the United States, presented four of her latest works yesterday afternoon in Carnegie Recital Hall. They were Fiesta, Dances and Intoxications for Piano (1961), Sonata for Violin and Piano (1962), String Quartet (1962), and Totengesange, a song cycle (1963).

The sonata was new to this city. The other works were being performed for the first time anywhere.

Miss Schonthal's parents were Viennese, and this heritage seems to play a major part in her style. This was true even of the Mexican-inspired Fiestas, the earliest and harmonically most conventional piece in the program.

The composer likes to enrich and thicken her harmonic scheme with added notes and then to simplify it again during the course of a work. Her music could be pleasantly Brahmsian or chromatic in the post-Romantic manner, and she was not above deliberate references, by quotation, to the works of earlier composers.

The most ambitious of Miss Schonthal's creations was the song cycle. In this the composer showed a gift for writing vocal lines that she let trail off at times into Sprechstimme as seductive as those of Richard Strauss. But the elaborate piano parts for the songs vitiated their initial dramatic impact through overextension.

Outstanding artists performed her music, including Herbert Stessin, pianist; Sonya Monosoff, violinist;

the York String Quartet, and Bethany Beardslee,
soprano.

Miss Schonthal herself was a pianist for the sonata
and song cycle. [Copyright © 1964 by The New York
Times Company. Reprinted by permission.]

Since economics are essential to everyday living expenses, Ruth Schonthal has always found it necessary to devote her energy to areas other than composing. She has
been accompanist for many dance troupes, performed in many
well-known night clubs under the name of Carmelita, has
taught piano privately and was a part-time member of the
faculty at New York University and the Westchester Conservatory. With a hectic teaching schedule along with other
additional responsibilities, Schonthal realized she could seldom
afford the luxury of a specific block of time that could be
devoted entirely to composing. So she disciplined herself to
use every scrap of time advantageously. If a student is 10
minutes late she spends that time working on scraps of her
compositions; she mentally occupies herself at all times. Her
evenings and weekends, with few exceptions, are devoted to
composing.

Awards and honors have not rained on Schonthal but
she feels her tremendously busy schedule is partly to blame.
She has received the Outstanding Alumni Award in music from
Yale University, numerous ASCAP Standard Awards and the
Delta Omicron Third International Award for her String Quar-
tet written in 1964.

The Crescent String Quartet recorded this piece on
Leonarda LP 1-111 after performing it in 1975. "Ruth Schonthal's quartet looks back to Schubert and to Tristan, but in
a more modernistic way than does another quartet included
on the same recording, and it only gradually reveals its
elusive goal," was the manner in which one reviewer described
the work. Another reviewer wrote, "Here is a disc that is
difficult to fault. I found it a joy throughout."

The first International Women's Year, 1975, was designated by the United Nations to call attention to the creative
talents of women which have been overlooked and generally
ignored for years. The same year, a concert dedicated to
the works of Ruth Schonthal was given at Carnegie Recital
Hall on Sept. 26. Works included Reverberations, Sonata
Concertanta, Sonatensatz and Song Cycle. As one music

critic noted, "Ruth Schonthal was best represented by herself at the keyboard and could pass with great honors as a
pianist and composer."

Also in the same year, Ruth Schonthal's music was
heard as part of "Hear America First" program in New York
City. Six compositions were programmed, all composed within
three years of each other and covered a wide range of contemporary styles from conservative to the most radical avant-
garde. The Schonthal piece Variations in Search of a Theme
was played by pianist Gary Steigerwalt and reviewed by Peter
G. Davis for a New York Paper: "Chaos and dissonace re-
solved into order and harmony is the structural idea."

This piece is included on a record featuring four of
Schonthal's works, Orion 81413. Other works are Sonata
Breve, Nachklange and Sonatensatz. Numerous reviews of
this recording have been issued and all have been positive.
The following was written for Fanfare, March-April, 1983 by
Walter Simmons.

> Schonthal: Sonata Breve, Reverberations, Sona-
> tensatz, Variations in Search of a Theme. Gary
> Steigerwalt, piano, ORION ORS-81413.
>
> This release offers a most impressive presentation
> of piano music by Ruth Schonthal, a New York based
> composer now almost 60 years old. The four works
> on this disc, most dating from the early 1970s, in-
> dicate a composer of real impressive impetus, with
> the technical command necessary to fulfill her inten-
> tions throughout a rather broadly based stylistic
> range. At one extreme is the seven-minute Sonata
> Breve--a warmly romantic work, rhapsodic in ges-
> ture but concentrated in its impassioned expression.
> This is the most immediately attractive work on the
> disc, and one that would easily appeal to many
> listeners.
>   Rather different is Reverberations, a collage-
> type piece for prepared piano, which suggests nos-
> talgic memories of a scene from ones past, recalled
> through veils of sadness and regret. The scene is
> the composer's native Germany, and wisps of Ger-
> man tunes are woven throughout the piece. The
> gentle clatter of the prepared piano evokes a sense

of desolation much the same way as does the unfor-
gettable Jesus' Blood never Failed Me Yet by Gavin
Bryars (Obscure-1), which has created such an
underground sensation. This is a very difficult
type of piece to shape effectively, but Schonthal is
remarkably successful.

Sonatensatz is another piece that combines very
simple, consonant sounds with jagged, angular ones
in a rhapsodic manner somewhat reminiscent of
Scriabin's Vers la flamme. Perhaps this one is a
bit too improvisatory, but it is effective nonetheless.

Variations in Search of a Theme is the least satis-
factory of the four pieces. This is a set of episodes that are to function as variations on an un-
stated theme. The cumulative effect of these episodes should imply a suggestion of the theme. This
is a promising idea, but the brief episodes are
closed, rather than elided, minimizing the desired
sense of accumulation, and emphasizing an unpleas-
antly choppy effect. Schonthal's manipulation of
the brittle gestures reveals solid control of dissonant
harmonic gradation, however.

This record provides convincing evidence that
Ruth Schonthal has a provocative compositional voice
worthy of further attention. Part of the credit for
its strong impact is due pianist Gary Steigerwalt,
who presents these pieces with technical competence
and expressive conviction. He is an intelligent,
adventurous pianist whose efforts merit considerable
praise. Orion supplies fine sound and surfaces.

The Beautiful Days of Aranjuez scored for orchestra
and harp was written in 1981. Sara Cutler, harpist, premiered the work with the Connecticut Chamber Orchestra
conducted by Sayard Stone in 1982. Lenny Cavallaro reviewed
the concert for the New Haven Register on Dec. 6, 1982:

PREMIERE HIGHLIGHTS CCO CONCERT

Real music is still being composed these days. That's
the only conclusion one could reach Saturday night
as the Connecticut Chamber Orchestra, under Sayard
Stone, premiered The Beautiful Days of Aranjuez by
Ruth Schonthal.

Schonthal combined touches of Ravel and Hindemith

with her own unique asthetic. By no means a de-
rivative composer, Schonthal is, on the contrary,
most original. She is also a highly communicative
and expressive voice writing exquisite music.

The piece featured a lengthy cadenza for harp,
realized by Sara Cutler, who successfully captured
the Spanish flavor. There were also prominent
solos by the violist Marvin Warshaw, whose lush,
rich tones merit special praise. Cellist Chris Adkins
likewise excelled in his important parts.

It was an excellent evening for the CCO, which
rose to yet greater heights. It was also a fortunate
occasion for those privileged to hear the marvelous
composition by Ruth Schonthal.

The National Musical Arts Ensemble performed the world
premiere of Schonthal's cantata The Solitary Reaper at the
National Academy of Sciences in Washington, D.C., in 1983.
This ensemble is noted for its diversity as well as its interesting and varied programs that adds very significantly to the
musical life in Washington. Schonthal chose Wordsworth's poem
about the power of music to stir feelings and memories as the
text for the cantata. It is an ideal text for music and she
scored the piece brilliantly for voice, flute, cello and piano.
The Solitary Reaper is a strong work easily followed by the
listener and is a clear indication of the compositional skills
of the gifted Schonthal.

Ruth Schonthal understands both the process and the
difficulty of establishing one's self as a 20th-century composer. That she has 14 pieces on recordings (with more
under consideration) is a noteworthy accomplishment. She
chose to use her energy to make recordings rather than to
follow an extensive concert schedule because recordings are
much more permanent. Schonthal realizes and appreciates
the work of the many talented musicians who have made these
recordings possible. She said "The artists who have recorded
my works are very very talented. I have had the finest
performers a composer could ever wish for."

Schonthal occupies a prominent position in the musical
life of this century. Determining one's cultural identity can
itself vastly enrich the resources upon which an artist draws
and this has been particularly true in Schonthal's career.
To be successful every composer must have a message and

she has developed the uncanny ability of writing beautiful,
lyrical music that is both sensitive and emotionally descriptive.

Ruth Schonthal is a remarkable woman who has contributed an important repertoire to 20th-century music.

Selected Compositions of Ruth Schonthal

Abbreviations used are given at the end of this section.

Stage Works

1955 Candide.
1963 The Transposed Heads.
1979- The Courtship of Camilla MS/AMC/CS.
  80

Large Orchestra

1945 6 Preludes RS.
1955 Candide Ballet Suite RS.
1957 Symphony 1 RS.
1963 The Transposed Heads Ballet Suite RS.

String Orchestra

1962 Serenade (Rental).

Orchestra with Solo Instrument

1942 Concerto Romantico RS.
1977 Concertos (2) CS.
1978 Music for Horn and Chamber Orchestra MS.
1981 The Beautiful Days of Aranjuez RS/CS.

Chamber Music

1945 14 Inventions a due voci MS/AMC/CS.
1962 Sonata MS.

1973 Sonata concertante MS/AMC/LP.
1975 4 Epiphanies LP.
1978 Fantasia in a Nostalgic Mood MS/AMC.
1978 Music for Horn and Piano MS.
1979 Loveletters MS/AMC/LP.
1980 Interlude MS/AMC.
1983 Quartets MS.

Piano Solo

1939 Sonatina RS.
1945 Capriccio español RS.
1945 Prelude and Fugue in b RS.
1945 Prelude and Fugue in f RS.
1945 6 Preludes RS.
1945 Bird Calls.
      Miniatures (3 Volumes).
      Minuscules.
      Near and Far.
      Potpourri.
1961 Fiestas y danzas MS.
1963 Blue Preludes.
1964 Sonata quasi un'improvisazione MS.
1973 Sonata breve LP.
1973 Sonatensatz (sonata movement) RS.
1974 Variations in Search of a Theme LP.
1967- Nachklange (Reverberations) MS/AMC/LP.
  74
1978 In Homage of... (24 preludes) MS/AMC/LP.
1978 11 Pieces (Gestures) MS.
1982 3 Elegies for a Murder victim MS.
1982 Fragments from a Woman's Diary MS/AMC/LP.
1984 14 Inventions a due voci MS/AMC/CS.

Voice and Chamber Ensemble

1956 3 Canciones (Homage a García Lorca) MS.
1960 9 Lyric-Dramatic Songs MS/CS.
1978 The Solitary Reaper MS/AMC/CS.

Voice and Piano

1939 3 Songs with Words by R.M. Rilke MS.

1942 3 Songs with Words by Lipo MS.
1943 2 Canciones (Garcĩa Lorca) MS.
1960 9 Lyric-Dramatic Songs MS/CS.
1963 Totengesange (Songs of Death) MS/AMC/LP.
1975 By the Roadside CS.
1977 7 Songs of Love and Sorrow MS/AMC/CS.

Selected Abbreviations

AMC--Available from American Music Center, New York City
CS--Cassette available from composer
LP--Recorded on long-playing disc
MS--Manuscript (of facsimile), available from composer for
     performance
Rental--Score & parts available for rental from composer
RS--Available from composer for research purposes only

Address of Publisher

American Music Center, 250 West 54th St., New York, NY
     10019.

For further Information contact: Ruth E. Schonthal, 12 Van
     Etten Blvd., New Rochelle, NY 10804.

Discography

Four Epiphanies, Paul Doktor, viola; Orion ORS 83444
Fragments from a Woman's Diary, Gary Steigerwalt, piano;
     Orion (forthcoming)
In Homage of..., for piano solo; Orion (forthcoming)
Loveletters, Michael Rudiakov, cello; Esther Lamneck, clari-
     net; Capriccio No. 1
Music for Horn & Chamber Orchestra, Rimon Meir, French
     Horn; Israel Philharmonic members (forthcoming)
Nachklange (Reverberations), Gary Steigerwalt, piano; Orion
     ORS 81413
Quartet 1, The Crescent Quartet, for string; Leonarda LP1-111
Sonata Breve, Gary Steigerwalt, piano; Orion ORS 81413
Sonata Concertante, for clarinet and piano, Esther Lamneck,
     clarinet; Gary Steigerwalt, piano; Opus One (forth-
     coming)

Sonatensatz (Sonata Movement), Gary Steigerwalt, piano;
        Orion ORS 81413
Totengesange (8 Songs), Berenice, Leonarda LP1-106
The Transposed Heads, ballet suite for orchestra, Branson,
        soprano; Schonthal, piano; Columbia Records
Variations in Search of a Theme, Gary Steigerwalt, piano;
        Orion ORS 81413

Addresses

Capriccio Records, 6192 Oxon Hill Road, Washington, D.C.
        20021.

Columbia Records, CBS Inc., 51 West 52nd Street, New York,
        NY 10019.

Leonarda Productions, Inc., Box 124, Radio City Station,
        New York, NY 10019.

Opus One, P.O. Box 604, Greenville, ME 04441.

Orion Master Recordings Inc., P.O. Box 4087, Malibu, CA
        90265-1387.

MARGARET SUTHERLAND, 1897-1984

Composer, Pianist, Teacher

Margaret Sutherland occupies a very special place in the
history of Australian music as the undisputed first lady of
Australian music as well as one of the earliest and most respected composers in the country. Music written in the 19th
century and earlier, from Great Britain and other European
countries, was the accepted and expected tradition on the
concert stage. It was only in the 20th century that works
written by native composers were being heard in the country.

Roger Covell, internationally respected authority on
the music of Australia, wrote in his book Australia's Music:
Themes of a New Society (Melbourne Sun Books, 1967):

> But it was a woman composer, Margaret Sutherland
> of Melbourne, who really naturalized the 20th-century
> in Australian music. Long before World War II she
> was writing music which paralleled the neo-classical
> reaction against Romantic styles in most European or
> Europe-derived societies.

Sutherland's contributions were not only in the field
of composing for she is generally recognized as the twentieth
century's leading pioneer of Australian music. She devoted
her long life to working for the acceptance of Australian music and the Australian composer. Her range of activities were
extensive including years of fighting for, promoting and
championing young composers and contemporary music as well
as leading the earliest movement for the establishment and
building of the Victorian Arts Centre.

She was born in Adelaide, South Australia, in 1897 and
moved with her family to Melbourne, Victoria, when she was

MARGARET SUTHERLAND   Photo by
                             James Murdoch

very young. Her childhood was spent in a very cultured
home unusual at that time in a country so geographically isolated. Her father was the leading writer for Age, a daily
newspaper, as well as a pianist. Her mother was a singer
and two aunts were performers (piano and lieder-singer),
while a third aunt was a painter. This proved to be a fine
home environment for the bright, sensitive, and artistic young
Margaret. At the age of 5 she could play the melody line in
octaves of Schubert's songs while an adult played the accompaniment part.

In 1914 she was awarded a scholarship to study piano
with Edward Goll and composition with Fritz Hart at the Marshall Conservatorium. Although both of these teachers were
to have an influence on Sutherland it was Henri Verbrugghen,
the Belgian conductor and violinist, who provided her with
the opportunity to hear live music, particularily chamber music, which developed and widened her creative talents. When
she was 19 years old he invited her to go to Sydney to perform the Beethoven G major Piano Concerto.

She spent a short period of time teaching piano and
theory at the Presbyterian Ladies College, working as an assistant to Edward Goll and performing piano recitals. But in
1922 she made a decision to pursue a career in composing,
an unheard-of profession at that time for a woman.

Sutherland left Australia in 1923 to study and write in
Paris, Vienna, and London. While in London she studied composition with Arnold Bax and completed her Sonata for Violin
and Piano. At the time Bax remarked that this was the best
sonata he had heard written by a woman. The sonata was
not published until 10 years later and Sutherland fully realized
that her dream of composing would be an almost impossible
battle.

When she returned to Australia in 1925 she had to survive for over 40 years with almost no encouragement. She
really lived during a period when there was no point in being
a composer in Australia; nobody wanted to hear new music.
It appears that she pursued the only avenue available to her
as a composer when she and friends arranged performances
of her music at musicales and soirees by societies in Melbourne. Being an active performer helped to assure that her
chamber music would be heard.

Although Margaret Sutherland married in 1926 and raised two children she continued to teach privately and taught at the Melbourne Conservatorium for almost a decade in addition to composing chamber music and pieces for her own children. Her output during these years was sparse but she continued as an active chamber performer with different ensembles that are now legendary in Melbourne. Her music was lean and reserved and the music critics did not know what to do with her. In retrospect she is now acclaimed as a true pioneer of Australian music.

During the frustrating early years of her career she did receive one small bit of recognition when her Sonata for Violin and Piano was published in 1935 by Louise Dyer in the Lyrebird Edition, a first for an Australian woman composer. However, this publication came some 10 years after the work was premiered. Some years later one Australian music critic wrote after hearing a performance of the piece, "this is a powerful mind at work here."

Sutherland was able to devote more time to composition when her children started to attend school. Suite on a Theme of Purcell was completed in 1935 and received many performances under the direction of George Szell. When Eugene Goossens programmed the suite at a much later date in Sydney, the critics wrote that Australia's contemporary music was advantageously represented by a work of commendable musical stature, a comment that certainly must have pleased the struggling Sutherland. Dithyramb composed in 1937 was performed by the Sydney Orchestra in the 1940s "to keen interest and acclaim" by the audience and critics. Other works completed during this period were, House Quartet, Pavan for Orchestra, The Soldier, String Quartet, and Prelude for Jig.

Throughout World War II Sutherland arranged for midday concerts of works by contemporary Australian composers for the Red Cross, all of which went unnoticed by the Australian Broadcasting Company, an organization that could have and should have provided more performance opportunities for their own composers. She was the most active member of the Council for Education, Music and the Arts and worked tirelessly for reform in Australian music education which she considered outdated, uninteresting and lacking any creative output. She was associated for years with the Australian

Advisory Committee for UNESCO and an active member of
the Advisory Board for the Australian Music Fund.

Perhaps her greatest contribution to her country, in
addition to her creative work, was begun in 1943 when she
and two other individuals formed a committee to ensure that
land on St. Kilda Road in Melbourne would be saved as the
site for the future Victorian Arts Centre. The struggle to
just set aside the land for this center would take over 10
years and Sutherland led the fight against the South Melbourne City Council who wanted to sell the land for industry.
Sutherland was a stauch protagonist for a combined arts
center and helped collect over 40,000 signatures on a petition
which was presented to the council that assured the land
would be designated for public buildings.

In 1982 The Victorian Arts Centre was completed and
during the dedication Sutherland was acknowledged for her
early vision. She had also served on the Board of Directors
for many years. The Arts Centre is unique in Australia in
that it combines all facets of the visual and performing arts
within walking distance from the central business district
and major hotels.

In a country where streets, buildings, parks, bridges
and squares are named after men who contributed to the
growth, development and future of Australia one has to wonder why Margaret Sutherland was not so recognized. Was it
because she was a woman in a man's world?

Supposedly there is a picture of Margaret Sutherland
somewhere in the Victorian Arts Centre but this visitor and
her tour guide could not find it. It has been said that only
one or two of the thousands of visitors to the center even
know what Margaret Sutherland accomplished. One can only
hope that this situation will be corrected, for she is a legend.

Margaret Sutherland wrote, "To pluck music from the
air was what made my heart beat faster and that was what I
longed passionately to have time and opportunity to do."
When she and her husband parted in 1948 Sutherland went
to Europe for a period of time and began the most productive
two decades of her creative life. During this time she composed nine orchestral works, 12 chamber works and a chamber
opera, in addition to many smaller keyboard and vocal pieces.

While in England a friend interested Boosey and Hawkes in publishing Concerto For String Orchestra which she had written in 1945 and signed M. Sutherland. Sutherland was elated with the prospect of having the piece published but was disappointed when the company refused publication upon learning that M. stood for Margaret. The concerto was performed by the Sydney Symphony Orchestra during their 1958 season along with the contemporary concertos written by Bartok and Bloch and the classical concertos of Telemann and Mozart. Reviewed in The Sydney Herald News on Feb. 17, 1958 (excerpt):

> Another concerto for strings by Margaret Sutherland of Melbourne as not out of place in this august company. Stylish and fresh in the Georgian manner of the Holst school, it said pleasant things that have been said many times by many another well-schooled composer of pre-Britten England.

During this same year the Concerto Grosso was recorded on ABC RRCS/145 by the strings of the Melbourne Symphony Orchestra with John Hopkins conducting. The soloists for the trio section were Sybil Copeland, violin, John Glickman, viola and Max Cooke, harpsichord. The work used the traditional form and is therefore in three movements. According to Sutherland she linked for form of the 18th-century with her ideas as a 20th-century composer and wrote two of the movements in an evocative and forthright manner while the middle section is tender to the point of being introverted.

In the same year Sutherland's Fantasy for Violin and Orchestra was one of the top four pieces selected as finalists in the Composers Competition Concert in Sydney. One music critic wondered how the judges decided on the winner since there was no comparison between the "light music with a work of such entirely different and more serious purpose as Margaret Sutherland's which seemed to be a far more finished and solidly inspired composition." She did not win the competition although the piece was described in one review as the most absorbing and genuinely modern work heard.

Sutherland composed the majority of her orchestral works during the 1950s and early '60s. Her tone poem composed during this period has had extensive performances and has been recorded. The Haunted Hills was premiered in 1951

by Eugene Goossens and the Sydney Symphony Orchestra
but received less than a positive review at the time. The
music critic felt the tone poem showed evidence of imagination
and sensibility but lacked formal cohesion and had a pianistic
approach to orchestration. When reviewed some 34 years
later the critic wrote, "Sutherland's Haunted Hills was a work
one seized with relief--this was a composer with something to
say, with a real sense of color creation and the ability to
convey shifting moods."

The Haunted Hills has been recorded by the Melbourne
Symphony Orchestra, John Hopkins, conductor, Festival Disc
SFC 800/20. According to notes by the composer, "haunted
hills" refers to the Dandenong Ranges located near Melbourne:

> These ranges are distinguished by a remarkable
> colour spectrum of reds and tangerines and are suf-
> fused with brilliant shafts of light. Set against a
> soft mountain mist, the effect on the senses some-
> times is that of a strange fantasy being enacted be-
> fore one's eye. This is the "argument" of the work.
> Haunted Hills falls into two parts, framing a
> short central meditative passage. The work opens
> with bold strokes, indicating the grandeur of the
> terrain. There follows a sturdy but uneven tune
> of some rhythmical power, which softens to a musty
> meditation on the antique land of an antique people.
> Marked scherzando, the second section takes a wing
> on a joyous flight of melody, to end the work with
> the strong jutting chords of the opening.

In 1958 Sutherland completed her orchestral suite,
Three Temperaments which was recorded in 1964 by John
Hopkins and the Melbourne Symphony Orchestra on A.B.C
RRCS/145. The following notes are reproduced with acknowl-
edgement to the Australian Broadcasting Company:

> Three Temperaments: The antique musical forms
> which Margaret Sutherland has chosen for the move-
> ments of this orchestral suite associate fittingly with
> antique concept of the "temperaments" which were
> supposed to rule the passions and behaviour of
> men. The composer, however, gives no indication
> as to whether this was in fact her intention. The
> first movement, Pavan, depicts a temperament that

is, in the composer's words, 'cool, detached, mysterious: controlled, even in a crisis.'

The second movement, titled Air, displays a temperament that is 'warm, affectionate, spontaneous, though not without human frailty.'

The third temperament is 'the complete extrovert, active, optimistic.' The movement is titled Canon.

Nineteen orchestral and chamber works written by Margaret Sutherland have been recorded either on disc or tape by the Australian Broadcasting Company. It is unfortunate that these discs and tapes are available only in approved circumstances for use in educational institutions, diplomatic and Broadcasting Union exchanges and internal A.B.C. usage. They cannot be purchased commercially.

The publication and recording of contemporary Australian music suffers the same fate as in other countries with small populations. In 1986 the population in Australia was a mere 15 million people making it economically not feasible to publish and record works of Australian composers. It is simply not a profitable business venture.

A limited number of recordings are made in the country but they are usually subsidized by government grants, individuals, or other organizations. Only a few recordings are issued and they are difficult to locate after a year or two.

There is no company in the country that publishes new contemporary music since J. Albert and Son deleted this division of their company in the 1980s. Fortunately some of Margaret Sutherland's music is available through Albert's, since it was published before the company made this decision. (Her music is also available through the Australia Music Centre, 80 George St., Sydney, 2000, Australia.)

Although Sutherland's largest group of orchestral works were written and performed during the 1950s she did not neglect her commitment to other Australian composers. During this time she organized the Camerata Society, a chamber group, devoted to the performance of Australian music. Sutherland realized the need for such an organization and knew that the only way composers grow and develop their style is to hear their works performed as quickly as possible. It was not an easy task to jolt the Australian public out of

its narrow provincialism into a cosmopolitan awareness and a
respect for the country's living composers. Sutherland knew
from experience that quality performances would gradually
win converts and she would not be denied. She devoted a
tremendous amount of energy to assure that younger Australian composers would have the opportunity to have their
music performed and would not need to struggle for years as
she had. The work of Sutherland and the Camerata Society
paved the road for an active decade of support for Australian
20th-century music.

In 1965 Margaret Sutherland collaborated with Lady
Maie Casey to write her only chamber opera, The Young Kabbarli. The opera is based on an episode in the life of Daisy
Bates, the pioneer worker among the Aboriginals. The preparation of Aboriginal girls for confirmation into the church is
re-enacted by Goondowell, elder of the tribe. He mistrusts
the ceremony and portrays it in a travesty of mime and dance
drama. Kabbarli, which means grandmother, understands the
ceremony and tries to explain to the monk the problems of
communication in race relations.

The opera was premiered at the festival of contemporary
music in Hobart during the same year in which it was written.
Sutherland scored the work for orchestra and involved mime,
film and passages from Aboriginal music and dance.

In 1972 the Intimate Opera Company received a grant of
$5,600 from the Australian Council for the Arts to present
the opera in Adelaide and Melbourne. The Young Kabbarli
and Margaret Sutherland were honored when the work was
selected as the first Australian opera recorded in Australia.
In addition it was the first recording made in quadraphonic
in the country in 1973.

If struggles are a part of the very nature of artistic
creation, then Sutherland epitomized for future Australians
that no artist should ever give up. She was 70 years old
before she received her first paid commission. In all her
years of composing she had never received more than $160
a year in royalties from performance. She did indeed struggle.

When asked how many compositions she had written during her career she laughed and said, "I've thrown so many
away I have no idea." Sixty-five of her works have been

documented and many of these can be found at the Australia
Music Centre.

During the last few years of her life she did receive
some recognition for her work in behalf of Australian music
that covered a period of over 55 years. At age 72 Margaret
Sutherland was awarded an honorary doctorate of music degree from the University of Melbourne and the following year
a Commonwealth recognition, the prestigious Officer of the
British Empire Order award.

Adele Sztar has produced a beautiful 16mm film titled,
Australian Women Composers. This documentary film looks
at Australian music history through the lives and work of
women composers including Margaret Sutherland, Ester Rofe,
Helen Gifford and Anne Boyd. This 45-minute film is dis-
tributed by Educational Media Australia, 7 Martin Street,
South Melbourne 3205, Australia. The film can be rented in
the United States for about $100 and is well worth the price.

On her 75th birthday Margaret Sutherland was recognized by the state and the institutions of her country which
owed so much to her. The Australian artist was honored in her
own country with a week of celebrations including concerts
of her chamber, orchestral and opera music at the Great Hall
of the National Arts Gallery in Melbourne. It must be noted
that the Melbourne Symphony Orchestra participated in the
celebration the first time in 13 years that the A.B.C. participated in a public tribute to an Australian composer. Among
the remarks made at the celebration were the following by
Dr. H. C. Coombs, then chairman of the Australian Council
for the Arts:

> Dr. Sutherland was one of the first practicing
> artists to proclaim the need for a unified vision of
> the arts. Margaret Sutherland is also in the very
> front ranks of those who ventured to be identified
> unequivocally as a modern Australian composer.
>   We are deeply indebted to Margaret Sutherland
> for her vision and her services to the arts as well
> as for the music she gave us.

Fortunately she lived to be 87 years old and her country
finally realized her great contributions and honored her many
times for her outstanding accomplishments. Perhaps James

Murdock best summed up Margaret Sutherland's career when he wrote, "If Alfred Hill is the Father of Australian music then Margaret Sutherland is the Matriarch."

Selected Works by Margaret Sutherland

Orchestral Music

1938	Pavan.
1939	Prelude and Jig, for strings.
1939	Suite on a Theme of Purcell.
1939	Concertino, for piano and orchestra.
1945	Concerto, for strings.
1945	Rondel.
1946	Adagio, for 2 violins and orchestra.
1947	Threesome, for junior orchestra.
1948	Ballad Overture, for junior orchestra.
1950	Bush Ballad.
1950	The Haunted Hills.
1953	Open Air Piece.
1954	Violin Concerto.
1955	Concerto Grosso.
1958	Outdoor Overture.
1958	Three Temperaments.
1959	Movement.
1961	Concertante, for oboe, strings and percussion.
1962	Fantasy, for violin and orchestra.

Chamber Music

1925	Sonata, for violin and piano, published by J. Alberts and Son.
1934	Trio, for clarinet, viola and piano.
1935	Fantasy Sonatina, for saxophone and piano.
1936	House Quartet, for clarinet, viola, French horn and piano.
1938	Rhapsody, for violin and piano.
1939	String Quartet no. 1.
1942	Sonata, for cello or saxophone and piano.
1944	Ballad and Nocturne, for violin and piano.
1945	Adagio and Allegro Giocoso, for 2 violins and piano.
1949	Sonata, for clarinet or viola and piano
1951	Trio, for oboe and 2 violins, published by J. Alberts and Son.

1953 Contrasts, for 2 violins.
1954 Discussion, string quartet no. 2.
1955 Quartet, for English horn and strings.
1956 Six Bagatelles, for violin and viola.
1957 Sonatina, for oboe or violin and piano, published by J.
         Alberts and Son.
1958 Divertimento, for string trio.
1960 Little Suite, for wind trio.
1960 Fantasy, for violin and piano.
1967 String Quartet no. 3.
1967 Quartet, for clarinet and strings.

Piano Music

1927 Burlesque, for 2 pianos.
1935 Two Chorale Preludes on Bach's Chorales, published by
         J. Alberts and Son.
1937 First Suite, published by J. Alberts and Son.
1937 Miniature Ballet Suite, published by J. Alberts and
         Son.
1939 Miniature Sonata, published by J. Alberts and Son.
1946 Six Profiles.
1956 Sonatina, published by J. Alberts and Son.
1957 Pavan, for 2 pianos, published by J. Alberts and Son.
1957 Canonical Piece, for 2 pianos, published by J. Alberts
         and Son.
1966 Sonata, published by J. Alberts & Son.
1967 Extension.
1968 Chiaroscuro I and II.
1968 Voices I and II.

Choral Music

1939 The Passing, for SATB choir and orchestra.
1966 A Company of Carols, Bassett, Casey, Dobson, Lindsay,
         for SATB choir and piano.

Vocal Music voice and piano unless otherwise indicated

1929 Songs for Children, Martyr.
1930 Three Songs, Thompson, for voice, violin and piano.
1936 Five Songs, Shaw Neilson, Published by J. Alberts &
         Son.

1938   The Orange Tree, Shaw Neilson, for voice, clarinet
           and piano, published by J. Alberts & Son.
1950   Four Blake Songs.
1960   The World and the Child, Wright, for mezzo soprano
           and piano or stringed quartet.
1964   Sequence of Verse into Music, Casey, for speaker,
           flute, viola, and horn.
1967   Six Australian Songs, Wright, published by J. Alberts
           & Son.

Opera

1965   The Young Kabbarli, Casey, in one act.

Addresses of Publishers

J. Albert and Son Pty. Ltd, 7-11 Rangers Road, Newtral
       Bay, NSW 2089, Australia.

Australia Music Centre, 80 George Street, Sydney 2000, Aus-
       tralia.

Discography

The Young Kabbarli, New Opera of South Australia, Patrick
       Thomas, conductor, EMI Q40ASO 7569.
Dithyramb, Australian Youth Orchestra, Sir Bernard Heinze,
       conductor, Philips S/10839/L.
The Haunted Hills, Melbourne Symphony Orchestra, John
       Hopkins, conductor, Festival Disc SFC 800/20.
Concerto Grosso, Sybil Copeland (violin), John Glickman
       (viola), Max Cooke (harpsichord), Strings of Mel-
       bourne Symphony Orchestra (John Hopkins, conduc-
       tor), ABC RRCS/387.
Three Temperaments, Melbourne Symphony Orchestra (John
       Hopkins, conductor), ABC RRCS/145.
Sonata for clarinet and piano, Jack Harrison (clarinet), Stephen
       Dornan (piano), Festival SFC 800/25.
Trio, Jiri Tancibudek (oboe), Sybil Copeland (violin), John
       Glickman (viola), Brolga BXM-02.
Six Bagatelles, Sybil Copeland (violin), John Glickman (violin),
       W & G AL/660.

Addresses of Recording Companies

EMI 301, Castlereagh Street, Sydney 2000, Australia.

Festival Disc Pty. Ltd, Miller Street, Pyrmont, NSW 2009,
Australia.

W & G Records, 17 Radford Road, Reservoir 3073, Australia.

Philips, 529 King Street, West Melbourne, Victoria 3003, Australia.

ABC Recordings, GPO Box 487, Sydney, 2001, Australia.

Brolga Records, out of business.

JOAN TOWER

Composer

"My life is evolving so fast these days it's unbelievable."
These words underscore the level of activity in Joan Tower's
musical life:

> This year alone, there are <u>nine</u> different orchestras
> performing my music and I'll be at all of them! After
> I stopped performing with the Da Capo Chamber
> Players in 1984, (with whom I had been a pianist
> for 15 years), I thought my schedule would be
> so much lighter but (lo and behold) all that perform-
> ing activity has been replaced by attending orches-
> tral performances of my own works. Something I
> couldn't have imagined even three years ago. But
> how lucky can you be? As a result of all this re-
> cent activity, I am commissioned up to 1990 to write
> four concertos and two orchestral pieces.

Tower has received numerous awards and grants throughout her career that are a testament to her creative skills.
She shared the Naumberg Award for Chamber Music as a
member and founder of the Da Capo Chamber Players, received the Academy-Institute Award for $5,000 and a CRI
recording from the American Institute and Academy of Arts
and Letters, four National Endowment of Arts Composers
Fellowships, a Guggenheim and Koussevitzky Foundation Grant,
commissions from the St. Louis Symphony Orchestra, Richard
Stoltzman, Carol Wincenc, Sharon Isbin, Maurice Andre Contemporary Music Society, The American Composers Orchestra,
Florida Orchestra and the Schubert Club. More recently she
had been asked by the Naumburg Foundation to write a
clarinet concerto for the winner of their clarinet competition
who was chosen in December 1985. In 1982 she was named

JOAN TOWER   Photo by
with Zubin Mehta   Kathleen M. Hat

Musician of the Month by <u>High Fidelity/Musical America</u> and
in 1983 WGBH-TV produced a special documentary on her life
for nationwide television. The film won Honorable Mention at
the American Film Festival in 1983. She has won numerous
other honors including a residency at the famous MacDowell
Colony, prizes and commissions from the New York State
Council of the Arts, the Jerome Foundation, the Massachusetts
State Arts Council and the Fromm Foundation, among others.

She was born in 1938, the daughter of Anna Robinson and George Tower in New Rochelle, N.Y. Tower grew up in South America, traveling from town to town because her father was a mining engineer. Perhaps to some degree her musical training suffered as the result of the continual moving, but her father, an amateur violinist from a musical family, realized his daughter was talented and he made sure there was a piano as well as a teacher for Joan wherever they lived. Living in various areas of Bolivia, Peru, and Chile over a period of nine years made it difficult for Tower to develop her musical talents with the same opportunities that were available in the United States. She was very involved in music as a performer but she had never met a composer nor did it occur to her that she could compose until she arrived at Bennington College in 1958. The Bennington years were both fruitful and productive for Tower and she reflects on that period of her life.

> At Bennington I was asked to write a piece and that got me hooked. Henry Brant, Louis Calabro, and Lionel Nowak were my teachers at that time.
> The first piece I ever wrote was performed at Bennington. It was scored for ten instruments and I recorded the performance. I just freaked out when I heard it. Probably vaguely sounded like what I had expected. (It was very much like Ravel's Bolero.)
> I was a composition major and it was wonderful to be there and make music and not just study about it. I made music from eight in the morning until midnight. I composed many pieces and they were all played so I could hear them and learn from them. I played a lot of piano with the students and the faculty and I loved it. I didn't want to leave when the three years were over.

Tower received her master of arts degree from Columbia University where she continued to study composition with Otto Luening, Jack Beeson and Chou Wen-Chung. The same University conferred a doctor of musical arts degree on her when she completed the required studies. She studied composition with Darius Milhaud at Aspen, Colo. and with Wallingford Riegger and Ralph Shapey.

"It may sound weird but I'm a self-taught composer," Joan says. She continues:

What I learned from my composing teachers was outside information. Henry Brant helped me develop
notationally and to think about instruments. Otto
Luening taught me what the world of music was all
about--he's the kind of person that has an overview
that is unbelievable.

But the material that I developed was very much
my own turf and had very little to do with what I
was learning in school or from any of the people I
was studying with.

Tower is the founder of and was pianist, up to 1983,
for the Da Capo Players, a highly acclaimed ensemble special-
izing in contemporary music. Founded in 1969, the ensemble
received the prestigious Naumburg Award for Chamber Music
in 1973. In the past 15 seasons, the group has performed
over 85 new works by contemporary composers, many of them
world premieres. They have recorded on Composers Recordings, Inc. (CRI) and Opus labels the music of Miriam Gideon,
Nancy Chance, Louise Talma, Ursula Mamlok, Shulamit Ran
as well as Tower's own compositions. Reflecting on the work
of the Da Capo Players she says:

I view Da Capo as my musical education. I wanted
to make music from both a playing and a compositional point of view. I couldn't wait around for
people to play my music so I formed my own group
which was the outgrowth of the Greenwich House
series. The instrumentation of the group just hap-
pened--I don't think I ever consciously thought of
certain instruments. I wanted to keep it small so
we would be mobile, and do between fifteen and
thirty concerts per year.

The membership of the Da Capo Players has
changed only twice over the years. Very few chamber groups come to mind that can earn a livelihood
just concertizing. Members must either teach or
free lance to financially survive.

The Da Capo Players are in residence at Bard
College so it is a fantastic experience for them, the
students, and myself. I have made a very difficult
decision--after fifteen wonderful years with the
group I have decided that I will no longer perform
publicaly with them. I need to devote my energies
to composing. I love to compose and it takes me a

long period of time to write a work, and a lot of un-
divided attention.

Part of Tower's work as pianist-composer with the Da
Capo Players consisted of writing a solo piece for each instru-
mentalist in the group. She feels a strong need for a dialogue between the composer and the performer which can
only strenghthen the contemporary music scene. She said,
"After all the Da Capo Players have performed together for
years I knew their techniques, what they like and what they
are good at."

Members of the Da Capo Players has changed only
slightly over a period of 15 years. One original member,
Helen Harbison, died and another member decided on a career
change. The group includes: Patricia Spencer, flute; Laura
Flax, clarinet; Joel Lester, violin; Andre Emelianoff, cello;
and Tower, piano.

One of Tower's solo pieces for a member of the Da
Capo Players was Platinum Spirals, for solo violin, written
for Joel Lester. It was written in memory of her father who
had spent his career as an engineer. Tower did some studying of metals and their characteristics and found that platinum was very malleable and stretchable and this became the
basis for the idea she wanted to project in the piece. According to Tower, the piece is a musical representation of
flexibility of the metal and therefore the piece covers the
entire range of the violin from the lowest register to the
very highest register. The Baltimore Sun, May 16, 1977
reviewed by Elliott W. Galkin (partial):

> Joan Tower's Platinum Spirals for solo violin, another
> high point of the program, is of a different and
> more overtly romantic musical world: neo-Berg-
> like, with all the lyricism of a baroque 'through-
> composed' rhapsody.
>
> Its materials seem fresh and personal in exploita-
> tion of elements reminiscent of those of Viennese
> expressionism. Yet it seems to follow no doctrinaire
> system.
>
> Its beauty of line, and pliancy of character, with
> its elegant contrasts of the different pitch registers,
> are individually crafted, intimately and evolving
> spontaneously. This is an interesting addition to
> the literature for violin.

It was played with warmth and obvious stylistic
empathy by Mr. Lester, his bow arm subtle, his use
of vibrato varied, his intonation secure, even in
the most jagged linear moments.

Platinum Spirals was performed at Tanglewood's Contemporary Music Festival in 1984 by Joel Smirnoff who at the
time was a member of the faculty at the Berkshire Music
Center. One reviewer described the piece by writing, "It
sounded full of intense private passion." Many of us in the
audience agreed with him.

Platinum Spirals has been recorded on CRI 517 by Joel
Smirnoff. The disc is the result of Tower being honored by
the American Academy and Institute of Arts and Letters Composer Award which provides a cash award of five thousand
dollars and a recording. Other pieces on the all Tower recording are Wings, Noon/Dance, and Amazon.

When Tower wrote Wings, for solo clarinet, for Laura
Flax, they had performed together for over eight years and
she knew all of Flax's exceptional capabilities on the instrument. Tower says, "Flax is an incredibly smooth player,
with extraordinary skills. I was looking for an idea to help
me express what I wanted to write and I was inspired by the
enormous flying/gliding capabilities of the falcon. When I
called Laura and told her of my idea she said, 'My god, have
you gone bananas?' " Whatever Flax's initial reactions might
have been she has performed Wings on numerous occasions
to the acclaim of the reviewing critics and has recorded the
piece on CRI 517.

Blakeman Welch, writing for Musical Notes in the Downtowner, Winnipeg on March 9-15, 1983 on the Da Capo Players concert at the Winnipeg Art Gallery (excerpt):

... The piece which made the most impact for me
was Wings, written by the ensemble's pianist, Joan
Tower. Laura Flax, for whom it was written, gave
a dazzling performance on solo clarinet. Most impressive was the dynamic switch in registers which
gave a Bach-like impression of part writing, as the
melodic line switched from high register to the low
chalumeau register and back again.

Tower's music has changed over the years and it has
been a slow evolution. Her style has evolved from virtuosic
serial pieces to equally brilliant but somewhat more Romantic
works. Pieces written before 1974 rely heavily on serial and
other more complex structural procedures which she refers
to as her early compositional "maps" (guides to laying out
her music). All of the pieces composed have nondescriptive
or abstract titles such as Hexachords, and Movements for
Flute and Piano, among others. According to Tower there
was a one-year (1974-75) hiatus between the writing of Breakfast Rhythms I & II. To her there is a different style that
evolves within the two movements although they are much
the same piece. "The first movement is a lean, agile work
which uses a hexachord or six notes, as the principal mo-
tive, and features various pedal points by the solo clarinet
and five instruments. The second movement is like Debussy
in a way; it's more colorful and has many pentatonic scales
and whole steps in it." The work has had numerous performances and excerpts from reviews written almost a decade
apart. Some examples follow.

Music Quarterly, LX, No. 4, October 1974, pages 625-
632, written by Gregory Levin for the ninth annual conference
of the American Society of University Composers in New York
City:

> Breakfast Rhythms is a stylish and elegant work,
> marked by great sectional clarity and nuance. Vari-
> ous transpositions of a single harmonic cell articulate
> phrase and sectional division, clarify the formal
> design of the one-movement work and give it unity.
> Piano and vibraphone announce the cell at the begin-
> ning of the work: the B-flat clarinet then restates
> the cell in an octatonic transposition. The pitches
> of this cell--transposition (G#/A/B/) return as a
> vertical sonority to give closure to the first section.
> In the interior sections of the work Ms. Tower at-
> tains great variety by distorting the proportions of
> the opening cell. The half-step, whole-step fragment
> reduces to a three-note fragment on the other ex-
> treme. By instrumental overlap and phrase exten-
> sion, these distortions result in variety of harmonic
> situations, including whole-tone clusters on the one
> extreme, and chromatic clusters on the other extreme.
> This procedure sets up one of the climactic moments

in the piece, in which the accompanying tutti presents two whole-tone trichords which together make up a chromatic hexachord.

The use of rhymes and partial rhymes and transpositions of the basic cell sets up a final harmonic witticism, a "wrong-key recapitulation." Almost at the end of the work the opening trichord appears vertically, and the clarinet, punning on the whole-step lower-neighbor-tone figure characteristic of the opening, returns to the gesture of the opening, but starts on A instead of B.

In 1983 Robert Black's New Music Group performed Tower's Breakfast Rhythms I & II at Carnegie Recital Hall. John Rockwell writing for the New York Times on Feb. 17, 1983 (Excerpt):

> ... The rest of the program was contemporary, and the best here was Jean Tower's Breakfast Rhythms I & II (1975), which ended the evening. These studies for clarinet (Laura Flax) and five other instrumentalists seem curiously diverse. The first is constricted, but the second opens up luxurious, full of drama and color. [Copyright © 1983 by The New York Times Company. Reprinted by permission.]

Breakfast Rhythms I & II has been recorded by the Da Capo Players on CRI 345, a listening must for all music lovers. (CRI recordings are of far more historical and aesthetic significance than a umpteenth recording of a 19th-century work since CRI brings to the listener the opportunity to hear music written by living composers.) Excerpt from Wilma Salisbury's review in the Cleveland Plain Dealer, May 8, 1977:

> Her Hexachords develops new techniques idiomatic to the solo flute into a clear structure of pitches, registers, timbres, dynamics, articulations and vibrato speeds.
>
> Despite the strictness of Miss Tower's compositional approach, her pieces are attractive, easily comprehensible to the listener and musically rewarding to the performer.

In honor of their 10th anniversary the Da Capo Players, with support by the New York State Council of the Arts, the

Meet the Composer program and the Fromm Foundation commissioned several distinguished 20th-century composers to write special pieces in tribute to the group's name. The commission requested that each composer work into their pieces the idea of Da Capo, a musical term which requires the repeat of some of the music already played and usually from the beginning.

The world premieres were played at a concert at Alice Tully Hall at Lincoln Center on March 23, 1980. Works included Joseph Schwantner's Wind, Willow, Whisper..., Shulamit Ran's Private Games, Charles Wuorinen's Joan (dedicated to Tower as founder and pianist of the group), George Perle's Scherzo, Philip Glass' (arranged by Moran) Modern Love Waltz and Joan Tower's Petroushskates. All of the compositions have been included on The Da Capo Players Celebrate Their Tenth Anniversary, CRI record SD-411.

Tower acknowledges strong influences by Beethoven and Stravinsky and she paid homage to the latter with Petroushskates. Robert Commanday writing for the San Francisco Chronicle on Feb. 7, 1982, said of the quintet, "It's an upbeat piece by a performer for performers, live and purposeful."

More recently, Tower has concentrated increasingly on the temporal aspects of music; in this regard, Messiaen's Quartet for the End of Time has been a seminal influence. Tower composes slowly, perhaps only one piece a year. Her modest but highly regarded output of chamber music has been performed with increasing frequency by leading chamber ensembles and most of her works have been recorded. This is an impressive accomplishment for a talented musician.

Tower said, "I've been in chamber music all my life and I know it inside out. But I was continually challenged by my colleagues and Imre Pallo, music director of the Hudson Valley Philharmonic, to write a transcription of my chamber piece, Amazon (1976) (scored for flute, clarinet, violin, cello and piano) for orchestra." Since orchestral writing was a genre she had no experience writing for, she followed her "time test route" of carrying on a dialogue with musicians who performed with orchestras. Again, it was important to Tower that composers be a living musician to performers. She was correct as evidenced by the success that has followed the premiere of her first orchestral writing Amazon II.

High Fidelity/Musical America, March 1980, written by
Neil Gould:

> Joan Tower, a young American composer of impres-
> sive gifts, has made a full orchestral setting of her
> quintet Amazon II, a tone poem that reflects the
> shifting moods of that mighty force of nature. The
> work in its original form was scored for violin, flute,
> viola, cello, and piano and was performed at Vassar
> College by the Da Capo Players, a chamber group
> founded by Miss Tower that has met with warm cri-
> tical reception. The conversion from chamber work
> to full orchestral palette was made at the urging of
> Imre Pallo, music director of the Hudson Valley
> Philharmonic and it was under his direction that
> the work had its premiere last November 10 at the
> Kingston Center for the Performing Arts.
>
> The aspect of Miss Tower's composition that most
> impresses is her ability to create a structurally
> cogent and moving work out of motivic materials
> that are concise and arresting to the ear. A basic
> melodic fragment is introduced in reduced orchestra-
> tion at the very beginning of the work and returns
> in various guises throughout its course. The motive
> is varied in its association with the shifting moods
> of the river, and is combined with groups of sonori-
> ties that are used as the structural underpinning of
> the work.
>
> Miss Tower has not yet found a completely ori-
> ginal voice with respect to orchestration. Early
> Stravinsky, Messaien, Mussorgsky, and Bartok are
> her models, and no doubt her original bent of mind
> will produce a more personal statement in the future.
> If there is a weakness in this work at all, it involves
> the transformation of triplets originally conceived
> for the piano into string figures. At the tempo
> demanded by this score these figures do not work
> and the result is a blurring of the rest of the score.
> But this is minor. Joan Tower is an artist of sta-
> ture and a welcome new voice in the developing
> canon of American orchestral composition.

Tower was later commissioned by the American Composers
Orchestra and her work Sequoia was premiered with Dennis
Russell Davies conducting in 1981. In 1982 Zubin Mehta

chose Sequoia for the New York Philharmonic series and also
as a representative American work on the televised program
that the Philharmonic played in honor of United Nations Day.
Headlines in one New York paper read, "Mehta helps Tower
tower." Joan explains:

> I wanted a big image for the Sequoia and started to
> look at nature. I was inspired by the majestic Cali-
> fornia redwoods. The piece is about a balancing-
> act, pedal points that go on each side. A lot of my
> music has been developed on this idea which I have
> been working on for a number of years. I was try-
> ing to figure out why these trees are so impressive?
> When you consider the height of them they defy the
> balance of nature. the trees are majestic, very
> quiet and elegant. Sequoia suggests power-grandeur.

Defying the rules of contemporary music programming,
the piece continues to have successive performances each
year. Dennis Davies took Sequoia to the West Coast for
several performances with the San Francisco Symphony.
Leonard Slatkin and the St. Louis Symphony Orchestra opened
their 1984-85 season with a performance and recorded it on
Nonesuch 9-79118-F. He also conducted it in his guest appearance with the Minnesota Orchestra and the National Symphony at the Kennedy Center in Washington D.C. Other orchestras to play this work were the Omaha Symphony, Bruce
Hangen, conductor and the Eugene Symphony, William Mc-
Glaughlin, conductor.

Allan Ulrich wrote about the West Coast premiere of
Sequoia in the San Francisco Examiner on Nov. 25, 1982:

> HALLELUJAH! A contemporary orchestral piece that
> an alert audience can experience without yawning,
> scratching its collective head in bewilderment or
> groaning under the weight of tired academic formulas.
>   That rare honor belongs to Joan Tower's Sequoia
> given its West Coast premiere at last night's San
> Francisco Symphony subscription concert under guest
> conductor Dennis Russell Davies, his only week with
> the full orchestra this season before moving on to
> the Symphony's New and Unusual Music series next
> Friday. Davies has devoted the remainder of the
> program to the first Symphony performance of Richard

Strauss' 1945 <u>Oboe Concerto</u> (with the Swiss virtuoso
Heinz Holliger in the solo spot) and Berlioz's <u>Harold
in Italy</u>, featuring principal violist Geraldine Walther.
   The best news came from the orchestra itself,
incisive and alert to Davies' style, which leans toward the volatile in virtually any repertoire. The
situation was worlds removed from the mushy, strings-
dipped-in-molasses response elicited last week by
other, and considerably lesser, conductorial hands.
   And Tower's piece, a formidable exercise, requires
nothing less than edge-of-the-seat playing from any
orchestra. <u>Sequoia</u> arrives in the Bay Area in such
a hailstorm of pre-publicity, that a bit of skepticism
is bound to color one's response.
   Judging from a tape of the 1981 <u>Sequoia</u> premiere
with the American Composers Orchestra, Davies led
an appreciably more translucent and compelling performance last night. Bassoonist Stephen Paulson's
work called for special commendation, and the 44-
year-old composer was on hand at Davies Symphony
Hall to accept a warm ovation.

   Tower's <u>Music for Cello and Orchestra</u> received its
world premiere in the opening concert of the Y Chamber Orchestra in October 1984. Andre Emelianoff, the Y Chamber
Orchestra's principal cellist, was soloist under the direction
of Gerard Schwarz. Conductor Schwarz and the Y Chamber
Orchestra opened the first program with two American works,
the <u>Notturno</u>, by Charles Tomlinson Griffes and the Joan
Tower's piece. An excerpt from a review written by Bernard
Holland for the <u>New York Times</u> on Oct. 2, 1983, read:

   Joan Tower's <u>Music for Cello and Orchestra</u>--with
   its angular sense of drama, bright primary colors
   and edge-of-the-chair intensity--had an altogether
   different feel. Miss Tower's piece, to borrow a
   phrase from Gertrude Stein, does not repeat, but
   insists. Repetitive figures in shifting instrumental
   colors begin it, but the movement is constantly
   altered by subtle changes of rhythm and phrase
   length.
      Andre Emelianoff, the Y Chamber Symphony's
   principal cellist, played the brutally wearing part
   with obvious enthusiasm and evident success. Mr.
   Emelianoff's part is high in oratory and ardent

declamation, though in the slower middle section
there were some delicate exchanges in harmonics
between his cello and Syoko Aki's solo violin.

At the end, Miss Tower's colors turned even
brighter and more fierce--with high-pitched wind
and percussion chords and evocative uses of mallet
percussion instruments. Music for Cello and Orchestra, a busy, tense, and very effective piece,
is dedicated to Mr. Emelianoff, Mr. Schwarz, and
the Y Chamber Symphony. This was its first performance. [Copyright © 1983 by The New York
Times Company. Reprinted by permission.]

Leonard Slatkin, conductor of the St. Louis Symphony
Orchestra, chose Tower's Sequoia as part of the festive program to open the 105th season at Powell Symphony Hall in
September 1984. Time magazine rated the St. Louis Symphony Orchestra second only to the Chicago Symphony Orchestra in the United States.

Slatkin liked the piece Sequoia so much that he and
the orchestra recorded it on the Nonesuch label, making the
work more permanent. "When I like something, I really push
it," Slatkin said. "Tower has a unique talent and writes like
nobody else." In his guest appearance, Slatkin conducted
the work with the Washington National Symphony Orchestra
and the Minnesota Orchestra. At a future date he plans to
conduct the piece with the Chicago Symphony Orchestra.

When Sequoia was performed by the Eugene Symphony
Orchestra conducted by William McGlaughin Feb. 16, 1985
Karen DuPriest the music critic for The Register-Guard wrote
(excerpt):

Sequoia is as massive as its namesake. It is a fe-
rociously difficult piece to play and demands rigid
concentration from performers and listeners alike.
Pulsing tones from the brass and woodwinds, hollow
percussive patterns and disjointed string melodies
move together in music of intense power.

The St. Louis Symphony commissioned Joan Tower to
write a new work for them. With her new schedule, she is
no longer playing piano professionally, and now teaches only
one day per week at Bard College, so she can now spend

her time composing about eight hours a day in her Manhattan
loft. Starting in September 1985, Tower will be composer-in-
residence with the St. Louis Symphony Orchestra.

Joan Tower is intensely dedicated to her support of
living composers. She is not afraid to be outspoken in situations where the composers are not treated as normal musical
beings. She is a strong advocate of a closer musical understanding between composer, performer and listener and has
spent countless hours as an active participant on numerous
boards and panels that foster and support contemporary music.

Her participation on the following boards and panels
attest to her unselfish concern for contemporary music and
for the people who compose it: The National Endowment for
the Arts, panel member for New Music Performance, Composers, Policy Panel, and Multi Presenters; New York Council
on the Arts, Music Panel; National Public Radio, Radio-visions
Project; Minnesota Composers Forum, Jury for Composers
Awards; Massachusetts State Arts Council, Jury for Composers
Awards; B.M.I Young Composers Award Jury; and more recently Chamber Music America and the N.Y. Foundation of
the Arts. Tower has been involved with Meet The Composer,
a primary composer funding and advocacy organization, since
its founding in 1974. She is also a member of the board of
the American Music Center, American Composers Orchestra
and the Fromm Foundation Advisory Council.

She is persistent in her quest that audiences and performers be in touch with composers. To her communication
is essential. She is a formidable music panelist who has won
the respect and admiration of her panel colleagues and fellow
musicians.

United Nations Radio presented <u>Women</u>, a program focusing on people, events and issues which affect lives and circumstances of women around the world. One segment featured Joan Tower and her orchestral work <u>Sequoia</u> performed
by the American Composers Orchestra. Tower responded to
an interview question during the program which asked whether
she had found it difficult to gain acceptance in the field of
composing where so few women worked at all, let alone have
some sort of prominence. Her answer:

The composer today is not as important as the

performer is. What you see on television, what's visible is the performer, the superstar, the Perlmans, the Pavarottis.... Then the woman composer is on the edge of that; I mean they're even smaller yet because there are so few of them, there are so few models around and I feel very, very lucky to be given these kinds of major performances because it sets an opening for other women. It becomes less of an event if one woman does it.

Joan Tower is a remarkable young composer as well as an articulate spokesperson for support of contemporary music. Few artists are willing to give of their time and energy for the development and promotion of other artists. The continued expression of her creative talents will eventually determine her final place on the roster of leading contemporary composers but her position at the present time is prestigious.

Selected Compositions of Joan Tower

Orchestral

1979 Amazon II, orchestra, published by Schirmer/AMP.
1981 Sequoia, orchestra, published by Schirmer/AMP.
1982 Amazon III, chamber orchestra, published by Schirmer/ AMP.
1984 Music for Cello and Orchestra, published by Schirmer/ AMP.
1985 Island Rhythms, on Rental AMP, Orchestra.
1985- Piano Concerto, Symphonic Work, Clarinet Concerto,
  89 Trumpet Concerto, Flute Concerto (future compositions).

Chamber/Instrumental

1963 Percussion Quartet, revision 1969, published by Music for Percussion, Inc.
1965 Brimset, 2 flutes, 2 percussion (MS).
1968 Movements for Flute and Piano, published by American Society of University Composers.
1970 Prelude for Five Players, flute, oboe (or violin), clarinet, bassoon (or cello), piano (MS).
1971 Six Variations for Cello (MS).
1972 Hexachords, solo flute, American Composers Edition (A.C.A.).

1974- Breakfast Rhythms I & II, clarinet and five instruments
75   (flute or piccolo, violin, cello, percussion, piano)
       Schirmer/AMP.
1976   Platinum Spirals, solo violin, published by Schirmer/
       AMP.
1976   Black Topaz, piano and six instruments Sonatina (Dis-
       tribution thru G. Schirmer).
1977   Amazon II, flute, clarinet, violin, cello, piano (Schirmer/
       AMP).
1977   Red Garnet Waltz, solo piano. C. F. Peters (Waltz col-
       lection).
1980   Petroushskates, quintet, G. Schirmer/AMP.
1981   Wings, solo clarinet. G. Schirmer/AMP.
1982   Noon Dance, sextet for flute, clarinet, violin, cello,
       piano, percussion, G. Schirmer/AMP.
1983   Snow Dreams, flute and guitar, G. Schirmer/AMP.
1983   Fantasy for Clarinet & Piano, G. Schirmer/AMP.
1985   Relojas, for solo guitar.

Addresses of Publishers

Principal publisher: G. Schirmer/Associated Music, 866 Third
       Ave., New York, NY 10022.

Some individual works published by: American Composers
       Editions, 170 W 74th St., New York, NY 10023. C. F.
       Peters, 373 Park Ave. South, New York, NY 10016.
       A.S.U.C. Study Score Series, c/o American Music
       Center.

Discography

Prelude for Five Players, Da Capo Players, CRI 302.
Hexachords, Pat Spencer, flute, CRI 354.
Breakfast Rhythms, Da Capo Players, CRI 354.
Movements for Flute and Piano, Pat Spencer, flute, Joan
       Tower, piano, Advance FGR-24S.
Red Garnet Waltz, Alan Feinberg, Piano, Nonesuch D-79011.
Black Topaz, Hodkinson, Ensemble, Pro Viva (in progress)
Snow Dreams, Carol Wincenc, fl, and Sharon Isbin, guitar,
       Pro Arte (in progress).
Wings, Noon Dance, Platinum Spirals, and Amazon with Col-
       lage & Da Capo as the CRI performers, CRI-517.

Sequoia, St. Louis Symphony Orchestra, Leonard Slatkin,
    Conductor, Nonesuch 9-79118-F.

Addresses

Advance Recordings, P.O. Box 17072, Tucson, AR 85710.

Composers Recordings, Inc., 170 West 74th Street, New York,
    NY 10023.

Nonesuch, 9229 Sunset Blvd., Los Angeles, CA 90069.

Pro Arte, 14025 23rd Avenue-North, Minneapolis, MN 55441.

Pro Viva, c/o Eastman School of Music, Rochester, NY.

GILLIAN WHITEHEAD

Composer, Teacher

When Gillian Whitehead graduated from the University of Wellington, New Zealand with a bachelor of music degree with honors in 1963 it was rare in her country for anyone to make a career in composing, especially a woman. It was necessary for her to leave New Zealand to pursue further graduate studies in composition because then there were no graduate programs in the country's universities.

In less than 20 years Whitehead established her credentials as a composer of distinct talent and individuality with a large number of significant compositions that have been performed, recorded, and broadcast on several continents.

Whitehead's first public performance was a choral work, Missa Brevis, performed by the Leonine Consort and directed by Charles Colman in 1965. The internationally recognized scholar and critic Roger Covell was in attendance for this performance. Some 20 years later he recalled how accurately that occasion promised that she would become a composer of stature. Dr. Covell was the first person to bring to my attention the music of the talented Whitehead. Part of the Missa Brevis has been recorded by the Dorian Singers on Kiwi record SLD-56 and published by Music Dei Gloria.

The following is an excerpt from Roger Covell's review published in the Sydney Morning Herald on April 24, 1965:

> Gillian Whitehead's Missa Brevis easily rose to the severe challenge of justifying its presence in an otherwise all Bach program. This young New Zealand composer now studying in Sydney obviously has a rare understanding of how to write for concerted

281

GILLIAN WHITEHEAD   Photo by
                                         Iona Chalmers

voices; everything she calculated on paper worked
in practice in this tenderly beautiful performance.

Gillian Whitehead was born in Hamilton, New Zealand in
1941 but spent most of her earlier life in Whangarei where
her musical parents Marjorie and Ivan Whitehead worked.
Her mother was a pianist and Gillian remembers as a child
being played to sleep every night by her mother. She said,
"Memories of Schubert, Beethoven and Bach have some quality
for me which is very strong. It is as if for me music is the
first language I learnt." Her father also taught music and
directed choirs. In the 1950s and 1960s he imported music
of all the classical repertoire as well as contemporary works
including those of Pierre Boulez and Karlheinz Stockhausen.
Whitehead was surrounded by music from a very early age
and always found the musical world of her parents a lot more
real than the world of school. She was aware even as a
child of what was happening on the musical scene and this
proved to be a valuable experience for a talented young girl
living on a geographically isolated island.

She studied piano, sang in choirs and played the violin.
In 1959 she entered the University of Auckland to study
arts but changed her degree to music, which included some
composition taught by Ron Tremain.

After completing her bachelor's degree at the Victoria
University in Wellington, she went to Sydney, Australia to
study with composer Peter Sculthorpe. Sculthorpe taught in
the department of music at Sydney University at a time when
a great interest in contemporary music was developing in the
country. For Whitehead, Australia was an exciting place to
be and she completed her master's degree with honors at the
university. During this time several of her compositions
were performed, such as the Missa Brevis, and they were
well received.

Whitehead composed Fantasia On Three Notes in 1966
on a commission by Tessa Birnie for the Australian Society
for Keyboard Music. It was premiered over Radio Turkey in
1967 by Tessa Birnie, recorded by her on Kiwi, SLD-19 and
published by Wai-te-ata Press. When pianist Birnie played
Fantasia On Three Notes at the Phillips Collection in the
United States the program was reviewed by Charles Crowder
for The Washington Post on Oct. 2, 1967 (partial):

The Whitehead piece is quixotic in mood, shifting in
sonorities and in the process using the keyboard
quite adroitly. It appeared to fall into a three-part
form and, in the context of such shifting sounds
returning to repeat, left an initial impression of
going on about three minutes too long. It was a
toss-up as to which was more interesting, the piece
or Miss Birnie's superlative playing.

Whitehead met Peter Maxwell Davies in Australia and
realized that his approach to analysis and self-discipline was
something that she needed. She went to the University of
Adelaide, where Davies was in residence, and completed the
most intense 10-week period of work she had ever undertaken.
It was here that she decided that she could make it as a contemporary composer. She said:

> Ron Tremain and Peter Maxwell Davies taught me
> the craft of music and some of their experiences
> obviously rubbed off. I admired Davies' music and
> his stringent craftsmanship and knew that was what
> I needed to study. At the time I could write a
> short piece of music and write another short piece
> of music but I needed to work toward longer time
> spans and I needed to better understand how to
> use my ideas. Peter Maxwell Davies helped me
> tremendously during my studies with him in Australia
> and when he left to go back to England he invited
> me to study with him there.

In 1967 Whitehead went to England to work and study
with Davies, who tutored her over the next two years, meeting occasionally to review her scores. He would look at the
scores objectively and analytically and make suggestions.
She said, "when I found myself totally knotted-up with a
particular piece he would throw me a life-line. He was excellent in finding the problem and helping me to understand
and develop my ideas."

Pakuru, scored for flute, clarinet, viola, cello, percussion and voice, was composed in 1967 by Whitehead to the
text of a love poem by Hone Tuwhare. The work was premiered by Mary Thomas with the Pierrot Players conducted
by Peter Maxwell Davies at the Berlin Akademie der Kunst
in 1968. One music critic wrote, "... the musical support

for the text, which is [as] mystically erotic as the Song of
Solomon became orgasmic, sultry and exotic."

A grant from the New Zealand Arts Council in 1968
and again in 1970 enabled Whitehead to spend a considerable
period of time in Portugal and Italy.   The grants permitted
her economic freedom to use all of her energy to compose.
This was a very productive period of time for Whitehead with
several of her pieces premiered by the Fires of London conducted by Peter Maxwell Davies.

She wrote her prize-winning string quartet, Te Ahua,
Te Atarangi, in 1970.   A string-quartet competition was sponsored by the New Zealand Broadcasting Company and the Australian Performance Rights Association with the cooperation
of the New Zealand Chamber Federation.   Thirty composers
submitted their works and Whitehead's quartet won the first
prize of $600.   The sponsors of this competition commissioned
Whitehead to write a chamber piece Whakatau-ki which she
scored for male voice, piccolo/flute/alto flute, oboe, bass
clarinet, horn, trumpet, trombone, violin, viola, cello, double
bass and percussion.   The work was recorded for NZBC by
Leslie Fyson and a wind ensemble conducted by William Southgate in 1974.

Te Tangi a Apakura for string orchestra was written in
1975 and first performed by the New Zealand Sinfonia conducted by Stephen Estall at New Zealand House in 1976.   The
performers were mainly New Zealand musicians who lived in
London.   Whitehead's piece was compared with Diversions for
String Orchestra.   Music critic Max Harrison credited Gillian's
Te Tangi a Apakura as the best piece on the concert program
and praised her ability to create a work, "so that mass and
line, colour and geometry, each heighten the effect of the
other."

During 1976 Whitehead went back to New Zealand for
the first time in 9 years.   She spent several months in her
home country composing, lecturing and attending concerts.
She has since made other visits home and reflects on those
experiences:

> I have written a lot of works that have Maori titles
> and the Maori culture has been a significant influence
> on my work.   There is not a literal drawing on

Maori music but I'm not totally convinced that there
isn't quite a bit of Maori there somewhere.

I feel very much that I belong in New Zealand
because the Maori part of me goes back further
than 1642. I think somewhere there are roots. I
wonder to what extent the fact that I write music
at all has something to do with that Maori background.
Perhaps its as simple as that.

My mother quoted a letter to me which I had
written when I was seventeen in which I said, 'I
want to be a composer. The kind of music I want
to write has something of the structure of Dufay,
the orchestration of Webern and a kind of Debussian
approach to harmony.' This was very much like I
was writing ten to fifteen years later.

In 1978, Northern Arts, the largest regional Arts
Council in England, inaugurated its first composer-in-residence
program with Gillian Whitehead as the two year recipient.
Her salary was 5000 pounds per year, quite enough to live
on in England during that time. In addition 2000 pounds
was available if the recipient wished further commissions.
The grant stipulated that Whitehead had to live somewhere
in northern England, and she could teach up to one day a
fortnight at the University of Newcastle of which she was a
Fellow. There were no other requirements. This grant probably the most valuable residence in the country, provided a
tremendous experience for the young Whitehead. In 2 years
she wrote 10 pieces and found that a life writing music full
time was totally satisfying. Most of the pieces she wrote during this period and over the next 10 years had some application of the magic square-idea, a principle which she had discovered for herself. She explains her work with the magic-
square ideas as follows:

> I continued using and adapting it in my own way,
> gradually simplifying my style. There was some-
> thing marvelous and very satisfying in the propor-
> tion of it, the balances and coincidences that just
> happened out of the various squares; the great
> variety of applications I was able to get out of them
> sometimes, for instance deriving every pitch from
> them, sometimes deriving only generative pitches
> and textural duration from them, sometimes letting
> the material from the squares assume its natural

proportions, sometimes forcing it into different shapes, or breaking it down, or breaking it up. Sometimes, as the Opera <u>Tristan and Iseult</u>, using their extra-structural connotations--battle scenes based on the square of Mars (nos. 1-25) love scenes on the square of Venus (nos. 1-49) and so on.

When Whitehead was asked to write an opera she found that it was a form that really excited her. She was especially interested in the interaction of characters, against a social background rather than considering a single character in isolation, which seemed to be the prevalent form of theater music at that time. Her first opera, <u>Tristan and Iseult</u>, a 65-minute music-theater piece with Malcolm Crowthers and Michael Hill as co-librettists, received its world premiere at the Auckland Festival of Opera in 1978. It was the first published opera in New Zealand. L.C.M. Saunders review was published in the <u>New Zealand Herald</u> in April 1978:

> The world premiere of <u>Tristan and Iseult</u>, an opera by New Zealand-born composer Gillian Whitehead, is one of the most significant musical events of this year's Auckland Festival.
>
> It took place at the Maidment Theatre last night, where the audience was warmly appreciative, though smaller than so notable an occasion warranted.
>
> In his <u>Tristan and Isolde</u> Wagner said the last word in sensuous romantic expression of the medieval Cornish story. The interest last night was to see what Gillian Whitehead would do with it a century later.
>
> Her achievement can be hailed with acclaim. As was to be expected, her approach is the antithesis of Wagner's musically and dramatically.
>
> In 13 concise scenes her story (the libretto is by Malcolm Crowthers and Michael Hill) covers much more ground in incidents, and is infinitely more economical in its musical material.
>
> It is all of a piece, an artistic whole that holds its grip of interest and atmosphere throughout the hour it lasts.
>
> Provided one approaches this 20th-century opera with an open mind, it can hardly fail to appeal, so imaginative are the touches of Rosalind Clark's production, in the simple yet amply effective setting,

the lighting, the costuming, and William Southgate's firm grasp of the music.

The orchestral score is a model of economy. A single instrument can graphically set up a mood, and, though the idiom has the contemporary tang, it blends most aptly with all the movement and mime on stage.

The action is divided between the singers, Graeme Wall and Jane Manning in the title roles, splendid vocalists both Roger Wilson (King Mark), Robert Oliver (Narrator), those who mime the story, and a pair of puppeteers.

The singing follows a beautifully plastic line, sometimes reminiscent of extended plainchant or very free recitative, sometimes developing into true lyricism, and always lying agreeably for the singers. [Reproduced by permission of the New Zealand Herald, Auckland.]

In 1979 Gillian Whitehead was awarded the Australian Performance Rights Association Award, a silver scroll, for her contribution to New Zealand music for Tristan and Iseult.

While Whitehead was composer-in-residence at Northern Arts, the New Zealand born poet, Fleur Adcock, became writer-in-residence and they worked together on Hotspur, the first of several collaborations. The piece is scored for clarinet/bass clarinet, violin, viola, cello, percussion and soprano voice. It was commissioned for soprano Margaret Field and the ensemble Gemini by Musicon with funds from the Northern Arts. The premiere performance was given in Durham in 1981 and conducted by Peter Wiegold with Margaret Field.

There were a series of five linked performances, three in the North and two in London, with one as the official presentation for Waitangi Day, New Zealand's National Holiday. The New Zealand Department of Foreign Affairs commissioned a backdrop and costume design from a leading New Zealand Painter, Gretchen Albrecht, who had done a series of panels, now on permanent display at the New Zealand National Gallery, as the backdrop for Tristan, and toured that as well. With five consecutive performances, rare for a piece of music, a high and exciting standard of performance was achieved.

The following are program notes on Hotspur:

> The piece concerns Harry Hotspur, one of the power-
> ful Northumbrian Percy family, and his involvement
> in the siege of Newcastle, the subsequent battle of
> Otterburn (in August, 1388), through the eyes of
> his wife, Elizabeth Mortimer (not Kate, as in Shake-
> speare's Henry IV Pt. I), and the text, except for
> the central mediative section and certain prophetic
> sections, is in ballad form.
>
> Writing Hotspur, not far from Otterburn in wild,
> high moorland, I became very aware of the effect
> of both the climate and the way of life on the quality
> of life in fourteenth century Northumbria. The cli-
> mate is sometimes benign, but often harsh or treach-
> erous, and until after the Scottish/English alliance,
> there was constant skirmishing between the Scots
> and the English, and opportunist cattle raiding be-
> tween the various feuding families. Something of
> the surroundings, the austerity, the sounds and
> silences, has coloured the pieces.
>
> Gretchen Albrecht's banners reflect some of the
> ballad's imagery. The central banners depict the
> Percy symbol the crescent moon; the silver one
> represents moonlight, the red one violence, battle,
> blood, and the blue one stands for Elizabeth herself.
>
> Hotspur falls into five sections: (I) Introductory
> ballad. (II) The siege of Newcastle. (III) Eliza-
> beth's meditation the night before the battle. (IV)
> The battle of Otterburn. (V) The death of Hotspur.

When Hotspur was performed in Sydney, Australia, with
Meg Chilcott, soprano and Graham Hair conducting the Conservatorium Contemporary Ensemble, Roger Covell reviewed
the performance for The Sydney Morning Herald, 1981 (excerpt):

> Hotspur deserves to win further admirers for this
> distinctive and gifted composer. She has a genuine
> creative power, one that sets up lingering reson-
> ances in the listeners' imagination ... she has the
> rare gift of knowing when to use nightmarish vehe-
> mence and when to be utterly straightforward.

In 1981 Gillian Whitehead spent nine months in Sydney

as a temporary teacher of composition at the New South Wales Conservatorium. It is one of the best tertiary music institutions in Australia with great strength among the composition teaching staff headed by Dr. Graham Hair. She obviously proved her strong teaching credentials, as member of the composition department, as she was appointed to a permanent position at the Sydney Conservatorium in 1982, a position she still holds. Since, June 1986, it's become possible for her to work there on a job-sharing basis, teaching for six months with freedom to compose and travel for the rest of the year. In 1985, she was acting head of the composition school.

Whitehead feels that her music changed when she moved to Sydney and she explains:

> For one thing I found that the magic squares that had still often been the basis of my music were somehow very much tied up with my life in Europe. It's not intrinsic to living here, so if I start with something like that I'll break it down, change it, alter it, obliterate it. I also find teaching, which I've done seriously in Australia for the first time in the last few years after freelancing for twelve years altered my work. I had found an optimum way of working, four days on and two days off which you can't fit into a teaching week. I found now that in lots of ways I am free-wheeling, writing far more instinctively like I used to, but with everything I've developed going through it. The logic goes into teaching. That's where things are now.
>
> Those European elements I'm not using now and because I'm writing in smaller segments, I'm writing in a totally different way. I don't think that that goes on forever. I know that things will change again.

Low Tide, Aramoana, for large mixed choir, mezzo-soprano, three trumpets, two trombones and timpani, with text by Cilla McQueen, was written in 1982 and commissioned by the Auckland Choral Society. It was premiered the same year with Ray Wilson, conductor, Anthea Moller, mezzo-soprano and the Auckland Choral Society. William Dart reviewed the premiere on Sept. 4, 1982, for the New Zealand Listener (excerpt):

Low Tide, Aramoana is an incisive piece of scoring with a strong emphasis on pointillistic writing for the five brass players coupled with equally imaginative stylings for the choral forces. From their very first utterance, "Sky with blurred pebbles, a ruffle on water," the Auckland Choral Society were in excellent form, as was Anthea Moller, her expert handling of the more florid writing reminding one of her Hotspur performance (which has now been broadcast over the Concert Programme).

Out of this Nettle, Danger, was written by Whitehead in 1983 on commission from the New Zealand Literary Fund. This monodrama based on Katherine Mansfield, with the text compiled from her writings, diaries and letters by Fleur Adcock, was performed by the Australian Contemporary Players at the Opera House Recording Hall in Sydney in 1985. David Vance reviewed the performance for The Sydney Herald News, on Oct. 29, 1985 (excerpt):

The most compelling work on the program was the premiere performance of Gillian Whitehead's Out of this Nettle, Danger (1983) a setting of a text, compiled by Fleur Adcock, drawn from the letters, diaries and writings of Katherine Mansfield.

The work documents the anguish of the writer, dying of tuberculosis, and is music that responds imaginatively to every image of the text.

An ensemble comprising flute, clarinet, trumpet, cello, piano and percussion accompany the vocal line given to a mezzo-soprano and sung on Sunday with unfailing sympathy by Anthea Moller.

Two particular sections stand out in what is a score of thorough craftsmanship: a centrally-placed chorale in which a melody of grave simplicity charts the loneliness of the isolated artist; and the final pages where nightmarish dreams are evoked by solo voice and percussion.

This work responds intuitively to the words of Mansfield, creating in its own way a piece as memorable as any of that writer's short stories.

Whitehead's chamber opera, The King of The Other Country, in two acts is some 90 minutes in length and was written in 1984. It was premiered the same year by the

Sydney Conservatorium Opera School and reviewed by Roger
Covell for The Sydney Morning News on June 8, 1984:

Feyness in its powerful as well as merely quaint
senses is a characteristic of the mood and subject
matter of Gillian Whitehead's work for the theatre.

In The King Of The Other Country she and a
fellow New Zealander, the poet Fleur Adcock, have
put together a new two-act opera of dream-like
strangeness and memorability.

It uses an old and recurring theme in folk tales
and ancient ballads: that of the mortal who is taken
off to be the consort of a supernatural being and
who returns home to discover that family and friends
have aged and died during what has seemed like no
more than a night of enchantment.

The opening scene of the opera, in which Isabel,
singing a lullaby to her baby, is taken off to another
world, is an interrupted idyll in which the narrative
elements, given shivers of premonition by the composer's calm vocal line and brilliantly poetic instrumental imagination, are stronger than those of
drama.

The scene of her preparation for her new marriage is a kind of tranced ritual. Even the beginning of the second act, in which she asks to see her
baby once more, and the first part of her homecom-
ing have the somnambulistic air of an enacted legend
(a description, not a complaint).

But then, as the unrecognized Isabel witnesses
the arrival of her aging husband's new bride, the
drama of loss and loneliness asserts itself. Librettist and composer have found words, cried, accents
and a timing and selection of events here that make
us attend to the action with concern and an awareness of emotional pressure.

Whitehead's vocal and instrumental writing seemed
to inhabit different, only partially related worlds.
The singing frequently has a timeless ballad-like
independence of any need for accompaniment. The
sounds of the 11 instrumentalists are as vivid as
they are economically disposed: drums speaking in
slithering volleys, fantastic whirls and spirals for
woodwind, incisively used and co-ordinated key-
boards.

Listeners who fear shrieking, aggressive, tune-
less operas can be assured the Whitehead's melodies
are approachable. It may give some idea of her
eclectic but personal vocabulary if I point out that
the musical refrain associated with Isabel's domesti-
city might have come out of the slow night music of
a Bartok piano concerto or that some of the choral
writing of the marriage ritual has just a touch of
Stravinsky's The Wedding to it.

Myer Fredman's musical direction is effective and
precise. Jane Manning's singing of Isabel's music
is a virtuoso performance.

Gillian Whitehead is a fine composer who communicates
her perceptions and emotions through music. Her creative
ingenuity provides the listener with new and exciting mediums
of expression and she is contributing an important repertoire
to 20th-century music. She has made a strong impact on contemporary music and it is hoped longevity will enable her to
continue to compose well into the 21st century. She may well
become the most prolific composer of our time. One can safely
predict that her accomplishments will be included in the history of music for she is simply too good to be denied.

Selected Compositions of Gillian Whitehead

Piano Solo

1966 Fantasia On Three Notes, published by Wai-te-ata Press.
1974 La Cadenza Sia Corta, published by Price Milburn.
1976 Voice Of Tane, published by Price Milburn.
1980 Tamatea Tutahi.
1981 Lullaby For Matthew.

Chamber Music

1969 Aria, for solo cello, Price Milburn Hire Library.
1970 Te Ahua, Te Atarangi, for string quartet, Price Mil-
        burn Hire Library.
1972 Piano Trio, Price Milburn Hire Library.
1972 Music For Christmas, for flute, clarinet, violin, violon-
        cello, double bass, guitar, piano/celesta, and marimba.
        Price Milburn Hire Library.

1974 Trio For Harpsichord, Violin and Cello, Price Milburn
      Hire Library.
1976 Moonstone, for viola and piano, Price Milburn Hire Li-
      brary.
1976 Ricercare, for solo viola, Price Milburn Hire Library.
1977 At Night The Garden Was Full Of Voices, published
      Price Milburn's recorder Book 2.
1977 The Children Of Rangi And Papa, for flute, oboe, bass
      clarinet, clarinet, bassoon, horn, trumpet trombone,
      piano, percussion, two violins, viola, violoncello and
      double bass, Price Milburn Hire Library.
1977 For Timothy, prelude and two pieces for guitar/arrange-
      ments of Northumbrian folksongs.
1979 Oue, for two flutes, oboe, bass, clarinet, bassoon,
      trumpet, violin, viola, violoncello and double bass.
1979 Okuru, for violin and piano, Price Milburn Hire Library.
1980 Antiphons, for three trumpets, two horns, three trom-
      bones and tuba, Price Milburn Hire Library.
1984 Ahotu (O Matenga), for flute, trombone, violoncello,
      percussion, keyboards (two pianos, celeste, harpsi-
      chord).
1986 Manutaki, for flute, clarinet, violin, viola, cello and
      piano.

Chamber Music with Voice

1967 Pakuru, for flute, clarinet, viola, violoncello, harps,
      percussion and soprano, Price Milburn Hire Library.
1970 Whakatau-Ki, for male voice, pic/a, flute, oboe, bass
      clarinet, horn, trumpet, trombone, violin, violin/
      viola, violoncello, double bass, and percussion,
      Price Milburn Hire Library.
1972 Three Songs of Janet Frame, for oboe, clarinet/bass
      clarinet, horn trumpet, trombone, guitar, double
      bass and soprano, Price Milburn Hire Library.
1973 Marduk, for flute, clarinet, violin/viola, violoncello,
      guitar, harpsichord/piano, percussion and soprano,
      Price Milburn Hire Library.
1974 Riddles 3, for soprano, flute, guitar, marimba and
      harpsichord.
1976 Wulf, for flute, clarinet, violin, violoncello, piano,
      percussion and female reciter, Price Milburn Hire
      Library.
1977 Riddles 2, for soprano and piano, five poems of Bill
      Manhire, Price Milburn Hire Library.

1980 Bright Forms Return, for string quartet with mezzo-
        soprano, Price Milburn Hire Library.
1980 Hotspur, for clarinet, clarinet/bass clarinet, violin/
        viola, violoncello, percussion and soprano, ballad
        by Fleur Adcock, Price Milburn Hire Library.
1981 Pao, for soprano, clarinet and piano.
1983 Out of This Nettle, Danger, for flute, clarinet, trumpet,
        violoncello, percussion and soprano, text by Fleur
        Adcock.
1983 These Isles Your Dream, for mezzo-soprano, viola,
        piano, poems by Kathleen Raine.
1985 Tongues, swords, keys, SSAATTBB, for percussion
        ensemble, text Randolph Stow.

Music for Stage

1975 Tristan and Iseult, for four singers, mimes and puppets,
        flute, flute/piccolo, oboe, bass clarinet, horn,
        trumpet, trombone, percussion, harp, two violins,
        viola, violoncello and double bass; libretto, Malcolm
        Crowthers and Michael Hill, Price Milburn Hire Li-
        brary.
1979 The Tinker's Curse, for six adult soloists, two child-
        ren's choirs string and wind quintets with children's
        percussion (six players) or piano, Children's Opera,
        libretto Joan Aiken, Price Milburn Hire Library.
1981 Requiem, for mezzo-soprano and organ, Price Milburn
        Hire Library.
1984 The King of the Other Country, Chamber Opera, for
        flute, clarinet trombone, two pianos, cello, violin,
        viola, violoncello, double bass, harp and percussion,
        text by Fleur Adcock.
1986 The Pirate Moon, chamber opera, six main roles, two
        smaller roles (chords of individual voices) for flute,
        oboe, clarinet/bass clarinet, trumpet, trombone,
        piano, two violins and viola, libretto Anna Maria
        dell'Oso.

Choir

1963 Missa Brevis, unaccompanied SATB, Price Milburn Hire
        Library.
1966 Qui Natus Est, carol, SATB, Price Milburn Hire Library.

1973   Riddles 1, choir SSA and harp, three poems of Bill
       Manhire, Price Milburn Hire Library.
1976   Five Songs of Hildegard Von Bingen, unaccompanied
       SATB, Price Milburn Hire Library.
1982   Low Tide, Aramoana, SATB large choir, mezzo-soprano,
       three trumpets, two trombones, tympani, text by
       Cilla McQueen.

Orchestra and Voice

1982   Eleanor of Aquitaine, chamber orchestra and mezzo-
       soprano, text by Fleur Adcock.

Choir and Orchestra

1970   Babel, for three eight-part choirs, orchestra, soloists,
       Price Milburn Hire Library.
1979   The Inner Harbour, SATB, chamber orchestra, two
       flutes, two oboes, two clarinets, two bassoons, two
       horns, two trumpets, strings and percussion, Price
       Milburn Hire Library.

Orchestra

1971   Punctus Solis, for piccolo/flute, alto/flute, flute, oboe,
       two clarinets, brass bass, four horns, two trumpets,
       trombone, tuba, two harps, strings, four percussion,
       four speaking voices, Price Milburn Hire Library.
1975   Te Tangi A Apakura, for string orchestra, Price Mil-
       burn Hire Library.
1976   Sinfonia, for three flutes, three oboes, two clarinets,
       bass clarinet, three bassoons, four horns, three
       trumpets, tuba, three percussion, harp and strings,
       Price Milburn Hire Library.
1978   Tirea, for oboe, violin, violoncello, harpsichord and
       strings, Price Milburn Hire Library.
1979   Hoata, for flute, two oboes, clarinet, bass clarinet,
       two bassoons, two horns, tympani and strings, Price
       Milburn Hire Library.

Addresses

Price Milburn Music Ltd, Box 995, GPO Wellington, New Zealand.

Book House, Boulcott Street, Wellington, New Zealand.

Boosey & Hawkes Pty. Ltd, 26-28 Whiting Street, Artarmon, NSW 2064, Australia.

Universal Edition, 2-3 Fareham Street, Dean Street, London, England.

Helen Lewis, First Floor, 56 Kellett Street, Potts Point, NSW, 2001, Australia.

Discography

Fantasia on Three Notes, Tessa Birnie pianist, Kiwi SLD-19.
La Cadenza Sia Corta, Bruce Greenfield pianist, Kiwi SLD-50.
Missa Brevis, (Sanctos, Benedict's, Agnus Dei only) Dorian
      Singers Kiwi SLD-56.
Qui Natus Est, University of Auckland Choir, Kiwi SLD-31.

Address

Kiwi/Pacific Records Ltd, 182 Wakefield Street, Wellington, New Zealand.

Adelaide Festival of Music 42, 67
Akin, Jim (Contemporary Keyboard Magazine) 136
American Composers Orchestra 264, 273, 275, 277
American Institute and Academy of Arts and Letters 190, 191, 192,
    264, 269
American Music Center 137, 196, 248, 277
American Women Composers News 140
Anderson, Beth see Vol. 2
Australia Music Centre 36, 55, 79, 177, 257, 259
Australian Broadcast Company 21, 24, 28, 67, 72, 73, 112, 171,
    253, 256, 257, 259

Bacewicz, Grazyna 1-17, 115
    Awards:
        Award of the Union of Polish Composers 9
        City of Warsaw Prize 5
        International Composers Contest 5, 6
        International Composers Tribune 8
        Minister of Cultural Arts 10
        Orchestral Division UNESCO 8
        Queen Elisabeth International Composers Award 10
        Radio and TV Prize 9
        Young Composers Competition 3, 5
    Celebration of Women Composers 5
    Compositional styles 4, 5, 6, 7, 8, 9, 10
    Concerts:
        Belgium 5, 6, 10
        Hanover 11
        London 5, 11
        New York 6, 8, 9
        Paris 3, 4, 5, 8
        Warsaw 4
    Compositions: 13, 14
        "Adventures of King Arthur" 9
        "Concerto for Stringed Orchestra" 5, 6
        "Concerto for Viola" 11
        "Contradizione" 11
        "The Desire" 11, 12
        "Music for Strings, Trumpet, Percussion" 8, 9, 10

"Olympic Contata" 5
"Overture" 5
"Pensieri Notturni" 10
"Piano Concerto" 5
"Quintet" 5
"String Quartets 1 through 10" 6, 8, 10, 11
"Symphony No. 4" 6
"Trio" 5
"Violin Concerto No. 7" 10
"Violin Sonata" 6
Congregation of the Arts 11
Dimov Quartet 10
Discography 15, 16, 17
Hopkins Center 11
Kletzki, Paul 3
Lodz Conservatory 3
Lutoslawski, Witold 1, 10
Marek, Tadeusz 7, 10
Polish Composers Union 9, 12
Polish Radio Orchestra of Warsaw 4
Publishers 17
Reviews:
    Etude 7
    Krakow 6
    La Libre Belgique 10
    Przeglad Kulturalny 8
    Ruch Muzyczny 9, 10, 12
    The New Yorker 5
    Washington Post 6
Szymanowski, Karol 3, 4, 5
Teachers:
    Boulanger, Nadia 3
    Flesch, Carl 3
    Jarzebski, Jozef 3
    Sikorski, Kazimierz 3
    Touret, Andre 3
    Turczynski, Jozef 3
Warsaw Conservatory of Music 3, 13
Bacewicz, Wanda 1, 7
Baculewski, Krzystol (Ruch Muzyczny) 93
Bai-Am, Benjamin (Jerusalem Post) 221, 222
Beath, Betty 18-36, 172
    Aronoff, Joseph 23, 24
    Australia Music Centre 36
    Australian Broadcasting Company 21, 24, 28
    Awards:
        Australian Broadcasting Company 21
        Literature Board of the Australian Council 24, 25, 26
        Southeast Asian Fellowship 24
        University of Queensland Music Scholarship 20, 21
    Brisbane Baroque Trio 30

Brisbane Radio Station   28, 29
Collins, Stuart   30
Compositions: List   33-36
    "Abigail and the Bushranger"   24
    "Abigail and the Rainmaker"   24, 25, 26
    "The Beasts Choir"   27
    "In This Garden"   23
    "Indonesian Triptych"   28
    "Marco Polo"   23
    "The Ninya"   32
    "Piccolo Victory, Images of Colonial Australia"   30
    "Raja who Married an Angel"   24, 25
    "Riddles"   24
    "Sea Watchers"   24
    "Spider"   23
    "Yunggamurra"   32
Concerts:
    A.B.C. National   24, 28, 73
    A.B.C. Queensland   28
    Brisbane Radio   28, 29
    Canada   23
    Dublin   27
    Jakarta   27
    New York   28
    Queensland Opera Company   23
    Queensland Orchestra   24, 28
Cox, David   22, 23, 24, 27
Discography   36
Gasztold, Carmen Bernos de   27
International Congress on Women in Music   28, 31, 33
International League of Women Composers   31
International Society of Contemporary Music   29
J. Albert and Company   23, 27, 36
Jakarta   24
Opus   3, 33
Poole, Jeannie   31, 33
Publishers   36
Queensland Conservatorium   22, 24, 27, 28
Queensland Opera Company   23
Queensland University   21
Reviews:
    The Courier Mail   30
    The Irish Times   27
    Opera Australia   24, 25
    Opera for Youth News   25, 26
St. Margaret's School   18, 21, 22
Sydney Conservatorium   21
Teachers:
    Baird, Nora   21
    Hutchens, Frank   21, 22
    Pollard, Lorna   20

Thorpe, Gary 28, 29
Berkshire Music Festival 167, 190, 224, 225, 229, 269
Berliner, Milton (Washington Daily News) 6
Bernstein, Leonard 215, 217
Black, Frederick (Terre Haute Star) 132
Blanks, Fred (The Sydney Morning Herald) 50, 73, 74
Bond, Victoria 9. See also vol. 1
Boulanger, Lili 5, 107
Boulanger, Nadia 3, 5, 200
Boyd, Anne 37-55, 259
    A.B.C. Children's Hour 38
    Adelaide Festival of Music 42
    Australian Ballet Orchestra 40, 42
    Awards:
        Australian Music Council 47, 49
        Commonwealth Music Award 52
        Commonwealth Overseas Grant 43
        Commonwealth Scholarship 40
        Frank Albert Prize for Music 41
        Newcastle City Council 50
        Radcliffe Trust 46
    Birtwistle, Harrison 45
    Blanks, Fred 50
    Compositions: 53, 54, 55
        "Air and Variation" 38
        "Alma Redemptoris" 42
        "Angklung" 46
        "As I crossed the Bridge of Dreams" 46
        "Coal River" 50, 51
        "The Creation" 42
        "The Death of Captain Hook" 48
        "Etenraku" 47
        "Exegesis No. I" 41
        "The Fall of the Icarus" 41
        "Kakan" 51
        "The Little Mermaid" 49
        "Metamorphoses of a Solitary Female Phoenix" 45
        "My Name Is Tian" 49
        "Nocturnal Images" 41
        "Rain Song" 52
        "Rose Garden" 45
        "Shineberg" 42
        "The Stairway" 42
        "Trio" 41
        "Tu Dai Oan" 43
        "The Voice of the Phoenix" 44
    Cage, John 42
    Dartington Summer School 45
    Davies, Peter Maxwell 49
    Discography 55
    Edinburgh Festival 46

Faber Music Ltd. 55
Feldman, Morton 44
Freda, Helen-Louise 52
Hornsby Girls High School 39
International Society for Contempory Music 42
John Alldis Singers 47
Kim, Don'o 47, 48, 49
Macnaghten Concerts 45
Maneroo 37
Medieval Aspects of Contemporary Music 42
Music Now 42
National Music Camp 41, 42
Pro Musica Society 42
Rands, Bernard 44
Publisher 55
Reviews:
    The Morning Sydney News 46, 49
    Music and Musicians 45
    Newcastle Morning Herald 50
    The Sydney Morning Herald 48
Seymour Group 49, 50
Sydney Opera House 49
Sydney University Musical Society Centenary Festival 47
Teachers:
    McMahon, Victor 40
    Mellers, Wilfred 43
    Peart, Donald 40, 42
    Rands, Bernard 43, 44
    Sculthorpe, Peter 40, 41
University of Hong Kong 51
University of Sussex 46, 47
University of Sydney 40, 47
University of Wollongong 49
York University Orchestra 43, 45
Brico, Antonia see vol. 1
The Brisbane Baroque Trio 30, 170, 171, 172, 173
British Broadcasting Company 8, 9, 94, 117, 118, 119, 206, 207,
    208
B.B.C. Philharmonic Orchestra 8, 9, 119, 120, 153, 158, 207
Britain, Radie see vol. 1

Caduff, Sylvia 56-66
    Barbirolli, Sir John 64
    Beecham, Sir Thomas 62
    Bern Conservatory 64
    Bernstein, Leonard 56, 60, 61
    Conducting Competitions:
        Dimitri Mitropoulos Conducting Competition 56, 59, 60
        Guido Cantelli Conducting Competition 39
        Nicoline Marro Competition 60

Lucerne Conservatory   57, 58
Orchestras:
   New York Philharmonic Orchestra   56, 60, 61, 62
   Orchestra da Camera   63
   Orchestra of the City of Solingen   56, 64
   Osnabrucker Symphony Orchestra   65
   Royal Philharmonic Orchestra   62
   Tonhalle Orchestra   59
Reviews:
   Daily News   63
   Neue Osnabrucker   65
   The New Yorker   60
   World Journal Tribune   61, 62
Sargeant, Winthrop   60, 61
Steinberg, William   61, 62
Teachers:
   Kubelik, Rafael   59
   Von Karajan, Herbert   58, 59
   Von Matacic, Lovro   59
Cage, John   42, 138
Caldwell, Sarah   5. See also vol. 1
Carnegie Hall   28, 104, 182, 219, 227, 241, 242, 271
Carr-Boyd, Ann   30, 31, 67-79, 174
   ABC   67, 72, 73
   Asian Composers League   76
   Awards:
      Children's Hobbies Exhibition   69
      Commonwealth Research Grant   70
      Maggs Award   72
      Sydney Moss Scholarship   70
   Blanks, Fred   73, 74
   Compositions: 76, 77, 78
      "Boomerang Chocolate Cake"   71
      "Catch 75"   72
      "Folk Songs"   72
      "Lullaby for Nuck"   71, 75
      "Music for Narjade"   73
      "Music for Sunday"   73, 74, 75
      "Patterns"   72, 73
      "Running"   68
      "String Quartet"   70
      "Suite for Veronique"   75
      "Symphony in Three Movements"   71
      "Theme and Variation"   71
      "Three Songs of Love"   71
      "Trois Leçons"   71
   Discography   78
   Fellowship of Australian Composers   76
   Goode, Robert   71
   International Congress of Women Composers   76
   Music Board of the Australian Council   73
   Musica Viva Festival   72

Parle, Nicholas 75
Publishers 79
Reviews:
   The Canberra Times 74, 75
   The Sydney Morning Herald 73
   The Sydney Morning News 73
   The First Hundred Years of European Music in Australia 70
Queensland Symphony Orchestra 72
Richardson, Marilyn 71
Royal College of Music 70, 71
State Archives Department 70
Sydney Opera House 67, 73, 74
Teachers:
   Fricker, Peter Racine 70, 71
   Goehr, Alexander 70, 71
   Peart, Donald 69
University of Sydney 69, 70
Cavallaro, Lenny (The New Haven Register) 244, 245
Celebration of Women Composers Concert 5
Cheltenham Festival 118, 207
Coates, Gloria 80-103
   Amerika Haus 87
   Awards:
      Ditson Fund 87
      Koussevitzky International Record Award 80
      National Federation of Music Clubs 82, 83
      Norlin Foundation Fellowship 96
   Bavarian Radio Orchestra 81, 94
   Compositions: 96, 97, 98, 99, 100
      "Chamber Symphony" 97
      "Dickinson Songs" 90
      "Five Pieces for Four Wind Players" 94
      "Music for Open Strings" 80, 81, 90, 93, 94, 98
      "Nonett" 96
      "Planets" 91, 92
      "Sinfonietta Della Notte" 94
      "String Quartet #2" 89
      "String Quartet #4" 90
      "Voices of Women in Wartime" 96
   Diary 86, 103
   Discography 100
   First International Festival of New Music, Moscow 88, 89
   Frau und Musik 88
   German-American Concert Series 89
   International League of Women Composers 34, 88, 92
   International Youth Orchestra 96
   Kronos Quartet 88
   MacDowell Colony 96
   Munich Ministry of Culture 87
   Mureca String Quartet 90
   Open House Broadcasts 88

Polish Chamber Orchestra   80
Publishers   103
Reviews:
    Arbetet   94
    Eastern Province Herald   95, 96
    Evening Post   96
    Frankfurter Allgemeine Zeitung   91, 98
    Hindustan Times   90
    Melos   91
    Neue Musikzeitung   92, 93, 96
    Passauer Neue Presse   92
    Ruch Muzyczny   93
    State Times   85, 86
    Suddeutsche Zeitung   97
    Sunday Morning Advocate   85
    Zeitschrift fur Musik   89, 90
Teachers:
    Beeson, Jack   86
    Brady, Mary   82
    Gunderson, Helen   86
    Klaus, Kenneth   86
    Luening, Otto   86
    Silverthorn, Elizabeth   82
    Tcherepnin, Alexander   84, 86
Warsaw Autumn Festival   80
Cole, Hugo (The Guardian)   124
Collins, Phillip (Santa Cruz Sentinel)   187
Copland, Aaron   225
Covell, Roger (Sydney Morning Herald)   46, 48, 49, 250, 281, 282,
    289, 292, 293
Cox, David   22, 23, 24, 27
Crawford, Ruth (Seeger)   see   vol. 1
Crowder, Charles (The Washington Post)   283, 284

Da Capo Players   193, 229, 264, 267, 268, 269, 271, 272, 273
Dartington Summer School   45
Davies, Dennis   273, 274, 275
Davies, Peter Maxwell   49, 284, 285
Diemer, Emma Lou   see vol. 1
Du Priest, Karen (The Register-Guard)   276

East, Leslie (Music and Musicians)   45
Edlund, Bengt   94
Emelianoff, Andre   268, 275, 276
Epstein, Selma   101-114
    Artist   114
    Australia   108, 111, 112
    Australian Broadcasting Corporation   112

Award:
   D. Hendric Ezerman Foundation Scholarship 104
Barzin, Leon 106
Boulanger, Lili 107
Brooklyn Museum Concert Series 106
Cannon, Phillip 111
Carnegie Hall 104
Concert Programs 108, 109, 110
Ella's Last Birthday Concert 112, 113
Grainger, Percy 112, 114
Grainger Society 112
International Congress on Women in Music 114
Klaus, Egge 111
Maryland Women's Orchestra 114
National Orchestra Association 106
New Zealand 108, 110, 111
Phillipines 108
Reviews:
   Grainger Journal 113, 114
   New York Herald Tribune 104
   San Diego Union 106, 107
   Wisconsin State Journal 110, 111
Teachers:
   Cowell, Henry 105, 108
   Dayas, Karin 105
   Esteban, Julio 105
   Isador, Philipp 105
   Lhevinne, Rosina 104
   Perin, Max 105
   Shehatovich, Stephanie 104
   Stevermann, Edward 104, 105
Ericson, Raymond (The New York Times) 241
Escot, Pozzi 5 See also vol. 2

Fine, Vivian see vol. 2
Flax, Laura 192, 268, 269, 271
Fromm Foundation 120, 167, 224, 229, 265

Galkin, Elliot W. (The Baltimore Sun) 268-269
Gardner, Kay see vol. 2
Gideon, Miriam 267 see vol. 2
Ginghold, David (City on the Hill) 187
Glackin, Bill (The Sacramento Bee) 140
Glagla, Gisela (Zeitschrift fur Musik) 89, 90
Glanville-Hicks, Peggy see vol. 2
Gojowy, Detlef (Frankfurter Allgemeine) 91
Gould, Neil (High Fidelity/Musical America) 273
Griffiths, Paul (The Times Saturday Review) 209
Guggenheim Fellowship 227, 231, 265

Hays, Doris see vol. 2
Hess, Myra 108, 147
Hillis, Margaret see vol. 1
Hoffmann, W. L. (The Canberra Times) 74, 75
Holland, Bernard (The New York Times) 275
Hopkins, Robin (Wisconsin State Journal) 110, 111

International Congress on Women in Music 28, 29, 32, 33, 76, 92,
    114
International League of Women Composers 31, 88, 92
Ivey, Jean Eichelberger see vol. 1

J. Albert and Company Ltd. 23, 27, 36
Jolas, Betsy see vol. 1

Kastendieck, Miles (World Journal Tribune) 61, 62
Kaul, Saloni (Hindustan Times) 90
Kletzki, Paul 3
Kolb, Barbara 227. See also vol. 1
Kriegsman, Alan M. (San Diego Union) 106, 107

La Libre Belgique 10
Landowska, Wanda see vol. 1
Lawrence, Richard (Music and Musicians) 118
LeFanu, Nicola 115-128, 149
    Allegri String Quartet 117
    Australia 125
    Awards:
        Cobbett Prize 117
        Fromm Foundation 120
        Gulbenkian Dance Award 120
        Harkness Award 120
        Mendelssohn Scholarship 120
        Radcliffe Trust 117
    Ballet Rambert 120
    Birmingham Symphony Orchestra 122
    Boston Symphony Orchestra 120
    British Broadcasting Corporation 117, 118, 119
    Camden Festival 123, 124
    Cheltenham Festival 118
    Compositions: 126, 127, 128
        "Anti World" 118, 119
        "But the Stars Remaining" 117
        "Chiaroscuro" 117
        "Christ Calls Man Home" 118
        "Columbia Falls" 122, 123, 126
        "Concerto for Double String Orchestra" 119

"Dawnpath" 123
"Deva" 123, 124, 125
"The Hidden Landscape" 118, 119, 120, 123
"The Last Laugh" 120
"The Old Woman of Beare" 125
"A Penny for a Song" 125
"Quintet for Clar. and Str." 117
"Rondeau" 118
"The Same Day Dawns" 120, 121, 122
"The Story of Mary O'Neil" 125, 126
"Stranded on my Heart" 125
"Variations for Oboe Quartet" 117
Conducting 120, 121, 122, 128
Discography 128
Dreamtiger Ensemble 122
Farnham Festival 117
Hilversum Oboe Quartet 117
Lumsdaine, David 116, 123, 125
New Opera Company 123
Promenade Concert 119
Publishers 128
Purcell Room 118
Royal Albert Hall 122
Reviews:
    The Boston Globe 121, 122
    The Guardian 124, 125
    Music and Musicians 118
    Western Mail 117
Royal College of Music 117
Teachers:
    Goehr, Alexander 115
    Kim, Earl 120, 126
    Petrassi, Goffredo 117
    Roberts, Jeremy Dale 115, 126
    Shifrin, Seymour 120
    Wellesz, Egon 115
University of London 123
Levin, Gregory (Music Quarterly) 270, 271
Limmert, Erich (Melos) 91
London Phil. Orchestra 155, 205
Luck, Ann (State Times) 85, 86
Lutoslawski, Witold 1, 10
Lutyens, Elizabeth 149

MacDowell Colony 96, 137, 265
McLean, Priscilla 129, 146
    American Society of University Composers 134, 143
    Antwerp 139
    Autumn Festival 137, 138
    Awards:

    American Music Center Grant 137
    MacDowell Colony 137
    Marcha Baird Rockefeller Grant 137
    Meet the Composer 137
    National Endowment for the Arts 137, 143
    National Symposium Award 132
    Resident Composer 135
  Bowling Green University 142
  Compositions: 144, 145, 146
    "A Magic Dwells" 141
    "Beneath the Horizon III" 138, 139
    "Dance of Dawn" 137
    "The Inner Universe" 138, 140, 141
    "Interplanes" 134
    "In the Wilderness is the Preservation of the World" 142
    "Invisible Chariots" 135, 136, 137, 141
    "Messages" 135
    "Night Images" 136
    "Songs of the Humpback Whale" 138
    "Spectra I" 136
    "Variations and Mosaics on a Theme of Stravinsky" 132, 141
  Gaudeamus Festival 138, 139
  Indiana University 131, 132, 133, 134, 135, 137
  Indianapolis Orchestra 132
  Louisville Orchestra 132
  McLean, Bart 130, 132, 133, 134, 135, 136, 143, 144
  The McLean Mix 137, 139, 140, 144
  New Music Festival 142
  Percussion Ensemble 136
  Publisher 146
  Pulitzer prize 132
  Reviews:
    American Women Composers News 140
    Contemporary Keyboard Magazine 136
    The Sacramento Bee 140
    Terre Haute Star 132
  Teachers:
    Beversdorf, Thomas 131
    Heiden, Bernhard 132
    Kent, Richard 131
    Xenakis, Iannis 133
  University of Hawaii 135
  University of Rhode Island 136
Macnaghten Concerts 149, 150
Maconchy, Elizabeth 115, 117, 126, 147-164
  Academy of St. Martin-in-the-Fields 156
  Albion Ensemble 157
  Allegri Quartet 152
  Allen, Sir Hugh 147, 149
  Awards:
    Birmingham Feeney Trust 155

    Blumenthal Traveling Scholarship   149
    Cheltenham Festival   154, 156, 157
    Chricklade Arts Festival   157
    Dorchester Abbey   154
    Evans Prize   152
    London Country Council   153
    Proms Commission   154, 157, 158
B.B.C.   153
B.B.C. Orchestra   120, 153, 157, 158
B.B.C. Scottish Orchestra   154
Britten, Benjamin   150, 155
Cheltenham Music Festival   154, 156, 157
Commander of the Order of the British Empire   156
Composers Guild   155
Compositions: 162, 163, 164
   "Concertino"   149
   "The Departure"   153
   "Epyllion"   156
   "Heaven Haven"   157
   "Heloise and Abelard"   156, 157
   "The Jesse Tree"   154
   "The Land"   149
   "Music for Strings"   158
   "Nocturnal and the Sirens' Songs"   156
   "Proud Thames"   153
   "Serenata Concertante"   155
   "String Quartet #1"   151
   "String Quartet #2"   152
   "String Quartet #3"   152
   "String Quartet #4"   152
   "String Quartet #5"   152
   "String Quartet #6"   152, 153
   "String Quartet #10"   154, 156
   "Three Donne Songs"   156
   "Three One Act Operas"   153, 154
   "Variazioni Concertante"   154
   "Wind Quintet"   157
Croydon Philharmonic Society   156
Discography   164
Hess, Myra   147
International Society for Contemporary Music   152
LeFanu, Nicola   149
LeFanu, William   149
London Philharmonic Orchestra   155
Lutyens, Elizabeth   149
Macnaghten Concerts   149, 150, 151
Marriner, Neville   156
Mendelssohn Scholarship   147-148
New Opera Company   153
Prague Philharmonic Orchestra   149
Proms   149, 154, 157, 158

Publishers   163
Reviews:
   Music and Letters   152, 153
   Musical Times   151
   Observer   157
   The Times   156
Royal College of Music   147
Royal Festival Hall   153, 157
Society for the Promotion of New Music   155, 156
Teachers:
   Alexander, Arthur   147
   Jirak, K. B.   149
   Williams, Vaughan   147
   Wood, Charles   147
Mageau, Mary   165-177
Awards:
   Australia Broadcasting Commission   171
   Australia Council Grant   171
   Gottschalk International Competitions   167
Berkshire Music Center   167
Brisbane Baroque Trio   170, 171, 172, 173
The Composer Speaks   174
Compositions: 175, 176, 177
   "Australia's Animals"   169
   "Concerto Grosso"   173
   "Elite Syncopations"   174
   "Forecasts"   169
   "Interaction"   169
   "Montage"   168
   "Pacific Portfolio"   173
   "Scarborough Fair"   172
   "Sonate Concertate"   171
   "Three Movements"   167
   "Variegations for Orchestra"   167
   "Winter's Shadow"   174
Contemporary Directions   167
Des Moines Symphony Orchestra   168
Discography   177
Duluth Symphony Orchestra   168
International Festival of the Arts   167
International Society for Contemporary Music   169
Kelvin Grove College   168
Publishers   176, 177
Queensland Symphony Orchestra   168, 170
Queensland Theatre Orchestra   173
Reviews:
   The Australian   169, 170, 171
   The Courier Mail   170, 171, 173
   The Piano Quarterly   169
Tanglewood   167.   See also Berkshire Music Festival
Teachers:

Bassett, Leslie 167
Crumb, George 167
Finney, Ross Lee 166
Schuller, Gunther 167
Stein, Leon 165, 166
White, Kenneth 165, 168
Maguire, James (The Irish Times) 27
Mamlok, Ursula 178-197, 267
American Academy and Institute of Arts and Letters 191, 192
Awards:
American Academy and Institute of Arts and Letters 190
Faculty Research Foundation 190
Martha Baird Rockefeller Recording Grant 190
National Endowment for The Arts Grants 190
National Federation of Music Clubs 181
Bennington College 183
Black Mt. College 181
City University of New York 194
Compositions: 194, 195, 196
"Capriccios for Piano and Oboe" 187
"Concert Piece for Four" 184
"Fanfare" 192
"Haiku Settings" 185, 186
"Panta Rhei" 187
"Sextet" 190, 191
"Sonar Trajectory" 186, 187
"Stray Birds" 183, 184
"String Quartet" 183
"Variations and Interludes" 189
"Variations for Solo Flute" 182
"When Summer Sang" 192, 193
Columbia Princeton Electronic Studio 186, 187
Da Capo Players 193
Discography 197
Ensemble Contemporana 187
Franklin String Quartet 182, 183
Krof, Anthony 184
Kolisch Quartet 181
Manhattan College 181, 182
Mumma, Gordon 187
Mamlok, Dwight 194
Music in Our Time 190
New Jersey Percussion Ensemble 189
New York University 194
Parnassus 184, 190, 193
Price, Paul 189
Publishers 196, 197
Reviews:
The Chautauguan 186
City on the Hill 187
The New York Herald 182, 183

Notes 190, 191, 192
Santa Cruz Sentinel 187
Teachers:
    Ernest, Gustav 178
    Giannini, Vittorio 182
    Sessions, Roger 181
    Shapey, Relph 185
    Szell, George 180, 181
    Wolfe, Stefan 182, 185
Mason, Colin (Musical Times, The Manchester Guardian) 63, 151,
    204
Mason, Eric (Daily Mail) 63
Mehta, Zubin 215, 220, 221, 273, 274
Mendelssohn Scholarship 120, 147, 148
Monson, Karen (High Fidelity/Musical America) 224, 226
Morgan, Martiza (The Chautauquan) 186
Musgrave, Thea 5, 119. See also vol. 1

National Endowment for the Arts 190, 264, 277
New York Herald Tribune 182, 183, 239

Oliveros, Pauline See vol. 1
Opera Australia 24

Papa, Jonathan (Opera for Youth News) 25
Peart, Donald 40, 69
Perkins, Francis D. (New York Herald Tribune) 104
Petrides, Frederique see vol. 2
Poole, Jeannie 31, 33
Porter, Andrew (The New Yorker) 5, 229, 230
Promenade Concert 119, 154, 157, 158, 207, 208, 209, 210
Ptaszynska, Marta see vol. 2
Purcell Room 118, 122

Queler, Eve see vol. 1

Rainier, Priaulx 198-214
    Alard Quartet 202
    Aldeburgh Festival 207
    Amadeus String Quartet 200
    Awards:
        Collard Fellowship 211
        Overseas Scholarship 199
    Bax, Sir Arnold 200

Boult, Sir Adrian 205
British Broadcasting Corporation 206, 207, 208
British Broadcasting Corporation Scottish Orchestra 209, 210
British Broadcasting Corporation Symphony Orchestra 207
Britten, Benjamin 202
Compositions: 212, 213
   "Aequoro Lunae" 207
   "The Bees Oracles" 207, 208
   "Concertante for Two Winds" 198, 209
   "Cycle for Declamation" 206
   "Dance Concerto Phala-Phala" 205
   "Duo Vision and Prayer" 208
   "Night Spell" 202
   "Organ Requiem" 208
   "Pastoral Triptych" 208
   "Ploermel" 208
   "Quanta" 198, 206, 207
   "Requiem" 203, 204, 205, 208
   "Sonata for Viola and Piano" 203
   "String Quartet" 198, 201, 202, 208
   "Suite" 203
   "Suite for Cello" 206
   "Three Greek Epigrams" 202
Discography 214
Fellow of the Royal Academy 203
Gertler Quartet 200
Glock, William 205, 206, 207, 211, 212
Groves, Sir Charles 209
London Contemporary Music Center 203
London Philharmonic Orchestra 205
Howarth, Elgar 208
Humphrey, Doris 202
Menuhin, Yehudi 206, 208, 209
National Arts Gallery 200
National Gallery Concerts 200
Pears, Peter 202, 203, 204, 206
Promenade Concerts 207, 208, 209
Publishers 214
Purcell Singers 203, 204
Reviews:
   The Financial Times 206, 209
   Manchester Guardian 204, 205
   Observer 201, 202
Royal Academy of Music 200, 203, 205, 206, 207
Royal Albert Hall 207, 208, 210
Royal Philharmonic Orchestra 209
South Africa 198
South Africa College of Music 199, 210, 211
Teachers:
   Boulanger, Nadia 200
   Woof, Rowsby 200

Tippett, Michael   202, 206, 211
Victoria and Albert Museum   203
University of Cape Town   211
Worshipful Company of Musicians   211
Ran, Shulamit   215-254, 267, 272
    Arnold Schoenberg Institute   223
    Art Series for Young Artists   215, 217, 223
    Avery Fisher Hall   217
    Awards:
        American-Israel Foundation Grant   231
        Chamber Music America   231
        Ford Foundation   223, 231
        Fromm Music Foundation   224, 229
        Guggenheim Fellowship   227, 231
        The Martha Baird Grant   231
        Meet the Composer   231
        National Endowment for the Arts   231
        W.F.M.T. Commissions   231
    Bernstein, Leonard   215, 217
    Brostoff Jewish Arts Ensemble   223
    Carnegie Hall   219, 227
    Columbia Broadcasting   219
    Compositions: 232-234
        "A Prayer"   229, 230
        "Apprehensions"   227
        "Capriccio"   217, 218
        "Concert Piece"   220, 221
        "Double Vision For Two Quartets and Piano"   225, 226
        "Ensembles for Seventeen"   224
        "Excursions"   230
        "O' The Chimneys"   222, 223
        "Piano concerto"   219
        "Private Games"   229, 230
        "Quartet for Flute, Clarinet, Cello, Piano"   219
        "Verticals"   230
    Contemporary Chamber Players   225, 226, 229, 230
    Da Capo Players   229
    Discography   233
    Israel Philharmonic   215, 220, 221, 222
    Kol Israel Orchestra   219
    Mannes College   218, 219
    Mehta, Zubin   215, 220, 221
    New York Music Ensemble   227
    Publishers   233, 234
    Reviews:
        Chicago Tribune   227, 230
        High Fidelity/Musical America   224, 226
        Jerusalem Post   221, 222
        The New York Times   219, 227
        The New Yorker   229, 230
    Shapey, Ralph   185, 222, 223, 225, 229

Tanglewood   224, 225, 229
Teachers:
    Boscovitz, Alexander   217
    Copland, Aaron   225
    Dello Joio, Norman   218
    Foss, Lucas   225
    The Laughing Man   219
    Reisenberg, Nadia   217, 218
    Shapey, Ralph   222, 223, 225, 229
    Taubman, Dorothy   218, 219, 224
  University of Chicago   222, 223, 229, 230
Richter, Marga   see vol. 1
Rockwell, John (The New York Times)   271
Royal Albert Hall   122, 153, 207, 208, 210
Royal College of Music   70, 71, 117, 147, 200, 203, 205, 206
Royal Philharmonic Orchestra   62, 209
Ruch Muzyczny   9, 10, 12, 13, 93

St. Louis Symphony Orchestra   264, 274, 276, 277
Salisbury, Wilma (Cleveland Plain Dealer)   271
Salzman, Eric (New York Herald Tribune)   182
Sargeant, Winthrop (The New Yorker)   60
Saunders, L.C.M. (New Zealand Herald)   287, 288
Schmidt, Hermann (Passauer Neue Presse)   92
Schonthal, Ruth   235-249
    Awards:
        ASCAP   242
        Delta Omicron Third International Award   242
        Outstanding Alumni Award Yale University   242
    Carnegie Recital Hall   241, 242
    Compositions: 246, 248
        "The Beautiful Days of Aranjuez"   244
        "Concerto for Piano and Orchestra"   238
        "Fiesta Dances and Intoxications for Piano"   241
        "Nachklange"   243
        "Reverberations"   243
        "Sonata Breve"   243
        "Sonata Concertante"   242
        "Sonata in Eb"   239, 240
        "Sonatensatz"   244
        "Sonatina in A"   237, 238
        "Song Cycle"   242
        "String Quartet"   241, 242
        "The Solitary Reaper"   245
        "Totensange"   241
        "Variations in Search of a Theme"   243, 244
    Connecticut Chamber Orchestra   244
    Crescent String Quartet   242
    Discography   248
    Hear America First   243

International Women's Year   242
Mexican Symphony Orchestra   238
Moscow Conservatory   237
National Musical Arts Ensemble   245
Placio de Bellas Artes   238
Publishers   248
Reviews:
    Fanfare   243
    New Haven Register   244, 245
    The New York Herald Tribune   239
    The New York Times   241
Royal Academy of Music   237
Steigerwalt, Gary   243, 244
Stern Conservatory   235
Stokowski, Leopold   238
Sweden   237
Teachers:
    Etthoven   237
    Hindemith, Paul   238, 240, 244
    Liljefors, Ingemar   237, 238
    Ponce, Manuel   238, 240
Town Hall   239, 240
Yale University   239, 240
Schreiber, Wolfgang (Suddeutsche Zeitung)   97
Schwemmer, Horst (Neue Musikzeitung)   92, 93
Sculthorpe, Peter   40, 41, 283
Seeger, Ruth Crawford   5. See also vol. 1
Shapey, Ralph   222, 223, 225, 229, 266
Siddell, Kevin (The Australian)   170
Simmons, Walter (Fanfare)   243
Slonimsky, Nicolas (Etude)   7
Smith, Julia   see vol. 2
Steinberg, Michael (Boston Globe)   121, 122
Stravinsky, Igor   3, 132, 219, 272, 293
Sutherland, Margaret   250-263
    Adelaide   250
    Australian Advisory Committee   253, 254
    Australian Broadcasting Company   253, 256, 257, 259
    Australian Music Centre   257, 259
    Australian Music Fund   254
    Australian Music: Themes of a New Society   250
    Australian Women Composers   259
    Award:
        Honorary Doctor of Music Degree   259
    Boosey and Hawkes   255
    Boyd, Anne   259
    Camerata Society   257, 258
    Composers Competition Contest   255
    Compositions: 260, 261, 262
        "Concerto Grosso"   255
        "Concerto for Stringed Orchestra"   255

  "Dithyramb" 253
  "Fantasy for Violin" 255
  "Haunted Hills" 255, 256
  "House Quartet" 253
  "Pavane for Orchestra" 253
  "Prelude for Jig" 253
  "Sonata for Violin and Piano" 252, 253
  "String Quartet" 253
  "Three Temperaments" 256, 257
  "The Young Kabbarli" 258
Casey, Lady Maie 258
Council for Education 253
Covell, Roger 250
Discography 263
Gifford, Helen 259
Gossens, Eugene 253, 256
Hill, Alfred 260
Hobart Music Festival 258
Hopkins, John 255, 256
International Opera Company 258
J. Alberts & Son 257
London 252
Lyrebird Edition 253
Marshall Conservatory 252, 253
Melbourne 250
Melbourne Symphony Orchestra 255, 256, 259
Murdock, James 259, 260
National Arts Gallery 259
Opera (first recorded in Australia) 258
Paris 252
Presbyterian Ladies College 252
Publisher 262, 263
Reviews:
    The Sydney Herald News 255
Sydney Orchestra 255, 256
Szell, George 253
Szter, Adele 259
Teachers:
    Bax, Arnold 252
    Goll, Edward 252
    Hart, Fritz 252
    Veebruuhen, Henri 252
Victorian Arts Centre 250, 254
Vienna 252
Swift, Richard (Notes) 190, 191, 192
Sydney Opera House 67

Talma, Louis 267. See also vol. 1
Tanglewood 167, 190, 224, 225, 229, 269. See also Berkshire Music
    Festival

Thrope, Gary 28, 29
Tjader, Marguerite (The Grainger Journal) 113, 114
Tower, Joan 192, 229, 264-280
    Alice Tully Hall 272
    American Composers Orchestra 273, 275, 277
    American Film Festival 265
    American Music Center 277
    Awards:
        Academy Institute of Arts and Letters 264
        Academy Institute Award 264
        The American Composers Orchestra 274, 275, 277
        Fromm Foundation 265, 277
        Jerome Foundation 265
        Koussevitzky Foundation Grant 264
        MacDowell Colony 265
        Maurice Andre Contemporary Music Society 264
        National Endowment of the Arts Fellowship 264, 277
        Naumberg Foundation 264, 267
        New York State Council of the Arts 271, 277
        Schubert Club 264
    Bard College 267, 276
    Bennington College 266
    Compositions: 278, 279
        "Amazons" 272, 273
        "Breakfast Rhythms" 270, 271, 272
        "Hexachords" 270, 271
        "Movements for Flute and Piano" 270
        "Music for Cello and Orchestra" 274, 275
        "Noon/Dance" 269
        "Petroushskates" 272
        "Platinum Spirals" 268
        "Sequoia" 273, 274, 275, 277
        "Wings" 269
    Carnegie Recital Hall 271
    Columbia University 266
    Da Capo Players 264, 267, 268, 269, 271, 272, 273
    Davies, Dennis 273, 274, 275
    Discography 279
    Documentary Video 265
    Emelianoff, Andre 268, 275, 276
    Eugene Symphony 274
    Flax, Laura 268, 269, 271
    Florida Orchestra 264
    Hudson Valley Philharmonic 272, 273
    Lester, Joel 268, 269
    Mehta, Zubin 273, 274
    Musician of the Month 265
    National Symphony 274
    New York Philharmonic 274
    Publishers 279, 280
    Reviews:

Cleveland Plain Dealer 271
Downtowner 269
High Fidelity/Musical America 273
Music Quarterly 270, 271
The New York Times 271
The Register Guard 276
San Francisco Examiner 274
The Sun 268, 269
St. Louis Symphony Orchestra 264, 274, 276, 277
San Francisco Symphony 274
Schwarz, Gerard 275, 276
Slatkin, Leonard 276
Smirnoff, Joel 269
Spencer, Patricia 268
Tanglewood 269. See also Berkshire Music Festival
Teachers:
    Beeson, Jack 266
    Brant, Henry 266, 267
    Calabro, Louis 266
    Luening, Otto 266, 267
    Milhaud, Darius 266
    Nowak, Lionel 266
    Riegger, Wallington 266
    Shapey, Ralph 266
United Nations Radio 277
Washington National Orchestra 276
Wen-Chung, Chow 266
Women 277
Y Chamber Orchestra 275

Ulrich, Allan (San Francisco Examiner) 274

Van De Vate, Nancy 33, 114. See also vol. 1
Vance, David (The Sydney Morning News) 291
Villaume, John (The Courier Mail) 30, 170, 171, 173
Von Karajan, Herbert 58, 59
Von Lewinski, Wolf Eberhard (Mainzer Allgemeine Zeitung) 95
Von Rheim, John (Chicago Tribune) 227, 230

Walsh, Stephen (The Times, Observer) 156, 157
Warren, Elinor Remick see vol. 2
Warsaw Musical Autumns 7, 93
Welch, Blakeman (Downtowner) 269
Western Mail 117
Whitehead, Gillian 281-297
    Adcock, Fleur 288, 292
    Albrecht, Gretchen 288, 289
    Auckland Choral Society 290, 291

Auckland Festival of Opera   287, 288
Australian Contemporary Players   291
Australian Performance Rights Association   285
Australian Society for Keyboard Music   283
Awards:
    Australian Performance Rights Association Award   288
    Northern Arts   286, 288
Birnie, Tessa   283
Compositions: 293, 294, 295, 296
    "Diversions for String Orchestra"   285
    "Fantasia on Three Notes"   283
    "Hotspur"   288, 289, 291
    "The King of the Other Country"   291, 292, 293
    "Low Tide, Aramoana"   290
    "Missa Brevis"   281, 283
    "Out of the Nettle, Danger"   291
    "Pakuru"   284, 285
    "Te Ahua Te Atarangi"   285
    "Tristan and Iseult"   287, 288
Conservatorium Contemporary Ensemble   289
Davies, Peter Maxwell   284, 285
Discography   297
Dorian Singers   281, 282
New South Wales Conservatorium   290
New Zealand Broadcasting Company   285
New Zealand Chamber Federation   285
New Zealand Sinfonia   285
Northern Arts Council   286, 288
Opera House Recording Hall   291
Phillips Collection   283
Reviews:
    New Zealand Herald   287, 288
    The New Zealand Listener   290, 291
    The Sydney Herald News   291
    The Sydney Morning Herald   281, 282, 289, 292
    The Washington Post   283, 284
Sculthorpe, Peter   283
Sydney Conservatorium   290, 292
Teachers:
    Davies, Peter Maxwell   284, 285
    Sculthorpe, Peter   283
University of Adelaide   284
University of Auckland   283
University of Newcastle   286
Victoria University   283
Waitangi Day   288
Wood, Marian (Sunday Morning Advocate)   85
Wordsworth, William (Music and Letters)   152, 153

Zaimont, Judith Lang   33.   See also vol. 2
Zielinski, Thadeusz (Ruch Muzyczny)   8
Zwilich, Ellen Taaffe see vol. 2